Gestalt in Social Work

Armin Schachameier • Ulrich Reichert
Tom Breitenfeldt

Gestalt in Social Work

Case Studies in Practice

Springer

Armin Schachameier
Department of Social and Educational Sciences
University of Applied Sciences Potsdam
Potsdam, Brandenburg, Germany

Ulrich Reichert
Irgendwie Anders GgmbH
Leipzig, Sachsen, Germany

Tom Breitenfeldt
Irgendwie Anders GgmbH
Leipzig, Sachsen, Germany

ISBN 978-3-031-95527-3 ISBN 978-3-031-95528-0 (eBook)
https://doi.org/10.1007/978-3-031-95528-0

English translation of the original German edition published by EHP – Verlag Andreas Kohlhage, Gevelsberg, 2025
The original submitted manuscript has been translated into English. The translation was done using artificial intelligence. A subsequent revision was performed by a third party to further refine the work and to ensure that the translation is appropriate concerning content and scientific correctness. It may, however, read stylistically different from a conventional translation.
Translation from the German language edition: "Praxishandbuch: Schlüsselsituationen der Sozialen Arbeit aus der Gestaltperspektive" by Armin Schachameier et al., © EHP – Verlag Andreas Kohlhage 2025. Published by EHP – Verlag Andreas Kohlhage. All Rights Reserved.

This Springer imprint is published by the registered company Springer Nature Switzerland AG.
The registered company address is: Gewerbestrasse 11, 6330 Cham, Switzerland

Preface

From the moment we began to develop our methodological approach, through the writing of this book, our central question was how we can understand and support the internal experience of people who express the desire to change and develop. As the authors of this book, we—Armin Schachameier, Ulrich Reichert, and Tom Breitenfeldt—have gathered many years' experience in facilitating experiential personal development workshops, grounded primarily in a Gestalt pedagogy approach, as well as in training Gestalt therapists. In this context, we reflect continuously on how to deal with inner blockages and resistance to change, especially among participants who show challenging behaviour and who have difficulty accessing their internal experience. Navigating such situations over and over again has shown us that establishing a trusting and constructive relationship with these participants is key, and that the Gestalt approach has much to offer in this regard. We have also observed that many of the inner and relational dynamics we encounter there are also relevant in the context of social work.

We hope that by passing on the knowledge and skills we have gained, this book will encourage students and practitioners to apply Gestalt-inspired relational work in various fields of social work. We also aim to convey an approach that explores and exemplifies dynamics between professionals and clients in a playful way, where fun, joy, and curiosity have their place. From our perspective, some of the most valuable learning can take place when the learner has the opportunity to gain insights through experimentation, reflection, and practice—and is not afraid when things don't 'work out' the first time. We advocate for a culture of permission to 'fail' together, again and again, in the search for solutions; this attitude is at the core of our methodology.

In short, we carried out our methodology as follows; we began by selecting scenes from encounters between clients and social workers in various different fields of social work practice and then re-enacted ('role-played') these scenes in order to reflect on them 'from the inside'. We then engaged in a process of developing these interactions through several rounds, modifying the professional's interventions according to our experiences in both roles. When we were satisfied with the insights and results we had gained, we created video recordings of the scenes in their latest iterations. The transcripts of these recordings, alongside theoretical references and discussion, form the chapters of Part III of this book, while access to the videos is detailed below.

It is important for us to emphasise that these are not intended as standard, off-the-shelf solutions. We show one possible way of acting in a particular situation. Naturally, other methodological approaches may also lead to success in the same situation. It is key to remember that people develop very individual patterns in their behaviour and thinking over the course of their lives. What fits for one person can be counterproductive for the next. Our examples are intended to provide suggestions for your own practice and experimentation. Replaying a situation several times deepens our understanding of the underlying dynamics and how to deal with them and allows our methodological repertoire to expand. If similar encounters with clients occur in practice, then these cases will have an increased familiarity and more routes of action will be available. At the same time, in practice, access to clients' individual experience and self-understanding must always be gained by way of an open and dialogical process; this is a core component of the Gestalt approach.

This dialogical process—or joint exploration—is an essential part of our working method, and one from which not only students of social work can benefit. Professionals can also apply these methods to address problematic cases in the context of team meetings or supervision, to find creative solutions which build relationships with this experiential and experimental approach. The case examples presented in the book are reflected on from the theoretical perspective of the Gestalt approach, and the ensuing impulses for intervention are then transferred back into practice. The selected scenes deal with practical questions and cross-sectional issues that are relevant in many fields of social work; we therefore advocate that our methodology be included from general-level study onwards.

We now provide an overview of the chapters. We begin with some notes on how to use this book when teaching social work methodology. We then address the question of the boundary between the roles of psychotherapist and social worker and present our underlying competence-oriented understanding of both professions. This is followed, in Part I, by an introduction to our working method, explaining its background in terms of didactics, epistemology, research, and theatre-based pedagogy. In Part II, we offer detailed description of important Gestalt-theoretical foundations that are relevant as we reflect on each of the practical cases. Building on these foundations, in Part III, we then present the case role-plays, addressing the topics of depression and suicide, addiction counselling including mandatory counselling in the context of a court order, co-dependency, parent counselling, psychosis including mandatory admission in an acute case, and trauma-based dissociation.

As the practical examples we present are designed for teaching methodology at degree level, we would like to begin by offering some advice on how they might be used most effectively.

General Instructions

Access to the Recordings

Naturally, this book can be worked through from beginning to end. Alternatively, however, we have designed it such that the reader can go directly to the case examples, returning to the theory sections later via the references in the case notes. The recordings of the role-plays can be found at: www.gestalt-socialwork.com.

Instructions for Use in Methodology Teaching

Each of the case role-play videos we recorded is limited to a maximum duration of 10 minutes. These excerpts are designed to highlight certain methodological aspects and portray fundamental dynamics. Due to their brevity, they cannot cover all of the practice-relevant details or possible case trajectories. Furthermore, we also invite the reader—particularly the experienced practitioner—to view our approach through a critical lens. This also applies to the application of the proposed Gestalt methods; refinements and further discourse are welcome. At the same time, we wish to underline two aspects: firstly, that the conversation sequences always focus on selected, case-specific aspects, and are therefore not to be seen as 'one-size-fits-all' solutions; secondly, that we strongly recommend that you, the reader, try out these methods yourself, experimenting with our way of working so as to assess the suitability of the approach we present in your own professional practice. In this vein, we would like to offer some advice to teachers or supervisors.

When using this book in social work teaching or supervision, it is of fundamental importance to create an atmosphere that allows students or practitioners to experience fun and enjoyment as they practice, so that they can adopt a playful, exploratory attitude. They should feel able to dare to try things out, make 'mistakes', and reflect on them in order to learn and grow. It should be conveyed that a change in perspective is sometimes necessary in order to better understand the inner experiences of our clients. Empathic imagination is an essential basis for building working relationships, and by training this skill, we believe the student will see an increase not only in their practical confidence, but also in their understanding of clients' individual patterns of thinking and behaviour.

In terms of practical didactic implementation, the following course of action has proven effective: first, the students or trainees (e.g., in the context of a Gestalt therapy course) approach the topic by way of a role-play between client and practitioner. Following this, students engage in an exchange around their experiences during the role-play and are sensitised to specific features of the case. After this, the videos can be viewed and the transcripts discussed. There should then be at least one practice role-play, ideally several, with time for reflective discussion between them.

Another possibility is to start with the videos; teachers should assess in advance which didactic approach is most appropriate to the setting. It should be considered that the experiential exercises might touch on students' unprocessed personal experiences; in a university context, it may be more fitting, at least with some topics, to approach a client's inner life through the videos alone, rather than through role-play, for example when it comes to the section on depression and suicidal thoughts. Therapeutic training groups represent a somewhat different context; here, there is an increased expectation on trainees to engage with their own biography, this being an essential component of the personal growth necessary for carrying out therapeutic work.

Furthermore, before engaging in role-plays, discussion is necessary on the importance of personal responsibility with regard to one's own boundaries. Students should pause or cease participation in role-plays if they feel overwhelmed, or become emotionally confused or unable to regulate themselves. In such cases, teachers are responsible for discussing, in a one-to-one setting, the extent to which the student might need support within or beyond the setting.

To conclude, teachers should always be mindful of creating a practice setting, and their choice of how to engage with the case examples should be sensitive to the context, for example, whether in higher education or in further training in counselling or therapeutic skills. This distinction is also connected to an important question that we wish to address in the first chapter. There, we will offer our view on the commonalities between psychotherapy and counselling or advisory roles within social work, as well as possible criteria for their differentiation.

Case Role-plays: Structure and Setup

The chapters in Part III deal with cases which have been selected from various fields of social work practice. For each case, we role-played an encounter between the client and counsellor. These conversations were video-recorded and then transcribed.

The videos can be found at www.gestalt-socialwork.com.

The transcript of each video is included in the discussion below, along with a commentary. For each case, the structure is identical. To begin with, the case is briefly introduced. We then present relevant aspects of the case through a Gestalt therapeutic lens, according to the following categories: *cognitions*, *emotions*, *physical sensations*, *longing* (the client's felt experience of their underlying need), *action and avoidance* (what the client is doing and avoiding), and *contact with the outside world* (which includes their relationships with others and to life itself). These are based on our experiences when role-playing the client. We then describe the internal parts which are relevant to the client's experience.

After this, the transcript of the role-play is included, annotated with descriptions of the counsellor's interventions (with references to the theory chapters) and of the internal effect of these interventions on the client. The latter is also based on our phenomenological experiences whilst playing the client role.

This is followed by a presentation of value squares (for a basic explanation of these, see the section of this name in the Chap. 7) and directions for development. Each case ends with a discussion, offering final thoughts and considerations as well as further theoretical references to the respective topic.

Throughout, key terms are printed in bold, and correspond to the headings in the theory section. For example, if the word **stagnation** is printed in bold in the explanations, it signposts the reader to the corresponding explanation under the same heading in the theory section.

Here is an overview of this structure:

1. Brief case presentation[1]
2. Experiences in the client role, according to the following: cognitions, emotions, physical sensations, longing, action and avoidance and contact with the outside world
3. Identified inner parts of the client
4. Transcript with notes on counsellor interventions and their effect on their client, with references to the theoretical background
5. Value squares and directions for development
6. Discussion: explanations and theoretical references

Potsdam, Germany Armin Schachameier
Leipzig, Germany Ulrich Reichert
Leipzig, Germany Tom Breitenfeldt

[1] The names of the protagonists in the case role-plays are fictitious. Any similarities with real-life cases are purely coincidental. The cases described were developed fictitiously on the basis of numerous practical experiences of the authors and take up recurring situations.

Acknowledgements

Special thanks go to Sarah Howard for the translation, Florentine Heimbucher for creating the graphics and Nicolai Jungk for his help in dubbing the videos.

Contents

About the Authors

Armin Schachameier, PhD is professor of theories and methods of social work since 2020 at the FH Potsdam, Germany. From 2010 to 2020 he headed the dual course in social services at the Berufsakademie Breitenbrunn. From 2004 to 2009, he was head of therapy at the Oberpfalz Rehabilitation Center—a sociotherapeutic addiction facility for addicts with chronic multiple impairments. He is a Gestalt therapist and completed his training at the Institute for Integrative Gestalt Weiterbildung (IGW).

Ulrich Reichert is the founder of Irgendwie-Anders Ggmbh. He completed an apprenticeship as a tool mechanic, studied medicine and trained as a Gestalt therapist. His training institutes were the Institute for Gestalt und Erfahrung (IGE) and the Center for Gestalt Therapy in Würzburg, Germany. He also completed Paul Rebillot's master class. He set up the Gestaltakademie from Irgendiwe-Anders and is also the training manager.

Tom Breitenfeldt completed training as a gestalt therapist at the Center for Gestalt Therapy in Würzburg, Germany. He completed experiential education training at Event Nature. From 2010 to 2020, he worked as an independent adventure educator for the Globetrotter Academy, among others. He runs his own practice for Gestalt therapy. He has been a seminar leader at Irgendwie-Anders since around 2010. He also works there in training and personnel development.

Part I
Didactic Concept

Chapter 1
Competence-Oriented Approaches

The Distinction Between Psychotherapy and Counselling in Social Work: Definitions

Humanistic approaches, including Gestalt therapy, view the relationship between the professional and the client—as experienced in the here and now—as playing a fundamental and special role. This applies both to the psychotherapeutic context and to counselling processes in social work.

In the case examples we re-enacted, our central consideration was how we can build good relational quality with clients—how understanding, trust and an authentic encounter can arise. At the same time, the professional has a mandate to fulfill and must respond appropriately to the client's concerns. This requires field-specific methodological competencies, an awareness of the boundaries of one's sphere of responsibility, and knowledge of referral pathways. Social workers must know the support system within which they operate, and if necessary, involve experts from other professions.

In the various practical situations that a social worker might encounter, the appropriate methodological approach is not always distinguishable from a psychotherapeutic intervention. A social work situation may necessitate the same conversational techniques that might be part of a therapy session. For example, imagine a traumatised client who is experiencing flashbacks and dissociation, and needs to be stabilised. In such a case, the methodological approach is identical regardless of the setting. Whether the setting is a psychotherapy practice or a consultation with a social worker in a residential home, the professional will try to help the client out of this unpleasant state.

Nonetheless, the mandates of the two professionals in their respective contexts and fields are different. For the social worker, the next goal may be to integrate the client into the daily routine of the residential home, supporting and intervening where necessary. There are usually other clients to care for and intensive individual

A. Schachameier et al., *Gestalt in Social Work*,
https://doi.org/10.1007/978-3-031-95528-0_1

support is not likely to be possible. This role has limits in terms of the amount of one-to-one support it can deliver, and the social worker might go on to recommend and arrange trauma therapy. This example illustrates that social work practice may demand certain methodological competencies which are shared by psychotherapists, while the distinction between psychotherapy and counselling in terms of boundaries and tasks is to be upheld.

Furthermore, it should be considered that certain fields of social work have a particularly close relationship to psychotherapy, in particular specialised counselling fields such as addiction or family counselling. As a rule, the professionals working in these fields also have additional qualifications, which further blur the differences between therapy and social work. At the other end of the spectrum are much more broadly acting social institutions such as social services, whose task is to oversee and deliver social support processes. But even in these contexts, relationship-building is of fundamental importance.

The situations or 'scenes' we have focused on are limited to around 10 min each. Distinguishing whether they constitute a psychotherapeutic process or a social work consultation is difficult, and arguably in many ways neither useful nor necessary. What is important to distinguish is the setting and the remit of the professional. For example, some sequences clearly show that further intervention in a psychiatric clinic or more intensive psychotherapeutic support are required as a next step.

Of central importance in these sequences are the basic assumptions of the humanistic and experiential approaches, especially with regard to the professional's attitude towards their client, and the way they engage in contact. In this respect, one could say that Gestalt therapeutic methods and techniques can shape, guide, and open the space for encounters between professionals and clients. In our view, working on the qualities of the relationship is fundamental to both relationships, and the distinction between counselling and therapy is of lesser relevance in this regard (e.g. cf. Krawitz, 1992).

In the literature, numerous attempts have been made to try to define and demarcate psychotherapy and counselling. Sickendiek et al. (2008, p. 15ff.) distinguish between psychological, social, socio-pedagogical, and psychosocial support. Similarly, Widulle (2011, p. 32) differentiates between "professional conversation skills in social work", "psychosocial advisory services" and "psychotherapy". He addresses the goals, processes, methods, settings, qualifications, ethical and legal framework of each. Like us, he emphasises that the respective context and remit are important rather than the skill sets per se.

These attempts at definition are important chiefly for theoretical discourse. However, when we refer to specific cases and contexts, the boundaries of these categorisations often begin to blur. Socio-pedagogical approaches can contain elements of psychological support. Psychosocial procedures sometimes integrate short psychotherapeutic interventions, etc. In practice, it is more important what the professional's mandate is within the specific situation, context and field; it is also important that they have an understanding of the boundaries of their responsibility, and knowledge pertaining to onwards referral, should this be necessary.

For this reason, the notes accompanying each of the case role-plays include additional information on the professional's field-specific task, as well as possibilities for further treatment. This clarifies responsibilities and makes boundaries visible. In our view, it is neither realistic nor advantageous to differentiate conceptually between psychological, psychosocial, social or socio-pedagogical support in advance, as the focus of our considerations and reflections is on the interventions, the relationship skills, and the task.

Given that we believe that any attempt at classification into general theoretical definitions and categories would quickly be relativised in practice, we see a strong argument for simplification. We will therefore mainly use the terms 'counselling in social work'and 'counsellor' from here on. In addition, in line with numerous other authors, we combine what in Germany developed as two separate traditions ('social pedagogy' and 'social work') under the term 'social work'(DBSH, 2016; Rauschenbach & Züchner, 2012; Scherr, 2012).

We now move on to the question of which methodological competencies are relevant in the respective practical situations and fields.

Personal Competencies in Social Work

Competence-oriented theories about the professionalisation of social work focus on the practical knowledge and abilities which are necessary in order to help people within support systems. According to Heiner (2010), "personal, case and system competencies" are of central importance in day-to-day practice, in dealing with both clients and colleagues. System competencies include cooperation with relevant welfare and support systems, the ability to cooperate within a team, and a clear understanding of one's professional role (Heiner, 2010, p. 63 ff.). It also includes knowledge about routes of onward referral, as described in the chapter above. Case competence, meanwhile, "includes the abilities needed for direct client work [...]" (Heiner, 2010, p. 62), for example forming and developing the quality of contact within the context of a working relationship.

These abilities are closely linked to personal competencies. Social workers should "be able to listen and feel into themselves to find out what they are experiencing internally [...] They can then analyse these feelings in terms of their causes and effects" and "have the capacity to influence their own patterns of emotional reaction and spontaneous impulses" (Heiner, 2010, p. 63). Ultimately, this leads to successful, healthy self-leadership, with good access to one's feelings and parts of one's personality; when these are controlled consciously and in accordance with the situation, the professional can master difficult interactions and conflicts with confidence (Dietz, 2007).

It is characteristic of social work that professionals often find themselves in a tense dynamic between two or more poles, and must take on a mediating role. Heiner (2004, p. 161) has tried to describe typical examples of such polarities through a framework model. One central and continuously resolving tension is the polarity between help and control. To operate effectively within this dynamic, the professional must hold well-developed personal, case and system competencies. For example, when clients experience confrontation with the legal system (state control), they may display very strong reactions; professionals tasked with supporting them may need strong internal boundaries in order to put their personal reactions—either to the client's behaviours or opinions, or to the legal framework—aside. But countless other topics which occur in contact with clients can also trigger personal reactions on the part of the professional. This is why internal boundaries, or maintaining healthy distance, is fundamental for building sustainable working relationships. Given its importance, we will look at this issue in more detail. Schulz von Thun writes the following:

> When setting boundaries, it is important to distinguish between external behaviour and internal dynamics. An exaggerated external boundary [...] is usually rooted in an internal susceptibility to being drawn in. [...] [T]he less the helper can endure witnessing the other person's suffering, the more brusquely, dismissively, aggressively they must present their refusal [...] Conversely, someone who has a strong internal boundary can let the person who is in need of help get much closer (Schulz von Thun, 2006, p. 89).

What, then, can those in helper roles do to improve their ability to set internal boundaries?

"First of all, it is important to know that when dealing with intense suffering (such as serious illness, pain, death and despair), the ability to endure another's suffering without intervening is usually of great help. [...] The more the helper has dealt with the issues they encounter (depression, abandonment, incurable states, death and dying...), [...] the less they will have to shy away, the less they will be infected by despair, and the more likely they will be the rock which lets the stormy waves come to it without being swallowed by them" (ibid., 92).

For these reasons, regular supervision and personal development are central pillars of social work. It is essential that future professionals engage with their own biographies. This is a prerequisite for being able to work professionally with clients, as a lack of conscious reflection about one's personal family background and socialisation can hinder and negatively influence the establishment and quality of professional working relationships.

According to Schulz von Thun, an overly empathic response to one's clients can be caused by a 'super-ego construct' (or moral standard), such as (to use the words of Goethe): "Man is noble, helpful, and good". Such parts of a person's personality try to control their own needs and drives, with the intention of insuring that neither their neediness nor aggression are externally perceived, which also precludes the possibility of verbalising them appropriately. This limits the extent to which the person then senses or expresses their so-called inner child, which is masked instead by external demonstrations of strength (ibid. 79). Schulz von Thun's 'personality square' shows the developmental journey from such denial towards an awareness of one's own unmet needs and vulnerability (ibid., 87); this in turn is vital for learning to express one's own needs for help and developing the ability to resolve one's aggression in a healthy way (ibid., 89). This is essential for ensuring the sustainability of work in any helping profession. It thus becomes clear that personal development is a crucial prerequisite for being able to build a good relationship with clients and cope well with challenging or stressful events.

Furthermore, as part of a competence-oriented understanding of the profession of social work, Heiner (2004, p. 88 ff.) advocates that professionals encourage participatory relationships with their clients, in order to activate the client's innate self-healing drive. This is also aligned with the assumptions of humanistic, experiential approaches (see the section entitled "Organismic Self-Regulation and Self-Actualisation"). In addition, skills should be developed to motivate clients and to be able to distinguish clearly according to the framework model (Heiner, 2004, p. 161) what the clients themselves are responsible for. The prerequisite for being able to implement both of these aspects is the development of the willingness and ability to clarify responsibilities transparently through dialogue and hand over responsibility where appropriate. The extent to which this succeeds depends on how solidly the corresponding personal competences have been developed.

"In order to be effective as a therapist [or social worker, A.S.], it is essential to take care of oneself in order to remain able to take care of clients" (Lambert & Barley, 2008, p. 130). Social workers must have the capacity to sense what is going on inside them. An ability for introspection must be developed in order to manage inner parts, feelings, and impulses, and to be able to set boundaries both internally and externally. This is an important step towards professionalism, as it enables the professional to better understand the inner experiences and behaviour of clients, and therefore support them more effectively.

In the following chapters, we will go into more detail about how such competencies can be developed, especially in the context of role-play, ideally in combination with other personal development exercises. First, though, we briefly explain the principles behind our work, and locate them within the theoretical research fields from which they stem.

References

DBSH. (2016). *Deutsche Übersetzung der Definition Sozialer Arbeit des FBTS und DBSH.* https://www.dbsh.de/profession/definition-der-sozialen-arbeit/deutsche-fassung.html (Stand 13.08.2023).

Dietz, I. (2007). *Selbst in Führung. Achtsam die Innenwelt meistern.* Junfermann.

Heiner, M. (2004). *Professionalität in der Sozialen Arbeit. Theoretische Konzepte, Modelle, und empirische Perspektiven.* Kohlhammer.

Heiner, M. (2010). *Kompetent handeln in der Sozialen Arbeit.* Ernst Reinhardt.

Krawitz, R. (1992). *Pädagogik statt Therapie.* Klinkhardt.

Lambert, M. J., & Barley, D. E. (2008). Die therapeutische Beziehung und der Psychotherapieeffekt—eine Übersicht empirischer Forschungsergebnisse. In M. Hermer & B. Röhrle (Eds.), *Handbuch der therapeutischen Beziehung.* dgvt-Verlag.

Rauschenbach, T., & Züchner, I. (2012). Theorie der Sozialen Arbeit. In W. Thole (Ed.), *Grundriss Soziale Arbeit* (pp. 151–173). VS Verlag für Sozialwissenschaften.

Scherr, A. (2012). Sozialarbeitswissenschaft. Anmerkungen zu den Grundzügen eines theoretischen Programms. In W. Thole (Ed.), *Grundriss Soziale Arbeit. Ein einführendes Handbuch* (pp. 283–296). VS Verlag für Sozialwissenschaften.

Schulz von Thun, F. (2006). *Miteinander reden: 2. Stile, Werte und Persönlichkeits-entwicklung. Differentielle Psychologie der Kommunikation*. Rowohlt.

Sickendiek, U., Engel, F., & Nestmann, F. (2008). *Beratung. Eine Einführung in sozialpädagogische und psychosoziale Beratungsansätze*. Juventa.

Widulle, W. (2011). *Gesprächsführung in der Sozialen Arbeit. Grundlagen und Gestaltungshilfen*. Springer VS.

Chapter 2
Method, Epistemology and Participatory Action Research

In this chapter we present our methodology and trace the path—both in conceptual and practical terms—that led to writing this book and creating the video recordings around which the book is centred. In the spirit of Gestalt therapy, this book was born of experimenting and then reflecting on these experiments together. We started by asking how methods and techniques from Gestalt therapy might be applied in the practice of social work. Our initial motivation was to try out ideas around certain dynamics which we were curious about, but we then continued to refine the results of this experimentation through continuous reflection. We began by replaying situations which we had experienced in various fields within our practice, and where we had noticed certain commonalities. We endeavoured to find out which elements of Gestalt therapy might be useful, and how they might be applied, to help clients. In particular, we found that our experiences in facilitating intensive personal development workshops and Gestalt therapy training at our institute *Irgendwie Anders*[1] were very useful. We noticed clear similarities between our experiences of and with participants (both in terms of their inner conflicts and the associated dynamics and tensions in their interactions with us as facilitators) and those encountered by social work practitioners with their clients or service users.

We cannot over-emphasise that we have not developed our videos to act as recipes or treatment standards. Instead, they represent ideas that emerged on the basis of many hours of practical exploration, which involved first trying out an approach, and then reflecting on it, modifying it, and trying it out again. The videos are designed to encourage viewers to think about what they see, and to start trying out and experimenting for themselves. Insights we have gained and shared in the recordings can of course be applied in practice, but we recommend that viewers first role-play and reflect on the situations themselves. This leads to a deeper understanding

[1] Irgendwie Anders is an institute that offers intensive workshops for creative personality development. The associated Gestalt Academy also offers training in Gestalt therapy (www.irgendwie-anders.de).

A. Schachameier et al., *Gestalt in Social Work*,
https://doi.org/10.1007/978-3-031-95528-0_2

of clients' inner experiences and how to deal skillfully with the respective topic, for example with depression. By experiencing underlying dynamics from the inside, practitioners can build confidence in navigating similar situations in real life.

Naturally, the individuality of each case—both in terms of the individual and the context—must always be considered. For this reason, the starting point of any role-play should always be a real-life situation that can be re-enacted through role-play and reflected on, taking into account the specific circumstances and character traits of the protagonists.

The learning process should always be accompanied by a curious, playful and exploratory attitude, such that fun can be had trying things out, making mistakes, reflecting on the approach together, and growing through the insights gained. Such an approach, with its deeply experimental orientation, has clear links both to the epistemological foundations of Gestalt theory and to participatory action research. We would like to discuss this briefly in the next section.

Epistemology and Participatory Action Research

Having engaged intensively with the epistemological considerations of Gestalt therapy, Mehrgardt (1995) developed two models.[2] In particular, we wish to highlight one fundamental idea which theoretically underpins our experimental approach. Mehrgardt (1995, p. 26) criticises the assumption in Critical Realism that describes the boundaries between the phenomenal and the transphenomenal world as "absolute, clear and immovable". He uses two different terms for reality (the German words *"Wirklichkeit"* and *"Realität"*) to describe phenomenal or perceived reality and the 'actual' reality of the transphenomenal world, respectively. Put simply, "*Wirklichkeit*" refers to our experiential reality—the constructions and personal ideas we hold about ourselves and the world. *"Realität"*, on the other hand, includes the objective world and the biological processes which happen inside people, independently of their awareness.

However, Mehrgardt sees the demarcation between these two worlds as untenable, and so instead proposes a dialectical view (ibid., 27). Put simply, for the context of counselling in social work, this means that the participants who may in the past have been viewed as subject and object, e.g. counsellor and client, are both participants in a process of exchange, and are constantly being influenced and therefore changing through the interaction. Constructions of perceived and unperceived realities are mutually dependent and influence one another. This is also the core idea of models that divide figure and background into phenomenal and transphenomenal areas, but only separate them with dotted lines (Mehrgardt, 1995, p. 32), which are intended to illustrate the permeability of the levels (see also Schachameier, 2021).

[2] This refers to the Onion model (1995, p. 32) and the Relationship model (2001, p. 496).

Clients are therefore seen not as the object of an intervention, but as partners who are dialogically involved in, and thus have an influence on, the process.

This epistemological paradigm is largely incompatible with the prevailing neo-positivist or rationalist paradigms of psychotherapy research, which view clients primarily as research objects, and where process-outcome research designs that measure pre-post change abound. Even in qualitative impact research, clients are researched as objects (see also Walter, 1996, p. 163 ff.).

Our experimental approach does not aim to carry out measurements and collect data. Nevertheless, we are researching practice-relevant realities. By stepping into roles on behalf of clients, we let the experience of both the counsellor and the client on the 'receiving end' of this intervention inform our reflection, with a view to finding solutions for certain practical questions. We enter into these role-play exercises with ideas about interventions and their impact—which constitute Mehrgardt's *Wirklichkeit*, or perceived reality—which we then try out and develop, and which can then inform and influence real-life dialogue (*Realität*, or transphenomenal reality) with clients in practice. This approach can also be linked to participatory action research.

Inherent to this form of applied social research is the rejection of a separation between theory and practice (Greenwood & Levin, 2005, p. 52). Instead, the exploration of the dialectical relationship between subject and object is central, leading ultimately to solutions to practical problems and generating corresponding "realities" (Freire, 1982, p. 30). This means that the "objects" or participants of the research are also involved in the research process and provide feedback; researchers and participants stand together in a process of reflection.

This approach is rooted in the tradition of pragmatism, established by William James and Charles Sanders Peirce and further expounded by John Dewey. "The guiding thought of pragmatic critique was the question of the significance of thought for the living environment; the practical consequences of applying certain philosophical thoughts, for human lives" (Neubart, 1998, p. 58). Action, dialogue, the resulting application and its practical consequences are all important for this approach in turn, meaning that changes which result from an action must be considered. Crucially, "the general concepts, ideas, and theories stemming from reason necessarily have consequences for future action" (ibid., 63). Constructivist implications unfold on the "ground of a realism which is both accepted and demanded" (ibid.). In other words, ideas from people that lead to actions change the world or other people. Theory and practice are therefore interconnected (Greenwood & Levin, 2005, p. 53). Thoughtful, collaborative reflection leads to practical action and thus changes the surrounding environment. In this way, both subjects and objects are involved in an ongoing process of change, with the aim of achieving certain desired practical results (ibid.).

The starting point of such democratic learning processes is always a concrete problem. In our project, these are the concerns brought by clients who come for counselling. This didactic principle stems from the pedagogy of John Dewey (Greenwood & Levin, 2005, p. 61). We explore in role-plays how to respond to specific requests for help. This means that the people playing both roles—practitioner and client—enter into a joint process of reflection to find out how best to build a relationship. This means that all participants are both teachers and learners at the same time (ibid.).

Kemmis and McTaggart (2005, p. 563) call this process a "spiral of self-reflective cycles". The following steps are continually repeated:

- "Planning a change.
- Acting and observing the process and consequences of the change.
- Reflecting on these processes and consequences.
- Replanning.
- Acting and observing again.
- Reflecting again…" (Kemmis & McTaggart, 2005, p. 563).

In summary, the following elements are essential for participatory action research:

- It is a social process that consciously examines the relationship between individuals and the social environment.
- It is practically and collaboratively oriented as well as involving emancipatory critique.
- Dialectical, recursive reflection plays a role of central importance, transforming theory and practice (Kemmis & McTaggart, 2005, pp. 566–567).

Our approach, which led to the development of the video recordings which suggest solutions for real-life problems, follows this process exactly. In the role-plays, we harvest experiences on behalf of clients, and then reflect on these whilst drawing on our knowledge of Gestalt therapy and counselling, and thus arrive at practice-relevant insights that can be tried out in practice and then reflected on again. The "external validity" is very high, as real-life practice can benefit from it directly: "External validity, in the context of action research, is the extent to which a result is meaningful for all participants. Collaborative, consensual articulation is the prerequisite to a result gaining the character of transparent reality" (Walter, 1996, p. 172).

The path to such insights leads through constant reflection on practical experiences. Schön (1983, 1987) has dealt with these processes in detail from a learning theory perspective. We will delve into this in more detail in the next chapter. Interestingly, he also bases his considerations on an understanding of research as both participatory and reflective: "Reflective research requires a partnership of practitioner-research and research-practitioners" (Schön, 1983, p. 323).

References

Freire, P. (1982). Creating alternative research methods: Learning to do it by doing it. In B. Hall, A. Gillette, & R. Tandon (Eds.), *Creating knowledge: A monopoly?* (pp. 29–37). Society for Participatory Research in Asia.

Greenwook, D., & Levin, M. (2005). Reform of the social sciences, and of universities through action research. In N. Denzin & Y. Lincoln (Eds.), *Handbook of qualitative research* (pp. 43–64). Sage.

Kemmis, S., & McTaggart, R. (2005). Participatory action research: Communicative action and the public sphere. In N. Denzin & Y. Lincoln (Eds.), *Handbook of qualitative research* (p. 559K603). Sage.

Mehrgardt, M. (1995). Erkenntnistheorie und Gestalttherapie: eine dialektische Erkenntnistheorie als Grundlage der Gestalttherapie. *Gesta, 9*, 20–35.

Mehrgardt, M. (2001). Erkenntnistheoretische Fundierung der Gestalttherapie. In R. Fuhr, M. Sreckovic, & M. Gremmler-Fuhr (Eds.), *Handbuch der Gestalttherapie*. Hogrefe.

Neubart, S. (1998). *Erkenntnis, Verhalten und Kommunikation: John Deweys Philosophie des "experience" in interaktionistisch-konstruktivistischer Interpretation*. Waxmann.

Schachameier, A. (2021). *Gestalttherapie und Soziale Arbeit. Ökonomische und ökologische Hintergründe*. EHP.

Schön, D. A. (1983). *The reflective practitioner. How professionals think in action*. Temple Smith.

Schön, D. A. (1987). *Educating the reflective practitioner*. Jos-sey-Bass.

Walter, H.-J. (1996). Zur Bedeutung der Aktionsforschung für Psychotherapie und Beratung. In H.-J. Walter (Ed.), *Angewandte Gestalttheorie in Psychotherapie und Psychohygiene*. Opladen.

Chapter 3
Reflections on Theories of Learning and Didactics

In this chapter, we elaborate on the reflection processes inherent in our working method. For this purpose, we use the terms "reflection-in-action", "reflection on action"and "reflection on reflection-in-action", as described by Schön (1983, 1987) and Tov et al. (2016).

Our role-plays started out as practical experiences. We used situations that we had experienced in real life, and in which the application of conventional "routine actions", by which we mean conversation techniques or strategies, were insufficient in supporting our clients. During these original conversations, we were already forced to reflect on our approach and look for alternative ways to respond appropriately to the client. Schön refers to routine actions as "knowing-in-action" (Schön, 1983, p. 54), and calls the immediate reflection on these actions, i.e. the confrontation with the situation *in* the situation, "reflection-in-action"(Schön, 1983):

> It is this entire process of reflection-in-action which is central to the 'art' by which practitioners sometimes deal well with situations of uncertainty, instability, uniqueness, and value conflict. (Schön, 1983, p. 50).

Many practical situations in social work are very complex, and professionals must continuously reflect on their actions. However, these internal processes happen very quickly in practice and can only to some extent be consciously described afterwards. Reflecting on action after the event allows evaluation and interpretation of the approach which was taken and any solutions which were found. After we have selected the practical situation we wish to focus on, such reflection is our first step. In particular, we consider the extent to which Gestalt methods were already applied, and how they could be used more extensively. We refer to this phase as "reflection-on-action". However, in order to make the emotional and physical experience and cognitions more conscious, we then proceed to re-enact the situation through role-play, reflect on our experiences immediately afterwards, and enter back into role-play to try out the new ideas which have arisen from reflection until we have reached a satisfactory result. We refer to this phase, which is repeated cyclically, as

A. Schachameier et al., *Gestalt in Social Work*,
https://doi.org/10.1007/978-3-031-95528-0_3

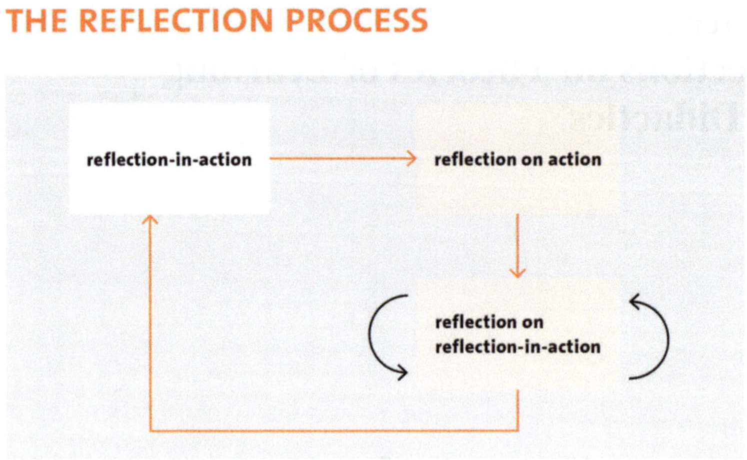

Fig. 3.1 Reflection on reflection-in-action

"reflection on reflection-in-action"in reference to Tov et al. (2016, p. 116) and Schön (1987, p. 31).

Figure 3.1 illustrates this process. Ultimately, the insights which are gained can be re-integrated into practice and then reflected upon again.

Process of Reflection

Repeated practice and reflection increases not only the awareness of internal cognitive-emotional processes, but also the level of practical confidence in future practice situations. By training certain modes of thinking and acting, informed by methods and techniques which are grounded in theoretical knowledge, new knowledge and skills are created. This cycle of knowledge transfer passes from the situational through the declarative and theoretical before returning once again to the practical situation (Kaiser, 2005, p. 186). Starting from an experience, a connection is made to Gestalt and other subject-specific explanatory approaches, which then in turn influence future experiences.

To use the terminology of the integrative learning model, there is an exchange between intentional, declarative, theoretical knowledge and extensional, practical, experiential knowledge (Kaiser, 2005, p. 46). At the same time, skills are being trained and optimised, and new action pathways created, to be used flexibly. In this context, Kaiser speaks of procedural and sensorimotor knowledge (Kaiser, 2005, p. 166 ff.). Such a process allows competence to be developed and integrated into the person as a "tool": "The integration takes place in such a way that individual actions are first practiced and then, so to speak, assembled into a whole. Once the competence is mastered, it sinks from consciousness into deeper layers, but can be accessed and used by the person at any time" (Spiegel von, 2018, p. 99).

Von Spiegel also distinguishes between the dimensions of knowledge and ability. The former includes, among other things, descriptive and explanatory knowledge; the latter includes, for example, the capacity for communicative methodological action and the ability to apply the "person as a tool". She also defines yet another dimension, namely attitude, referring to reflective work on one's own professional attitude and the orientation towards professional value standards (Spiegel von, 2018, pp. 97, 98). In our view, however, the distinction between attitude and ability is not always clearly defined. Our dialogical and phenomenological approach is a method that is simultaneously associated with a certain inner attitude (see the chapters "Phenomenology", "Existentialism" and "Dialogical Attitude").

By using the reflection cycle as described above, our approach allows us to establish connections to Gestalt theory and to make it practically usable. It can also be viewed from the perspective of a reflective understanding of professionalism (Dewe, 2009). From this vantage point, the relationship between theory and practice or the interplay of the competence dimensions of knowledge and ability must be related:

> At the centre of professional action is not scientific knowledge as such, but rather the ability for discursive interpretation of everyday difficulties and individual cases with the aim of opening up perspectives or justifying decisions under conditions of uncertainty. From my understanding of scientific theory, this means that theory is not *applied* in practice, but is rather *related* by the "reflective professional": this person reflects on their professional experience and the problems and uncertainties to be dealt with in communication with his client using a multiple knowledge base. (Dewe, 2009, p. 107, emphasis in original).

Essentially, this corresponds with both our transfer strategy and our understanding of how learning processes can be managed and designed. By reflecting on practical situations and applying (or relating) the findings in further practice units, students gain more confidence in their practice. They can access methodical concepts and techniques from Gestalt therapy as well as other theoretical knowledge in specific situations and use this knowledge in a way which is flexible and situationally appropriate. The reflective practitioner benefits from methodological training and can draw on knowledge and strategies for action which have been practised as part of the process of "reflection on reflection-in-action".

However, performance in practice or exercise situations can also be understood as a kind of production, as a performance of internal parts and roles. This will be the subject of the next section.

Drama-Based Pedagogy: The Production

In this section we will describe the drama-based pedagogical background which underpins our approach. All three of us, as authors, also have extensive practical experience in facilitating intensive personal development workshops which are grounded in both drama-based pedagogy and Gestalt. A key methodological component is the exploration of old and new behaviours through role-play. In particular, participants are encouraged to identify, embody and empathise with inner parts (Link & Schachmeier, 2016; Schachameier, 2016; Schachameier & Link, 2016, 2017).

These workshops were developed conceptually by Paul Rebillot. In the genesis of Rebillot's seminal workshop 'The Hero's Journey', as well as his various other structures for initiating and supporting processes of transformation and transition, certain phases of Rebillot's personal biography were particularly relevant, especially those centred around the subject of theatre. He had a "lifelong passion for the dramatic arts," studied theatre, and had experience in acting, directing, and production (Grof, 1992, p. 10). Kabuki and Noh theatre were also sources of inspiration (ibid.). Rebillot saw great potential in theatre for initiating and supporting personally significant processes of change and personal development. He founded the *Gestalt Fool Theater Family* in 1968 as a forum for self-awareness. This platform was inspired by Jacob Levy Moreno's psychodrama and drama therapy, which is why therapy, ritual and theatre became core elements of Rebillot's workshops. The basic theoretical assumptions of drama-based pedagogy, such as the educational value of aesthetics in theatre, as well as an artistic and educational theoretical positioning (Czerny, 2004, p. 67ff.), are reflected in the concept of the Hero's Journey.

During this 6-day structured process, as if they were in a play, each participant plays the role of the hero (representing the desire for change) as well as their nemesis, the demon (representing inner resistance to change), filling both roles with biographical and individual content (Rebillot & Kay, 2011, p. 38). As a result, the Hero's Journey resembles a play; the participants grasp the meaning of their own life story, their own 'personal drama', with their mind, emotions and body (ibid., 36).

Fritz Perls, the co-founder of Gestalt therapy, also had a passion for theatre. Working as an extra while still a schoolboy, he became acquainted with the theatre culture of Max Reinhardt; during his time in New York at the end of the 1940s, he identified with the *Living Theater* movement (Hartmann-Kottek, 2004). "Both Perls and Moreno experienced firsthand that improvised role-play contains a healing and therapeutically usable component due to the inherent expression involved when real aspects are also enacted. They met twice at the end of the 1940s and exchanged ideas around their methods"(ibid.).

Gestalt therapy has, in other words, adopted elements of improvisation and impromptu theatre. This involves playful experimentation and exploration, and finding joy in the freedom of play. This type of play represents an environment where the individual can connect to their internal experience fearlessly, enabling growth and development (ibid.). The unconscious inner self is allowed to take the lead in shaping the act of expression (ibid.)

Inspired by Rebillot, we founded *Irgendwie Anders*, an organisation which is based in Germany and runs workshops and training courses centred around Gestalt and drama-based pedagogical methods; as such, we are very familiar with this way of working. From this perspective, human behaviour and expression are viewed as productions, similar to theatre productions; in other words, the way in which a person presents themselves in certain life situations, or the roles that they play. A key principle is: "You can't *not* act yourself." In other words, however a person presents themselves, it is always an aspect of themselves that they are presenting, because they cannot be anyone else. An individual perceives, assesses and interprets every interaction they have in their own particular way, viewed through their respective "lens of consciousness". Each person responds to and processes the events and circumstances of their life individually and develops their own character traits and patterns of action.

As such, productions are presentations of different behaviours that can be chosen, comparable with roles. What is often referred to as "authentic behaviour" is in fact a habitual role or behaviour that is associated with a particular emotional experience. New roles, or forms of action, are often experienced initially as alien, as not being in keeping with our nature. The possibility exists, however, to try out and integrate these new behaviours so as to be able to react more adequately in certain situations (see the chapter on "Incongruence and Flexibility"). From this perspective, there is no real difference between "experimenting" and "exploring" in the context of workshops and in "real" life. This also corresponds to various sociological approaches. For example, Goffman (1969) views everyday life situations as a production by actors who present their inner states and thoughts about themselves and the world as if they were on a stage.

"Staging, therefore, is not a *special* thing, everyday dramaturgy is not an *unusual* type of behaviour, acting is not a *specific* form of human coexistence, but a basic condition of the 'conditio humana' on the one hand, and a rather banal, everyday matter on the other; we all aim to be perceived by others in a certain way through our self-presentations, to appear before others in a certain light" (Soeffner, 1989, p. 157 cited in Hitzler, 1992, p. 457; emphasis in the original). The staging or role behaviour is always situation-specific, that is to say that adjustments are made according to the expectations of others depending on the circumstances and the actors involved. According to symbolic interactionism, an interpretive negotiation process in which meanings are attributed to the actions of other people underlies all such interaction (Blumer, 1981, p. 81). Schütz and Luckmann (2017) speak in this context of the social construction of reality, a 'reality' which could be constructed in infinite iterations. Meanings are internalised, sorted through an internal communication process with oneself, and checked and adjusted in the next encounter with other people (Blumer, 1981, p. 84). People go through internal and external interaction processes cyclically, and these influence each other.

Anyone who has participated in a systemic family constellation will know that it involves taking on a role based on certain information about the person who is to be role-played; after stepping into this role, the role-player then experienced emotions and impulses vicariously. Interaction and negotiation processes take place in a matter of seconds and the communication structures of the wider family system become apparent. This generally happens automatically; the ability to empathise with other people and anticipate the expectations of others who are involved in the interaction is a central mechanism of interpersonal interaction.

Empathy seems to be of great importance in this context. Rizzolatti and Sinigaglia (2008) postulate that mirror neurons are "the biological basis of compassion". Häusser writes:

> The phenomenal experience of the same feelings, the creation of a common intersubjective 'experience space', finds its neuronal equivalent in the synchronisation of neuronal activation. The functioning of mirror neurons is therefore a necessary prerequisite for recognising the emotional situation of other people. [...] The presence of mirror neurons suggests that people quite simply participate in the experiences of others. (Häusser, 2012).

These considerations help answer the question of how re-enacting key social work situations can provide important insights for practice. We slip into roles and become performers of a psychotic or depressive person. The more encounters we have had with these clinical pictures in our private or professional environments, the better we can play these roles. Our mirror neurons enable empathetic compassion for the emotions of the other. This gives us an idea of how the person with typical symptoms feels, or at least allows us to approach this experience as closely as possible. During the role-plays, the protagonists always produce their own individual version of a role, but these individual productions relate to certain underlying personal experiences, such as the experience of depression within the context of a certain life situation. As with family constellations, role-playing an individual allows increased access to their inner experience. In particular, by adopting a certain body posture, corresponding sensations arise. When playing a role, an individual interpretation of the role is presented; in these moments, the difference between "re-enacting" and "reality" disappears.

As such, the typical dynamics at play within the corresponding individual cases become visible. We can try out potential strategies for action or conversation and better understand clients' inner experience. In practice, of course, we must always respond to the peculiarities of the individual and situation. However, when professionals or students are familiar with basic underlying dynamics, it is easier to deal with these and adjust interventions accordingly, or to find out which intervention clients are receptive to and will find supportive.

The drama-based pedagogical background outlined in this chapter forms an essential basis of our methodological approach; the re-enactment and thereby experiencing of practical situations through role-play is at its core. These re-enactments are viewed and reflected on from a humanistic and experiential perspective. The necessary theoretical knowledge for such a perspective will be described in the next chapter (Chap. 4).

References

Blumer, H. (1981). Der methodologische Standort des symbolischen Interaktionismus. In Arbeitsgruppe Bielefelder Soziologen (Ed.), *Alltagswissen, Interaktion und gesellschaftliche Wirklichkeit*. Rowohlt, Reinbek.

Czerny, G. (2004). *Theaterpädagogik. Ein Ausbildungskonzept im Horizont personaler, ästhetischer und sozialer Dimension*. Wißner-Verlag.

Dewe, B. (2009). Reflexive Sozialarbeit im Spannungsfeld von evidenzbasierter Praxis und demokratischer Rationalität—Plädoyer für die handlungslogische Entfaltung reflexiver Professionalität. In R. Becker-Lenz, S. Busse, G. Ehlert, & S. Müller-Hermann (Eds.), *Professionalität in der Sozialen Arbeit* (pp. 95–116). VS Verlag für Sozialwissenschaften.

Goffman, E. (1969). *Wir alle spielen Theater. Selbstdarstellungen im Alltag*. Piper.

Grof, S. (1992). Vorwort. In P. Rebillot & M. Kay (Eds.), *Die Heldenreise. Das Abenteuer der kreativen Selbsterfahrung* (pp. 9–13). Eagle Books.

Hartmann-Kottek, L. (2004). *Gestalttherapie*. Springer.

Häusser, L. F. (2012). Empathie und Spiegelneurone. Ein Blick auf die gegenwärtige neuropsychologische Empathieforschung. *Praxis der Kinderpsychologie und Kinderpsychiatrie, 61*(5), 322–335.

Hitzler, R. (1992). Der Goffmensch. Überlegungen zu einer dramatologischen Anthropologie. *Soziale Welt, Jg., 43*, 449–461.

Kaiser, H. (2005). *Wirksames Wissen aufbauen. Ein integrierendes Modell des Lernens*. hep.

Link, P.-C., & Schachmeier, A. (2016). Werde wieder der Regisseur deines Lebens! Die Heldenreise: Theaterpädagogik und Gestaltarbeit im Dialog. *Zeitschrift für Theaterpädagogik, 10*(69), 70–72.

Rebillot, P., & Kay, M. (2011). *Die Heldenreise. Das Abenteuer der kreativen Selbsterfahrung*. Eagle Books.

Rizzolatti, G., & Sinigaglia, C. (2008). *Empathie und Spiegelneurone. Die biologische Basis des Mitgefühls*. Suhrkamp.

Schachameier, A. (2016). Humanistisch-experientielle Persönlichkeitsbildung am Beispiel des gestaltpädagogischen Seminars die Heldenreise. *Neue Praxis. Zeitschrift für Sozialarbeit, Sozialpädagogik und Sozialpolitik., 3*(16), 263–279.

Schachameier, A., & Link, P.-C. (2016). Humanistsch-experientielle Veränderungsprozesse am Beispiel des theater- und gestaltpädagogischen Seminars "Die Heldenreise". *Thepakos. Interdisziplinäre Zeitschrift für Theater und Theaterpädagogik, 09*(31), 4–16.

Schachameier, A., & Link, P.-C. (2017). "sich des Dunkeln bewusst werden"—Theater- und gestaltpädagogische Schattenarbeit. *Thepakos. Interdisziplinäre Zeitschrift für Theater und Theaterpädagogik., 33*, 16–28.

Schön, D. A. (1983). *The reflective practitioner. How professionals think in action*. Temple Smith.

Schön, D. A. (1987). *Educating the reflective practitioner*. Jos-sey-Bass.

Schütz, A., & Luckmann, T. (2017). *Strukturen der Lebenswelt*. UVK Verlagsgesellschaft mbH.

Soeffner, H.-G. (1989). Handlung—Szene—Inszenierung: zur Problematik des "Rahmen"-Konzeptes bei der Analyse von Interaktionsprozessen. In H.-G. Soeffner (Ed.), *Auslegung des Alltags—Der Alltag der Auslegung. Zur wissenssoziologischen Konzeption einer sozialwissenschaftlichen Hermeneutik* (pp. 140–157). Suhrkamp.

Spiegel von, H. (2018). *Methodisches Handeln in der Sozialen Arbeit*. Ernst Reinhardt.

Tov, E., Kunz, R., & Stämpfli, A. (2016). *Schlüsselsituationen der Sozialen Arbeit. Professionalität durch Wissen, Reflexion und Diskurs in Communities of Practice*. hep Verlag.

Part II
Theoretical and Methodological Background

Chapter 4
Gestalt Theory and the Basic Assumptions of Humanistic Psychotherapy

Since the aim of our book is to convey actionable knowledge in a practical and user-friendly way, we refrain from complicated expositions and try to present the relevant background as simply and briefly as possible. In the following chapters, we will discuss Gestalt theory. Starting with the general principles of humanistic approaches, we identify the special characteristics of the Gestalt approach and begin to establish connections between these and our case examples. In particular, we explain the philosophical roots of the Gestalt 'attitude', personality development processes and methodological approaches. The theoretical presentations refer to Gestalt therapy. In the practical section of the book, we discuss their significance for counselling in social work contexts.

Humanistic Psychotherapy

Gestalt therapy is one of a number of approaches to psychotherapy labelled as humanistic. These share a focus on supporting "psychological growth (in terms of personal development and differentiation in social contexts) by activating specifically human resources (potential), allowing these to unfold towards a meaningful, self-realising, authentic life" (AGHPT, 2012, p. 24). Promoting "self-actualisation"stimulates clients' creativity and vitality, and thus strengthens their ability to design and structure their reality and to regulate themselves (AGHPT, 2012, p. 26). Humanistic psychology sees the striving for growth and self-realisation as a trait shared by all humans (ibid., 24); this process of personal development can be supported by certain methods and techniques.

The existentialist justification of humanistic approaches is reflected in their central goal of promoting the individual's ability to conceptualise and perceive, thereby increasing both their behavioural possibilities and their awareness of the inherent responsibility for themselves, others and the environment that such freedom entails

A. Schachameier et al., *Gestalt in Social Work*,
https://doi.org/10.1007/978-3-031-95528-0_4

(ibid., 26). The aim of counselling is to "help the client gain a sense of their identity, boundaries, and sovereignty within their social contracts, as well as to define, protect and expand these, in order to build a fulfilling and purpose-oriented path in life" (ibid.). This process can bring about "centeredness, clarity, direction, and grounding" (ibid.).

These basic assumptions can be found in both Gestalt therapy and Gestalt pedagogy. However, certain characteristics of Gestalt approaches distinguish them from other humanistic approaches; in particular, the experiential and processual nature of Gestalt, with its focus on emotional experience, is of importance in therapy, pedagogy and counselling. In the literature (Cooper, 2012; Cooper et al., 2010; Elliot et al., 2013), explorations of these concepts can be found using terms such as "humanistic", "experiential", "experience-oriented", "process-oriented", or "emotion-focused".

Contact Phases

To introduce the theoretical foundations of Gestalt therapy in which our methods and techniques are grounded, we start by describing the contact phases, both in their ordered and disordered states, and the process model of holistic change. In so doing, we refer to Fig. 4.1, which depicts the different phases of the contact cycle model by comparing them to the phases of food intake.

The starting point for this model is the idea that each person has needs which come to the fore depending on the moment-to-moment situation; for example, if a person's organism demands food, they may notice a feeling of hunger. Alternatively, a psychological need may surface, such as a desire for closeness to another person.

The perception of this need is the first phase in this four-stage model, also known as *pre-contact*. On perceiving a need, the next step is to orient oneself in the 'outside world', i.e. to see where this need can be met—for example, where there is food to

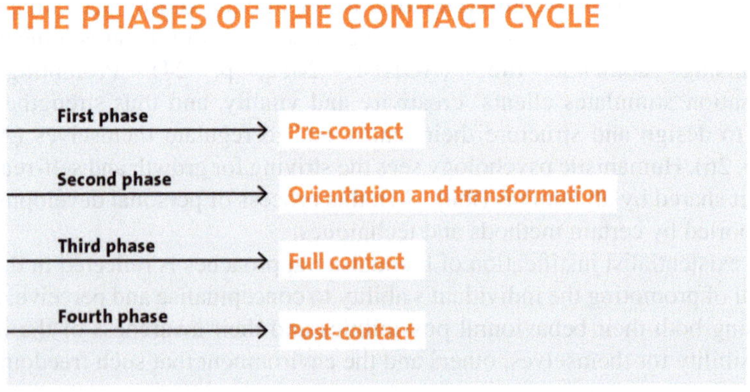

Fig. 4.1 The phases of the contact cycle (Based on Dreitzel, 2004, p. 37)

eat or someone to make contact with. Once located, the person may then move towards this potential source of fulfillment, for example by going to the fridge or approaching another person who might be able to participate in closeness. This corresponds to the second phase, namely of *orientation and transformation*.

Next, in our examples, the food is ingested and chewed, or tenderness is exchanged with another person. This phase is described as *full contact*. The last phase involves digestion, i.e. in relation to food, the absorption of nutrients and the excretion of the 'non-useful'. In contact with another person, this might involve tuning in to the experience, letting it 'land', in hindsight. This phase is called *post-contact*.

Blocks to the satisfaction of needs can occur during any of the four phases. To stay with the example of food intake: a person may have difficulties in perceiving their hunger or in orienting towards something edible, or may not chew or digest appropriately. Similarly, in the example of needing closeness, a person may find it difficult to recognise or perceive this need, or to approach another person, to really engage in contact, or to allow the experience to sink in after it has happened.

In Gestalt therapy, we engage in a kind of experiential research with our clients to find out where and how clients block the process of satisfying their needs. When needs arise, they always occur within a context of past experiences which constitute the individual's biography. As such, the emerging need can be seen as the *foreground*, or *figure*, and unavoidably arises against a *background* of the person's life experiences. The foreground or figure is both influenced by this background, and only comprehendible when seen in the context thereof. This interplay between figure and background can be referred to as a 'Gestalt'.

In Gestalt counselling, the aim is to make conscious the ways in which a person cognitively, emotionally, and physically blocks this process of satisfying their needs. Often, particular aspects of the person's background that cause a behaviour or a typical figure in the foreground are not initially conscious. In contrast, a healthy organism develops good figures, meaning that the organism perceives its needs and performs behaviours which satisfy these needs appropriately; we can describe this as the ability to *self-regulate* in exchange with the environment.

Gestalt counsellors view 'misguided' attempts at need satisfaction not as a deficit or disorder, but rather as adaptation mechanisms that were vital in an earlier phase of life in a specific environment in order to avoid having to repeat painful experiences again and again. For example, if a child's desire for more closeness to their caregivers is continuously denied, they develop strategies to compensate for this repeated frustration and experience of lack. In so doing, they are adapting to their social environment.

This brief introductory explanation contains essential aspects of the foundations of Gestalt therapeutic theory. The example of food intake and its comparison with the assimilation of psychological needs was used originally by Perls (2002a, b, p. 52). Many authors who have written about Gestalt therapy refer back to this, including Dreitzel (1992, pp. 45, 46); in his presentation of the phases of the contact cycle, he emphasises the positive aspects of aggression. This refers to the energy that is necessary to be able to influence the environment (Dreitzel, 2004, p. 101).

Starting with the example of hunger, if followed through, a person will move into the phase of "manipulation of the environment" (ibid.). In breaking bread, carving meat or mashing potatoes, a "dismantling, crushing, breaking down into its components, a de-structuring" takes place (Dreitzel, 1992, pp. 45, 46). Nature is "processed" (ibid.) and made usable for the individual.

> This aggressive process continues through biting, chewing and swallowing. In the pleasurable act of tasting and chewing, the contact process reaches its climax; the entire sensorimotor attention of the organism is now focused on the mouth, the current point of contact between organism and environment. Finally, a feeling of satiation sets in, and the figure (the need for food) fades away as the excitement of the organism subsides and finally disappears completely. The organism can now integrate that which is assimilable and excrete the rest. (Dreitzel, 1992, pp. 45, 46).

Dreitzel describes the process of exchange between an organism and its environment, emphasising the positive aspect of 'dental' aggression. The use of the term 'aggression'in this context may be perceived as problematic by some, as aggression is usually negatively or destructively connoted in our culture. However, in both Gestalt pedagogy and Gestalt therapy, the term aggression has a specific meaning. It is understood as an energy that is necessary for an organism to fulfill its needs and to engage constructively with its environment. Perls describes it as follows:

> Aggression is not only a destructive energy, but the force which is behind all our activities, without which we could do nothing at all. Aggression not only makes us attack, it also makes us tackle things; it does not only destroy, it also builds up: it not only makes us steal and rob, it also lies behind our endeavors to take hold and to master what we have a right to. (Perls, 1992, p. 43).

Both Dreitzel and Perls wish to make clear with these comparisons that the organism must critically engage with the information from the environment, with the 'psychic nourishment'; only in this way is healthy development possible. Dental aggression allows for a testing, or figuratively speaking, a dissection and chewing, of what has been taken in. For example, it can be problematic if information or messages from the environment are 'swallowed' and adopted without question. At the very latest, the post-contact phase offers the opportunity to review the content, categorise it, evaluate it, and decide what is to be integrated and what is to be discarded.

The individual's personal background plays an important role in determining their ability to make contact; it can either support or hinder therein. The relationship of a figure to its background gives the Gestalt its meaning (Perls, 2005, p. 94). Those who grew up in a pleasant family climate, were well cared for, and received a lot of affection, usually also form more positive self-concepts. On the other hand, those who had to spend their childhood in an environment of disinterest, rejection or violence were and are disadvantaged, as they simply had fewer supportive experiences. Corresponding background structures are formed accordingly.

Gestalt Psychology: Figure and Background

The Gestalt theoretical terms 'figure' or 'foreground', and 'background' or 'ground' come from the Berlin School of Gestalt Psychology, whose most important representatives were Wertheimer, Koffka, and Köhler (AGHPT, 2012, p. 23). Kurt Goldstein, who was closely connected to them, describes the principle of self-actualisation of an organism (Goldstein, 1934). Alongside the findings of the Berlin Gestalt psychologists, these concepts form an essential framework of Gestalt therapy as developed by Fritz and Laura Perls.

In their foundational work "Gestalt Therapy", Perls et al. (1985, p. 13) thus see the interplay between figure and ground as being at the core of their theory of Gestalt therapy. They distinguish between healthy and disturbed figure/ground processes. The former are represented by attention, concentration, interest, concern, excitement and grace; the latter by confusion, boredom, compulsions, fixations, fear, amnesias, stagnation and self-consciousness. A blockage is always connected in some way to the background; figure formation is always related to the life experiences which form the background. "The concept of a Gestalt is thus a concept of experience, it means the way we experience "world" as what we encounter in the organism/environment field." (Dreitzel, 1992, p. 46).

According to Hartmann-Kottek (2004), the term "Gestalt" can be used synonymously with "wholeness" (Hartmann-Kottek, 2004, p. 49). A "Gestalt" is a structural unit that at the same time represents more than the sum of its parts. This basic idea is also found in the philosophical school of thought of holism according to Smuts (1926).

The "Gestalt" is an "indivisible but transposable relationship structure", such as "a melody, a behavioural pattern, or a self-image" (Hartmann-Kottek, 2004, p. 49). It is a figure which exists against a background. "Gestalt" also means a "dynamic unity" or a "creatively changing form" (ibid.).

Organismic Self-regulation and Self-actualisation

Perls (1980) speaks of a basic law of organismic self-regulation, as the dynamics of figure and ground ensure that only one event is ever in the foreground at one time and can determine the situation (Perls, 1980, p. 97). This means that when a person is bothered by a topic which is causing them problems, they can be supported through therapy or counselling through the figure-ground process being 're-activated', by being made conscious, so that blockages can be resolved. Through dialogue and other interventions to raise the person's level of awareness on a cognitive, emotional, and possibly also physical level, therapists or counsellors enable clients to come up with their own solutions. The organism self-regulates and self-actualises.

According to the principle of the tendency towards conciseness, the organism always pursues the intention of finding a creative, 'good' Gestalt (Hartmann-Kottek, 2004, p. 55). This can be understood as the individual's attempt to engage constructively with their living environment. So-called 'open Gestalts' push for closure, which in Gestalt jargon is often referred to as 'unfinished business'. This means that a "Gestalt which is blocked during formation, and therefore unfinished" naturally drives towards conclusion; examples of such situations could include the sudden or inexplicable ending of a relationship, an interrupted professional career, a failed attempt at reconciliation with a dying person, a staved-off grieving process etc. "Unfinished Gestalts" become fixed in place, hold on; completed forms drop away like ripe fruit into the background of a person's biography. Recognising, closing and letting go of Gestalts is liberating, and enables new, full engagement with life in the here and now" (Hartmann-Kottek, 2004, p. 49). This process of self-actualisation is a fundamental humanistic principle (Sanders, 2015, pp. 30, 31; Perls, 2002a, b, p. 23, Rogers, 2009, p. 183). Inner processes, perceptions and insights are integrated into the person's self-concept, and they grow.

References

AGHPT. (2012). *Antrag der AGHPT an den Wissenschaftlichen Beirat Psychotherapie auf wissenschaftliche Anerkennung des Verfahrens "Humanistischen Psychotherapie"*. https://aghpt.de/antrag-wissenschaftliche-anerkennung/ (Stand 20.07.2019).

Cooper, M. (2012). *Existential counselling*. PCCS Books.

Cooper, M., Watson, J. C., & Hölldampf, D. (2010). *Person-Centered and experiential therapies work. A review of the research on counseling, psychotherapy and related practices*. PCCS Books.

Dreitzel, H. P. (1992). *Emotionales Gewahrsein. Psychologische und gesellschaftliche Perspektiven in der Gestalttherapie*. Deutscher Taschenbuch Verlag.

Dreitzel, H. P. (2004). *Gestalt und Prozess. Eine psychotherapeutische Diagnostik oder: Der gesunde Mensch hat wenig Charakter*. EHP.

Elliot, R., Greenberg, L. S., Watson, J. C., Timulak, L., & Freire, E. (2013). Research on humansitic-experiential psychotherapies. In M. J. Lambert (Ed.), *Bergin & Garfield's handbook of psychotherapy an behaviour change* (pp. 495–538). Wiley.

Goldstein, K. (1934). *Der Aufbau des Organismus*. Nijhoff.

Hartmann-Kottek, L. (2004). *Gestalttherapie*. Springer.

Perls, F. S. (1980). Gestalt—Wachstum—Integration. Aufsätze, Vorträge, Therapiesitzungen. In H. Petzold (Ed.), *Integrative Therapie*. Junfermann.

Perls, L. (1992). In J. Wysong (Ed.), *The gestalt approach: Living at the boundary. Collected works of Laura Perls*. The Gestalt Journal Press.

Perls, F. S. (2002a). *Gestalt-Therapie in Aktion. Konzepte der Humanwissenschaft*. Klett-Cotta.

Perls, F. S. (2002b). *Grundlagen der Gestalttherapie. Einführung und Sitzungsprotokolle*. Klett-Cotta.

Perls, L. (2005). Leben an der Grenze. Essays und Anmerkungen zur Gestalttherapie. In M. Sreckovic (Ed.), Bergisch Gladbach: EHP.

Perls, F. S., Hefferline, R. F., & Goodman, P. (1985). *Gestalt-Therapie. Wiederbelebung des Selbst*. Ex Libris.

Rogers, C. R. (2009). *Die klientenzentrierte Gesprächspsychotherapie. Client-Centered Therapy*. Fischer.

Sanders, P. (2015). *Person-centred counselling*. PCCS Books.

Smuts, J. C. (1926). *Holismus and evolution*. Macmillan.

Chapter 5
Contact Functions and Interruptions

Every person must adapt to their environment throughout their life. As part of this process of socialisation, patterns of thought and behaviour are acquired in order to navigate familial, educational, professional and other 'life worlds', as well as to interact appropriately within them. This requires certain adaptive 'contact functions'which, although necessary, can also be over-applied, leading to over-adaptation and inappropriate processing of life events. Such instances can be referred to as 'contact interruptions'.

From a Gestalt theory perspective, the way in which these mechanisms block contact in the here-and-now is significant (Stein, 2005, p. 67). The contacts functions are to be understood not only as stemming from the person's biography or as a defense against inner and intrapsychic conflicts, "but rather more comprehensively as a person's creative, meaningful reaction within the framework of their individual biography" (ibid.).

As described in the section above, a contact process is divided into pre-contact, orientation and transformation, full contact, and post-contact (Dreitzel, 2004, p. 37 ff.). Disturbances can occur during any of the phases, thus preventing contact from being appropriately carried out. Gestalt theory speaks of the contact functions and disturbances, which occur through introjection, retroflection, deflection, confluence or projection. We will briefly discuss the meaning of these terms below.

Introjection

Through the lens of Gestalt therapy, the contact function of introjection describes the way in which a person may unconsciously adopt and internalise values, attitudes and perspectives from their environment, which may in turn hinder or even block the satisfaction of their own needs (Stein, 2005, p. 68). According to Stein, introjection does not involve a conscious process of assimilation, but rather involves "a

A. Schachameier et al., *Gestalt in Social Work*,
https://doi.org/10.1007/978-3-031-95528-0_5

passive acceptance and adoption of what the environment provides in terms of norms, ideas, emotional concepts, etc." (ibid.). Such introjects are experienced as belonging to one's own being, meaning that the contact boundary becomes elusive. Introjects have a particular significance for the transgenerational transmission of values and culture, and can be seen as having a "culture-forming function" (Gremmler-Fuhr, 1999, p. 369) which ensures the transmission and adoption of knowledge and rules. Typical examples of introjects are sentences often heard in counselling sessions: "I should..." (Stein, 2005, p. 68).

Example: Chapter on Co-Dependency.

Retroflection

Unlike introjection, the contact function of retroflection involves a stronger demarcation between the person and the environment: "Impulses directed towards the outside are restrained and instead directed against one's own organism" (Stein, 2005, p. 71). Through this contact function, the person learns to relate to themselves as they would like to relate to their fellow human beings, or relate to their fellow human beings as they would like to be treated themselves (ibid.). This means that an inner impulse which was originally directed outwards is retroflected, or addressed to oneself (ibid.). Stein also identifies a culture-forming function of this contact mechanism, because "the restraint of aggressive impulses, but also the restraint of affection and expressions of love [fulfil] important cultural functions for living together in our society" (ibid., 72). Negative consequences can, however, be an "inappropriate demarcation and restraint in the situation" as well as a "fixation of this contact function and a blockage of opposing, non-delineating functions" (ibid.).

Example: Chapter on Parent Counselling.

Deflection

In the case of deflection, the exchange processes between the person and the environment are blocked or reduced (Stein, 2005, p. 73). From the person's point of view, contact can only be allowed in a weakened form or may even be (un)consciously avoided. Avoidance of eye contact, chronic jocularity or irony can all be expressions of deflection (ibid.). According to Stein, people usually rely on deflection when they have experienced "that contact with people was associated with emotional injury. It therefore seems better to avoid (close) contact in future, in order not to find oneself sustaining new injuries" (ibid.).

Example: Chapter on Addiction

Confluence

Confluence refers to a merging between the organism and the environment. This is accompanied by the lack of ability to distinguish between oneself and others or to tolerate these boundaries. Whilst the capacity to connect and empathise with others is an important function in order to be able to engage actively in contact (Dreitzel, 2004, p. 64; Stein, 2005, p. 70), it becomes problematic when one's own feelings and needs are no longer clearly perceived and this results in an inability to articulate them (ibid.). In such cases, a person's experience of their own needs is weak and diffuse, if indeed they perceive them at all. The boundary to the environment, including other people, is very permeable and blurred (Dreitzel, 2004, p. 65).

Example: Chapter on Co-Dependency

Projection

In projection, people experience something as being outside although it actually belongs inside (Dreitzel, 2004, p. 56). Emotions, impulses, thoughts, and ideas are shifted onto other people because the person cannot accept or bear them in themselves. The contact boundary thus moves 'inside' one's own organism, and one's own parts are split off (Stein, 2005, pp. 69, 70; Gremmler-Fuhr, 2001, p. 370). In projection, formative experiences that we have had with significant people in our biographies can be projected onto therapists or other people (Dreitzel, 2004, p. 57).

Example: Chapter on Chronic Psychosis.

In the context of counselling, it is possible for clients to become aware of their inner processes, recognise forms of contact interruption, and integrate alternative patterns of thinking or behaviour that correspond more to their own life goals and needs. This process of change and growth often follows very specific phases in practice; these will be the subject of the next chapter (Chap. 6).

References

Dreitzel, H. P. (2004). *Gestalt und Prozess. Eine psychotherapeutische Diagnostik oder: Der gesunde Mensch hat wenig Charakter*. EHP.

Gremmler-Fuhr, M. (1999). Grundkonzepte und Modelle der Gestalttherapie. In R. Fuhr, M. Sreckovic, & M. Gremmler-Fuhr (Eds.), *Handbuch der Gestalttherapie* (pp. 345–392). Hogrefe.

Gremmler-Fuhr, M. (2001). Grundkonzepte und Modelle der Gestalttherapie. In R. Fuhr, M. Sreckovic, & M. Gremmler-Fuhr (Eds.), *Handbuch der Gestalttherapie*. Hogrefe.

Stein, R. (2005). *Einführung in die pädagogische Gestaltarbeit und die gestalttheoretische Sicht von Störungen*. Schneider-Verl. Hohengehren.

Chapter 6
Holistic Change Processes

Over the course of his therapeutic work with clients, Perls (2002a, b, p. 63) was able to observe certain typical phases of change, which he referred to as the ‘layers of neurosis’. Staemmler and Bock rely on this model and have described the following characteristic steps of change based on their practical experiences and observations (see Fig. 6.1):

In the first phase, *stagnation,* no change takes place; personal complaints and the situation are often considered unchangeable, and the client feels dependent on help from the outside to change anything (Staemmler, 1987, p. 33). As awareness of the

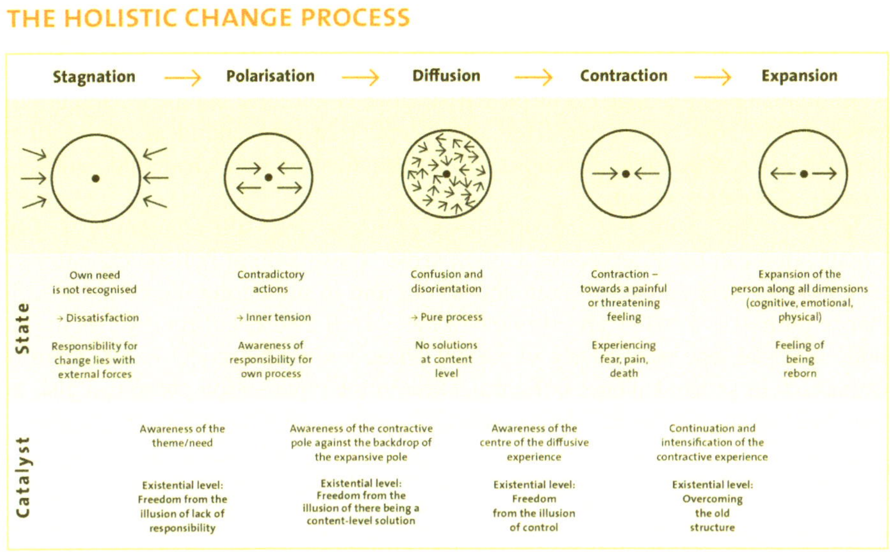

Fig. 6.1 The Holistic Change Process (based on Staemmler & Bock, 1998, p. 121)

A. Schachameier et al., *Gestalt in Social Work*,
https://doi.org/10.1007/978-3-031-95528-0_6

theme is gained, the client may transition into the second phase, namely *polarisation.* Not only does the client's underlying need become clear, but so too does the way in which they themselves are blocking (avoiding) this need; the client tries to solve the problem on the content level (ibid. 33 ff.). In the third phase, *diffusion*, the client 'loses the plot', as cognitive understanding dissolves and the poles blur; the client lets go of the fixation with solving the problem on the content level (ibid.). Staemmler and Bock see this as an important turning point; this is where the client enters the stage of *contraction* or *implosion.* Here resides fear, helplessness, the feeling of being frozen, dead, or dissolving; the organism experiences a holistic contraction (ibid.). Through the intensive holistic experience of this state, the client passes into the fifth phase, *expansion,* and a creative solution is born. This phase is often associated with the feeling of happiness, relief, liberation, or inner peace (ibid.).

In this process, the person's own healing potential is activated, complete with its individual resources, and a solution arises as if by itself—this is what is meant by the term organismic self-regulation. Change occurs not through effort, but through conscious experience.

This apparent paradox is an essential part of Gestalt therapeutic theory, because "change happens when someone becomes what they are, not when they try to become something they are not" (Beisser, 1997, p. 139). For this to occur, it is necessary to "fully engage in one's present being" without trying to force a change (ibid.). Ultimately, the "self-organising wisdom" of the organism can activate self-healing capacity and bring about a more suitable alignment of the self (Bohart & Tallman, 2010, p. 93).

The phases of a holistic change process as described by Staemmler and Bock are primarily observed in the context of in-depth therapeutic sessions. However, its core principle is transferable to the context of counselling in social work, namely that even small steps of change occur primarily when cognitions, emotions, and bodily sensations are consciously perceived and accepted. Insights and ideas for solutions can then emerge, possible directions for development become clear, and pathways towards solutions open up.

In our video examples, the principles of organismic self-regulation or self-actualisation can be observed on a small scale. These are not holistic change processes as we have described them above; our aim in presenting the entire holistic change process is to allow an overview of the overall theoretical context. As for the video material, one particularly important phase within the model is the phase of stagnation. In some sequences, the transition to the polarisation phase can also be seen. We therefore cover these two phases in more detail in the following section.

Stagnation

The starting point for any kind of change is dissatisfaction. This means that certain needs are not being met (Staemmler & Bock, 1998, p. 81). It is for this reason that people engage in counselling or therapy processes. The affected individuals may be suffering from symptoms of depression or addiction, often in connection with the failure of social relationships such as marriages or friendships (ibid.). "All these symptoms are perceived more or less as something that 'happens' to the person, that 'befalls' them from the outside; they sees themselves more as a victim rather than the master of their own fate" (ibid., 81). In our examples, for instance, a man experiencing difficulties with his son comes to parent counselling. His initial wish, however, is that someone talks to this child; there is no obvious motivation for change on his part.

Typically, people attempt to "influence the environment and other people in such a way that they contribute to an improvement of their own situation" (ibid.). Internally, the affected individuals "fixate" on the situation, which from their perspective is caused by external circumstances. They await "impulses from the outside" that will lead to a solution (ibid.). "The phase of stagnation is characterised by the fact that the person no longer senses themselves as a possible agent of change in their situation, but instead attributes the power for this change to external forces, upon which they then naturally experience themselves as being dependent. In this state, the person may be able to do a lot externally, on a motor level, but in terms of a possible change, they remain motionless in their status quo" (ibid., 81).

At this point, we would like to briefly point out a special feature that often occurs in social work. Unlike psychotherapy, which clients generally choose voluntarily, clients in certain fields of social work are forced to partake in counselling. In one of our cases, a court ordered a cannabis user to attend addiction counselling sessions. The principle of stagnation becomes even more apparent here, as the youth attending mandatory addiction counselling sessions sees the problem as solely external. The pathway to an internal change process nonetheless remains the same as in voluntary counselling, as both require the individual to make decisions and take responsibility.

In the next phase, which is also of importance in some of the video sequences, a process of gaining awareness begins, enabling the individual to experience their actual underlying need more clearly.

Polarisation

When clients realise that it is not—or at least only partially—the external circumstances that are keeping them trapped in stagnation, but that there is in fact scope for manageable action, this represents a decisive step in the process of change (Staemmler & Bock, 1998, p. 84). The person becomes aware that they can take responsibility for themselves. They no longer see themselves only as a victim of the situation, but understand that it is possible to influence the situation in an active and creative way (ibid.). At this point, something new enters consciousness: the need, the longing, the desire to change something specific and to take responsibility for the necessary action. Staemmler and Bock refer to this as the "expansive" pole (ibid.). At the same time, however, the other side of the coin appears: the inner resistance to this desire for change, the so-called "contractive" pole. This can be due to a fear of change or unease because another basic need—the desire for the security of the status quo—is threatened (ibid. 83). When both poles enter conscious awareness, this often leads to a state of inner tension (ibid., 84) hence the name of this stage, *polarisation*.

> The essence of the polarisation phase thus lies in the simultaneous occurrence of an expansive and a contractive action, which results in both actions cancelling each other out in their effect. (Staemmler & Bock, 1998, p. 84).

Both types of action, which are known as the expansive and the contractive pole, are necessary and must be experienced in the further change process. It is not possible to "maintain one pole and eliminate the other" (ibid.), given that both are needs.

In the example with addiction counselling, the client feels a desire to reduce his consumption. At the same time, however, he is also aware that this would necessitate great change to aspects of his everyday life which currently bring him joy. It is as if the expansive and contractive poles turn to face each other internally.

We do not describe the further phases of the model in more detail here, as they are not relevant to the video examples; moreover, the diffusion phase at the very latest involves an intense, emotionally charged process which should be worked through in an appropriate context such as with a trained psychotherapist.

However, counselling processes in social work can still make use of the earlier stages of this model to support clients to grow personally and find solutions for current problems. Often, a central goal is to increase the person's awareness of inner parts of themselves which may be helpful, or to develop new perspectives on a current problem. This process of self-actualisation, as outlined by humanistic psychology, can also be understood as personality development. The following chapter (Chap. 7) deals with this in more detail.

References

Beisser, A. R. (1997). Die paradoxe Theorie der Veränderung. In A. R. Beisser (Ed.), *Wozu brauche ich Flügel? Ein Gestalttherapeut betrachtet sein Leben als Gelähmter*. Wuppertal.

Bohart, A. C., & Tallman, K. (2010). Client as active self-healers. Implications for the person-centered approach. In M. Cooper, J. C. Watson, & D. Hölldampf (Eds.), *Person-Centered and experiential therapies work. A review of the research on counselling*. Monmouth PCCS Books.

Perls, F. S. (2002a). *Gestalt-Therapie in Aktion. Konzepte der Humanwissenschaft*. Klett-Cotta.

Perls, F. S. (2002b). *Grundlagen der Gestalttherapie. Einführung und Sitzungsprotokolle*. Klett-Cotta.

Staemmler, F.-M. (1987). *Was ist was? Das Vokabular der Gestalttherapie. PBZ Publikation Heft 5*. Waschkowski/PBZ.

Staemmler, F.-M., & Bock, W. (1998). *Ganzheitliche Veränderung in der Gestalttherapie*. Peter Hammer Verlag.

Chapter 7
Incongruence and Flexibility

To quote the diagnostic book by Dreitzel (2004) of the same title, "the healthy person has little character"! Ideally, a person can adapt to a wide variety of internal or external circumstances; however, success in mastering new situations necessitates a certain inner flexibility. A rigid character structure can be a hindrance in many cases, and can even lead to a crisis. To cope with an internal or external conflict or challenge, self-concepts which are obstructive, inappropriate or rigid may need to be softened and new behaviours integrated.

Schulz von Thun, who was heavily influenced by humanistic psychology, illustrated such processes of personal development with the aid of 'personality value squares'or the 'inner team' (Schulz von Thun, 2006a, b, 2012).

Value Squares

According to Schulz von Thun, humans often have not only a rather underdeveloped part of their personality, but also a too strongly expressed pole, which can lead to either inauthentic or situationally inappropriate behaviour and experiences. The goal is therefore to become more flexible again, gaining access to the appropriate resources for the respective situation (ibid.).

The "authentic, self-aligned" pole stands for characteristic aspects of a person, which, if they are very strongly developed, can be inappropriate in some situations. The "situationally appropriate"pole refers to adaptive behaviours that, if leaned into too heavily, can lead to over-adaptation, or a person holding back their thoughts and emotions in interpersonal interactions to a degree which becomes self-denying.

In Table 7.1, for the purpose of clarification and illustration, polarities which are relevant in the case studies in Part III are summarised according to the four categories of the value square (see Fig. 7.1), namely:

A. Schachameier et al., *Gestalt in Social Work*,
https://doi.org/10.1007/978-3-031-95528-0_7

Table 7.1 Polarities value squares

"Off-track": Situationally Inappropriate	Both/and: Situationally appropriate or authentic, self-aligned		"Off-track": Self-denying over-adaptation
Despair	Scepticism	Trust	Blind Optimism
Helplessness	Delegation of responsibility	Personal responsibility	Self-importance
Isolation	Withdrawal	Contact	Confluence
Self-denial	Calm	Awareness of the problem	Depressive brooding
Confluence	Harmony	Confrontation	Aggression
Addiction	Relaxation	Engagement	Over-exertion
Fear	Concern	Safety/security	Excessive naivety
Isolation	Autonomy	Connection	Symbiosis
Insanity	Deviation	Grasp of reality/ normality	Over-adaptation
Resignation	Relaxation	Engagement	Over-exertion
Helplessness	Openness	Competence	Perfectionism
Abdicating responsibility	Accepting help	Personal responsibility	Self-importance
Overwhelm	Confrontation	Acceptance	Indifference
Neglect	Self-determination	Leadership/ Support	Control
Isolation	Withdrawal	Contact	Confluence

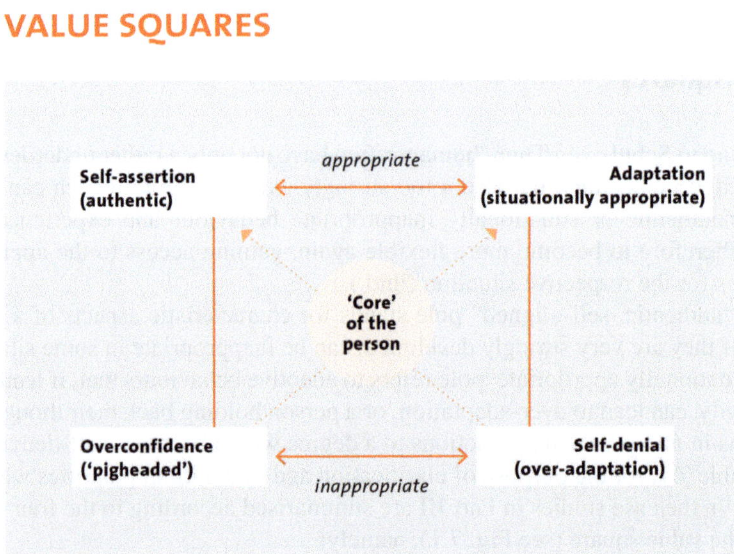

Fig. 7.1 Value Squares (based on Schulz von Thun, 2012, p. 68)

1. Situationally inappropriate
2. Situationally appropriate
3. Authentic, self-aligned.
4. Self-denying over-adaptation.

Further examples can be found in Schulz von Thun (2006a).

Schulz von Thun's central thoughts on the subject of personal development are similar to those of Perls. He sees the fundamental teaching of Gestalt therapy as being on the differentiation and integration of the self (Perls, 1980). Perls writes: "Differentiation as such leads to polarities. As dualities, these polarities can easily come into conflict and paralyse each other. By integrating opposing traits, we make people whole again. For example, weakness and tyrannical behaviour integrate as calm firmness" (Perls, 1980, p. 155; translated from the German edition). In order to behave in a way which is authentic *and* appropriate to the situation, a person must be aware of their various inner parts and decide which should be brought into contact with the outside world.

According to the Gestalt therapist Joseph Zinker (2005), a person with a healthy self-concept is aware of many opposing forces within themselves. They are willing to see themselves "in a multitude of "contradictory" ways", experience relationships between different inner parts and can bring these parts into contact as they choose (Zinker, 1977, p. 198). This can mean a whole conglomerate of different polarities, such as sentimentality versus callousness or control versus impulsivity (Zinker, 1977, p. 198). A person with a pathological self-concept, on the other hand, sees themselves "in a unilateral stereotypical manner"; they are "always this and never that", and their awareness of the multitude of inner forces and feelings which inhabit them is very limited (Zinker, 1977, p. 199). Such a person has a large blind spot and is unable to accept or perceive many parts of themselves (ibid., 199).

A term coined by Rogers in this context is so-called "incongruity" (Rogers, 1959). This refers to a discrepancy in the way a person experiences themselves, as their ideal self comes into conflict with their lived experience of their real self. This perceptible difference makes people more susceptible to mental illnesses (Rogers, 1959). Perls formulates it this way: "*Many people dedicate their lives to actualize a concept of what they should be like, rather than to actualize themselves. This difference between self-actualizing and self-image actualizing is very important" (*Perls, 1976, *p. 20; emphasis in the original).*

In relation to the graphic by Schulz von Thun (Fig. 7.1), this could mean, for example, that a person is almost always understanding and helpful, but finds it very difficult to set boundaries. The need for boundaries and feelings like anger or rage, are suppressed, but still perceived. This leads to a state of incongruity and to inner conflict. A solution might consist of acknowledging these unwanted parts and integrating them, in order to be able to react more appropriately to the situation. Schulz von Thun speaks of an "inner team" of inner parts, some of which can also turn out to be inherited from one's parents (Schulz von Thun, 2006b, p. 223). It is important that all inner parts "have their right, have their say, have their place.

Finding this inner balance is important for mental health. The banishment of often unwanted and also often unconscious parts can lead to illness" (ibid. 228). "For example, if parts are chronically not recognised, tremendous emotional muscle power is often needed to maintain the facade; the use of medication, drugs and alcohol can only delay the collapse. In people with a very strong constitution, this state can also become eternal" (Schulz von Thun, 2006b, p. 229). Healthy self-leadership goes hand in hand with good access to feelings and parts of the personality, which, when brought into operation consciously and appropriately to the situation, enable confident mastery of potentially difficult interactions and conflicts (Dietz, 2007).

Supporting clients therapeutically with their experiences can enable personality development processes as they have been described here. In so doing, the Gestalt therapist's *attitude* is crucial. The Gestalt attitude has philosophical roots, which will be explained in the next section.

References

Dietz, I. (2007). *Selbst in Führung. Achtsam die Innenwelt meistern*. Junfermann.

Dreitzel, H. P. (2004). *Gestalt und Prozess. Eine psychotherapeutische Diagnostik oder: Der gesunde Mensch hat wenig Charakter*. EHP.

Perls, F. S. (1976). *Gestalt therapy verbatim. An action approach to deepening awareness and living fully in the here and now, as experienced in workshops at Esalen institute*. Bantam Book & Real People Press.

Perls, F. S. (1980). Gestalt—Wachstum—Integration. Aufsätze, Vorträge, Therapiesitzungen. In H. Petzold (Ed.), *Integrative Therapie*. Junfermann.

Rogers, C. R. (1959). A theory of therapy, personality and interpersonal relationships, as developed in the client-centered framework. In S. Koch (Ed.), *Psychology: A study of science, Bd. 3: Formulations of the person and the social context* (pp. 184–256). McGraw-Hill.

Schulz von Thun, F. (2006a). *Miteinander reden: 2. Stile, Werte und Persönlichkeits-entwicklung. Differentielle Psychologie der Kommunikation*. Rowohlt.

Schulz von Thun, F. (2006b). *Miteinander reden: 3. Das "Innere Team" und situationsgerechte Kommunikation. Kommunikation, Person, Situation*. Rowohlt.

Schulz von Thun, F. (2012). *Miteinander reden: Fragen und Antworten*. Rowohlt.

Zinker, J. (1977). *Creative process in gestalt therapy*. Brunner/Mazel.

Zinker J. (2005). *Gestalttherapie als kreativer Prozeß*. Paderborn: Junfermann Verlag.

Chapter 8
Philosophical Roots

Phenomenology and existentialism are two significant philosophical approaches that have had a strong influence on the theoretical foundation of Gestalt therapy and humanistic psychology. These schools of thought are woven not only into the Gestalt attitude and methods, but the way Gestalt practitioners (and indeed other humanistic psychologies) conceive of humanity itself.

Phenomenology

In their work with clients, Fritz and Laura Perls, the founders of Gestalt therapy, were primarily concerned with increasing their clients' awareness for their actions and behaviours. Accordingly, in Gestalt therapy, clients are "taught to experience themselves" (Perls et al., 1985, p. 36); the aim is that they come to feel what is present (Perls et al., 1985, p. 43ff.).

> But whenever we speak of the present, we shall mean the immediate, here-and-now present—the time of your present attention-span, the time that is *right now!* Remembering and anticipating are actual, but when they occur, they occur in the present (Perls et al., 1951, p. 32; emphasis in the original).

When re-enacting and reflecting on practical situations, as emphasised in our method, it is important that the actor comes into contact with their inner experience, i.e. their thoughts, feelings and bodily reactions. This encounter with our inner life always takes place, in spatial terms, where we are currently located (Zinker, 1977). That which is problematic arises in the here and now, albeit in an updated form. Grawe (2005) sees this as an important factor in psychotherapy, and we believe it also has significance in this context.

A. Schachameier et al., *Gestalt in Social Work*,
https://doi.org/10.1007/978-3-031-95528-0_8

Gestalt therapists work on the assumption of a 'continuum of awareness', a constant stream of experience that is perceptible from moment to moment. They encourage their clients to focus their attention again and again, and as holistically as possible (i.e. through cognitions, emotions and physical sensations), on this ongoing internal process (Staemmler, 2001, p. 446). The focus is therefore on the client's subjective experience of their life (Cooper, 2012, p. 13; Sanders, 2015, p. 21; Fleming Crocker, 2017, pp. 32, 33). The question of "how?", rather than "why?" is therefore of particular importance. By helping clients to describe and experience *how* they deal with a problematic life situation, the client can gain awareness—on cognitive, emotional and behavioural levels—into their own patterns.

This interest in perceivable, present-moment phenomena can be traced back to the founder of the school of phenomenology, Husserl (2018), who criticised the objectivist, natural-science-based mindset of his time. The individual's subjective experiences and perspectives are at the heart of Husserl's approach, along with the possibilities of insight offered by the contents of consciousness. Husserl sees consciousness as both intentional and always focused on contents. In order to apprehend the essence of a thing, he developed the method of phenomenological and eidetic reduction. Starting with the inquiry into objects in the world of our immediate experience, he focused on human perception of these objects' metaphysical existence. Only the phenomena as they appear in consciousness *through perception or memory* are the subject of analysis. Phenomenological inquiry is thus synonymous with our conscious sensory experience of the world; it thus necessitates the withholding of all theories, assumptions, and prejudices about the world and things.

The practical significance of this phenomenological reduction lies in the continuous feedback to the individual's immediate experiences, to the contents of consciousness, as they appear to the client in the here and now. According to Husserl, it is absolutely necessary to ask the person repeatedly—and in various ways—about their immediate experience of the phenomena around them, so as to discover patterns of 'interconnected essences'. The guideline is their actual experience, otherwise there is the risk of getting lost in fantasy (Fleming Crocker, 2017, p. 36). Through a descriptive enquiry from moment to moment, the essence of the contents of consciousness can be grasped and recognised (ibid., 33).

In other words, the current figure (i.e. the topic of the counselling process) is explored, experienced and expressed in relation to the background (current and past life situations); this allows what is obvious and essential to be revealed and grasped. In both the role-plays and our reflections on them, we repeatedly ask about the individual's feelings, physical reactions, and thoughts. The initial aim is simply to perceive what is really there, to find out the contents of the person's consciousness as they appear in the here and now. This reveals what is essential for understanding the situation in the specific context. This can be described as a phenomenological knowledge process.

Existentialism

Such questioning and exploration increases awareness among those concerned, in turn shedding light on alternative courses of action. Clients can then choose between different behavioural possibilities, and thus take more responsibility for their action or non-action. Perls et al (1951, p. 23) describe this as follows:

"One cannot on any rational ground take responsibility for what one is not in contact with. This applies to happenings in distant places of which perhaps one has never heard, but it also applies equally to events taking place in one's own life if one is not aware of them. If one makes contact with them and becomes intimately aware of what they are and how they figure in one's functioning, then one becomes responsible for them—not in the sense of now having to assume some burden that was not there before, but rather in the sense of now recognizing that it is oneself who determines in most instances whether they shall or shall not continue to exist."

The possibility of "taking responsibility"can also be considered in connection with the existential philosophical roots of humanistic approaches. These are based on the anthropological assumption that "existence precedes essence" (Sartre, 2007, p. 10). According to Sartre, a main exponent of existentialism, human life is not pre-determined, and neither is human nature unchangeable; in his words,

> Man is free, man is freedom. ... We are left alone, without excuse. That is what I mean when I say that man is condemned to be free. Condemned, because he did not create himself, yet is nevertheless at liberty, and from the moment that he is thrown into his world he is responsible for everything he does. (ibid.).

Perls formulates it similarly: "But responsibility is really response-ability, the ability to choose one's reactions." (Perls, 1973, p. 78). In this respect, clients have the opportunity to decide how they want to act in a similar situation in the future. This freedom to choose, to make a decision, is what is meant by taking responsibility.

We will supplement this phenomenological-existentialist perspective with some empirical findings in the next section.

References

Cooper, M. (2012). *Existential counselling*. PCCS Books.

Fleming Crocker, S. (2017). Die phänomenologische Methode bei Husserl und in der Gestalttherapie. *Gesta, 31*(1), 26–45.

Grawe, K. (2005). Empirisch validierte Wirkfaktoren der Psychotherapie. *Report Psychologie, 2005*(7/8), 311–315.

Husserl, E. (2018). *Die phänomenologische Methode*. Reclam.

Perls, F. S. (1973). *The gestalt-approach & eye witness to therapy*. Science and Behavior Books.

Perls, F. S., Hefferline, R. F., & Goodman, P. (1951). *Gestalt therapy. Excitement and growth in the human personality*. Julian Press.

Perls, F. S., Hefferline, R. F., & Goodman, P. (1985). *Gestalt-Therapie. Wiederbelebung des Selbst*. Ex Libris.

Sanders, P. (2015). *Person-centred counselling*. PCCS Books.
Sartre, J.-P. (2007). *Existentialism is a humanism*. Yale University Press.
Staemmler, F.-M. (2001). Gestalttherapeutische Methoden und Techniken—Der Geist der Gestalttherapie in Aktion. In R. Fuhr, M. Sreckovic, & M. Gremmler-Fuhr (Eds.), *Handbuch der Gestalttherapie*. Hogrefe.
Zinker, J. (1977). *Creative process in gestalt therapy*. Brunner/Mazel.

Chapter 9
Experiential Confrontation

In their well-known meta-analysis, Orlinsky et al. (1994) described a central factor of experiential humanistic approaches as being so-called "experiential confrontation". When the client's attention is guided towards their "immediate, processual experience and behaviour" (Strümpfel, 2012, p. 283) in the here and now, this is associated with a positive therapy outcome.

This speaks particularly to the phenomenological, hermeneutic methods and existentialist justifications at the root of Gestalt therapy. This includes the experiential or immediate, conscious, experiential exploration of one's own experience. By activating the person's awareness of their holistic (physical, mental and emotional) experience, confrontation with own individual situation becomes possible (Pernter, 2008, p. 115).

Fritz Perls also emphasises that "phenomenology is the most important and indispensable step we must take in order to know what is to be known" (Perls, 1981, p. 72; cit. According to Hartmann-Kottek, 2004, p. 133). When the client is guided to focus on their actual lived experience of relevant areas of their life, holistic awareness is created by directing their attention to their inner impulses, emotions, and accompanying body sensations or breathing. The attention is shifted from the topsoil – the topic of conversation – to the person's bodily expression and accompanying feelings, which often leads to a sort of emotional intensification (Strümpfel, 2012, p. 265). Mahrer et al. (1991, 1992) have shown that this process can initiate important moments in therapy.

Strümpfel (2012) summarises a series of process-outcome studies by Greenberg and colleagues (Greenberg, 1983, 1992, Clarke & Greenberg, 1986, Paivio & Greenberg, 1995, Greenberg & Foerster, 1996, Watson et al., 2010) that show the correlation between the *process variables* "depth of experience", "emotional activation" and "awareness of feelings" and the *outcome variables* "conflict resolution", "therapeutic goals" and "symptom change" (ibid., 280). It was found that the forms of therapeutic dialogue found in Gestalt therapy lead to a greater depth of

A. Schachameier et al., *Gestalt in Social Work*,
https://doi.org/10.1007/978-3-031-95528-0_9

experience, emotional activation, and awareness of feelings than client-centered mirroring or cognitive understanding (Strümpfel, 2006, p. 12).

From these studies, it was inferred that the successful resolution of an internal or external conflict can be predicted based on the presence of the following process variables during a session: "building of oppositional tension, emotional activation of the conflicting parts of the self, alternating representation of the conflicting parts of the self, access to the underlying (primary) feelings and needs" (Strümpfel, 2012, p. 288). In other words, a primary factor for effectiveness in therapeutic work is the clients' conscious experience of their internal processes. Our didactic concept with its focus on experiential case studies (see chapter "Reflections on Theories of Learning and Didactics") is based on these findings.

In another study, Elliot et al. (2004) repeatedly demonstrated that depth of experience is associated with a better therapy outcome. It is now generally accepted across the spectrum of psychotherapeutic schools of thought that emotional engagement and deep, experience-based exploration and reflection (Watson & Bedard, 2006) are associated with positive therapy outcomes. Herein lies the strength of the humanistic, emotion-oriented, experiential approaches, as they enable a deeply holistic experience and process.

The next chapter (Chap. 10) explores the basic attitude which lies at the root of the humanistic, experiential approaches.

References

Clarke, K. M., & Greenberg, L. S. (1986). Differential effects of the Gestalt two-chair intervention and problem solving in resolving decisional conflict. *Journal of Counseling Psychology, 33*(1), 11–15.

Elliot, R., Greenberg, L. S., & Lietaer, G. (2004). Research on experiential psychotherapies. In M. J. Lambert (Ed.), *Bergin & Garfield's handbook of psychotherapy and behavior change* (pp. 493–540). Wiley.

Greenberg, L. S. (1983). Toward a task analysis of conflict resolution in Gestalt therapy. *Psychotherapy: Theory, Research and Practice., 20*(2), 190–201.

Greenberg, L. S. (1992). Task analysis: Identifying components of intrapersonal conflict resolution. In S. G. Toukmannian & D. L. Rennie (Eds.), *Psychotherapy Process Research: Paradigmatic and Narrative Approaches* (pp. 22–50). Sage Focus Editions.

Greenberg, L. S., & Foerster, F. (1996). Resolving unfinished business: The process of change. *Journal of Consulting and Clinical Psychology, 64*, 439–446.

Hartmann-Kottek, L. (2004). *Gestalttherapie*. Springer.

Mahrer, A. R., White, M. V., Howard, M. T., & Lee, A. C. (1991). Practitioner methods for heightening feeling expression and confrontational strength. *Psychotherapy in Private Practice, 9*(2), 11–25.

Mahrer, A. R., White, M. V., Howard, M. T., Gagnon, R., & Mac Phee, D. C. (1992). How to bring about some very good moments in psychotherapy sessions. *Psychotherapy Research, 2*(4), 252–265.

Orlinsky, D., Grawe, K., & Parks, B. (1994). Process and outcome in psychotherapy – noch einmal. In A. E. Bergin & L. Garfield (Eds.), *Handbook of Psychotherapy and Behavior Change*. Wiley.

Paivio, S. C., & Greenberg, L. S. (1995). Resolving 'unfinished business': Efficacy of experiential therapy using empty chair dialogue. *Journal of Consulting and Clinical Psychology, 63*, 419–425.

Perls, F. S. (1981). *Gestalt-Wahrnehmung. Verlorenes und Wiedergefundenes aus meiner Mülltonne*. Verlag für Humanistische Psychologie.

Pernter, G. (2008). *Spiritualität als Lebenskunst. Gestalttherapeutische Impulse*. EHP.

Strümpfel, U. (2006). *Therapie der Gefühle. Forschungsbefunde zur Gestalttherapie*. EHP.

Strümpfel, U. (2012). Forschungsstand der Gestalttherapie. In L. Hartmann-Kottek (Ed.), *Gestalttherapie*. Springer.

Watson, J. C., & Bedard, D. (2006). Clients' emotional processing in psychotherapy: A comparison between cognitive-behavioral and process-experiential psychotherapy. *Journal of Consulting and Clinical Psychology, 74*(1), 152–159.

Watson, J. C., Greenberg, L. S., & Lietaer, G. (2010). Relation Process to Outcome in person-centered and experiential psychotherapies. The role of the relationship conditions and clients' experiencing. In M. Cooper, J. C. Watson, & D. Hölldampf (Eds.), *Person-Centered and Experiential Therapies Work. A review of the research on counselling, psychotherapy and related practices*. PCCS Books.

Chapter 10
Dialogical Attitude

The formation of a working relationship is fundamental in both psychotherapy and social work. At the beginning of work together, alongside contracting, anamnesis and diagnosis, a trusting relationship must simultaneously be established. Gahleitner (2017) summarised research findings on the initiation, formation and importance of relationships, as studied in pedagogy, psychotherapy, attachment and network research, and other disciplines. According to these findings, a relationship should be "authentic," "emotionally sustainable," "personally shaped," and yet still wholly "reflective and professional" (ibid., 305). It is crucial that the professional not only acts in their social role, but also shows up as a person. This enables trust to be established (ibid., 103). The client's experience of a sincere, personally shaped, human encounter can be seen as the key factor of effectiveness among and indeed connecting various different disciplinary concepts (ibid., 133, 140).

This is very close to the Gestalt therapeutic understanding, as this considers contact in the here and now as fundamental, and attributes special importance to that which can be phenomenologically experienced. The focus is on recognising and expressing what is experienced—felt, sensed and thought—from moment to moment. Counsellors offer their own personal phenomenological experience ('resonance') to the client and formulate questions that can lead to a deeper understanding or awareness of the ongoing process. The counsellors give structure to the session and offer phenomenology-based impulses. They act partly from a role, but—in accordance with the principle of selective authenticity—there is a large scope for "real encounters" or "personal encounter moments" (ibid.).

Such moments are referred to by Gestalt therapy and pedagogy as "I-Thou contact", a term coined by Martin Buber. He distinguishes between a more distant, "thing-like" "I-It contact", for example in the context of data collection during anamnesis, and a more direct, personal encounter between two people. We may alternate between the two qualities of contact within a conversation:

A. Schachameier et al., *Gestalt in Social Work*,
https://doi.org/10.1007/978-3-031-95528-0_10

> Man becomes an I through a You. What confronts us comes and vanishes, relational events take shape and scatter, and through these changes crystallizes, more and more each time, the consciousness of the constant partner, the I-consciousness." (Buber, 1970, p. 39).

Sometimes, the counselling professional leaves behind their distancing, objectifying role towards their client. A "meaningful phonetic event" takes place, "whose meaning is found neither in one of the two partners nor in both together, but only in their physical interplay, in their between" (Buber, 1984, p. 276 cited in Staemmler, 1993, p. 48). Buber means that this relationship to the *Thou* is direct and unmediated:

> Nothing conceptual intervenes between I and You, no prior knowledge and no imagination; [...] No purpose intervenes between I and You, no greed and no anticipation; [...] Every means is an obstacle. Only where all means have disintegrated, encounters occur. (Buber, 1970, p. 31).

According to (Buber, 1983, p. 12), the basic word 'I-Thou'is where the world of relationships begins. Yontef (1993) calls such an encounter an existential dialogue, a meeting between people that occurs within the realm of their personal existence. Amongst other things that contribute to the creation of this relational quality, he particularly emphasises the counsellor's respectful entering into the client's phenomenological experience, accepting this phenomenological world as it is. Thus, the client too is accepted as they are (Yontef, 1993). The counsellor is present with their true self and surrenders to the dialogue (ibid.). (Staemmler, 1993) speaks in this context of the counsellor "offering personal contact".

The relationship unfolds within a figure-ground dynamic. Counsellors encounter their clients from the "middle mode", which allows oscillation between mindful, directed attention and awareness on the one hand, and a more intuitive, undirected openness on the other (Stein, 2005, p. 38; Hartmann-Kottek, 2004, p. 278). This means that during conversation with clients, counsellors are flexible in terms of where they direct their attention, either applying it specifically to certain aspects, or following the client's utterances with a more open perceptual awareness. Human consciousness is designed both for narrowing and widening (Hartmann-Kottek, 2004, p. 135), and counsellors can decide consciously which form they employ in any moment.

The encounter takes place in the here and now: "The process of moving from moment to moment reflects the existential view that whatever exists, only exists now. Flux is basic to experience; so if one can allow each experience the reality it seeks, it will fade into the background in its turn, to be replaced by whatever next has the force to appear in the foreground" (Polster & Polster, 1973, p. 48).

When working with clients, counsellors can provide a space that allows for the emotional expression of what is currently important. If counsellors follow this figure-ground process and meet clients authentically, then I-Thou moments as described by Buber arise naturally, and can lead to growth, awareness, and insight: "The man who steps out of the essential act of pure relation has something more in his being, something new has grown there of which he did not know before and for whose origin he lacks any suitable words." (Buber, 1970, p. 76).

Healing or growth occur above all through the experience of I-Thou relationships. I-It and I-Thou naturally oscillate; at the beginning of a working relationship, an I-It relationship is more in the foreground, but over time, more and more I-Thou encounters may arise due to increasing openness and familiarity. When we see clients as objects to be diagnosed and treated, this corresponds to Buber‘s conceptualisation of I-It contact. However, it is also possible to experience moments of personal encounter, or I-Thou contact, in the initial phase of work with a client.

Buber‘s understanding of the dialogical encounter, as well as its role in leading to new insights and self-actualisation, is somewhat more differentiated than comparable concepts in other humanistic therapies, such as that of Carl Rogers. Rogers (1959, 2009) examined the importance of three basic variables which he saw as fundamental in all humanistic therapy approaches, both for the therapy process and the therapeutic relationship. These three variables—empathy, unconditional positive regard and congruence—were found to be positively correlated with therapy outcomes. These findings can also be applied to counselling processes.

Congruence, in this context, means that counsellors are able to respond authentically and be open to their own experience in the here and now (Sanders, 2015, p. 51). Unconditional positive regard refers to acceptance and respect of the client and their experience, without judgment (ibid., 58). The third basic variable, empathy, describes the attempt to attune to the inner experience, feelings, and experiences of the other person and to reflect this back, also known as active listening (Rogers, 1959, p. 213). Rogers describes it thus: "Being empathic is to perceive the *internal frame of reference* of another with accuracy, and with the emotional components and meanings [...] as if one were the other person, but without ever losing the 'as if' condition" (Rogers, 1959, p. 210; emphasis in the original).

As stated above, Gestalt therapy is built upon the foundation of Buber‘s concept of the dialogical attitude rather than Rogerian concepts. It employs Buber‘s own terms rather than Rogerian ones. The differences between the two may not be as substantial as some would make out, but we nevertheless try to present Buber‘s perspective in such a way that these subtle differences become clear.

Inclusion

Buber uses the term "Umfassung", which is translated in the literature either as 'inclusion' or as 'embracement'. Both terms are fitting, and emphasise slightly different aspects of Buber‘s original meaning. Inclusion emphasises the dialogical inclusion of the other and a sense of mutual recognition, both of which are central to the I-Thou relationship. Embracement conveys the emotional warmth and comprehensive acceptance that characterises Buber‘s idea of deep encounter. We have decided to use the term 'inclusion' in the following, as it best suits the context of social work. Whilst empathy is an important concept to Buber, inclusion goes further than empathy in his eyes. He describes it as "the back-and-forth movement of being centered in one's own existence, and yet being able to go over the 'other side'… Inclusion is … a turning of one's *entire* existence to the other and the concentrated attempt to experience the other person's experience *as well as* one's own" (Hycner, 1993, p. 616, emphasis in the original). Inclusion, like an "I-Thou"moment, cannot be forced; rather, it requires a continuous effort to grasp the other's as well as one's own side of the dialogue (Hycner, 2003, p. 74).

Using the relationship between educator and pupil as an example, Buber (1970, p. 87) expounds upon what Inclusion can mean. In his eyes, the educator should try to encounter the pupil in such a way that they can realise their "best potential". To do this, the pupil must be addressed "as this particular person, both in [their] potentiality and in [their] actuality". To do this, the educator must not regard the pupil "as a mere sum of qualities, aspirations, and inhibitions", but must rather "apprehend [them], and affirm [them], as a whole", experiencing the situation "in all its aspects not only from [their] own point of view but also from that of [their] partner" (ibid).

This attitude can be transferred to the counselling context. Counsellors can see their clients' abilities as well as their possibilities for development. They encounter them with an attitude which aims to both affirm and promote their potential.

Confirmation

Buber uses the term "confirmation"to go beyond what is meant by "unconditional positive regard" in the Rogerian sense. Unconditional positive regard is part of confirmation: "**Confirmation, on the other hand, recognizes and affirms this person's existence even while perhaps saying that his current behavior is unacceptable**" (Hycner, 1993, p. 657). A dialogical encounter on this basis means that disagreements, differences of opinion, and conflicts are all possible without ceasing to confirm the other in their existence (Hycner, 2003, p. 74).

It is therefore perhaps the particular emphasis on the existence of the other that accounts for the difference between Rogers'empathy and unconditional positive regard and Buber's confirmation. Such an emphasis means above all that conflicts can be carried out in a therapeutic or counselling context, such as when a counsellor confronts a client in terms of a certain behaviour; while the behaviour is confronted, the person is nonetheless affirmed in their existence and dignity.

The goal of a therapeutic process should be that as much mutuality as possible arises within the encounter, a largely mutual, dialogical relationship (Hycner, 2003, p. 77). In many fields of social work in particular, clients may have limited capacity for communication on an equal footing. The professional has a special responsibility here, and can see themselves as the guardian of the dialogue. As such, in many fields of practice mutuality is more of a direction than a goal, and it is about finding a realistic degree of reciprocity.

The attitude described here, as based on Buber and his concepts of inclusion and confirmation, can be understood as an underlying method of Gestalt therapy, on the basis of which specific techniques are applied.

References

Buber, M. (1970). *I and thou*. Charles Scribner's Sons.

Buber, M. (1983). *I and thou*. Schneider.

Buber, M. (1984). *The dialogical principle*. Lambert Schneider.

Gahleitner, S. B. (2017). *Soziale Arbeit als Beziehungsprofession. Bindung, Beziehung und Einbettung professionell ermöglichen*. Beltz Juventa.

Hartmann-Kottek, L. (2004). *Gestalttherapie*. Springer.

Hycner, R. (1993). *Between person and person: Toward a dialogical gestalt therapy. Kindle edition*. Gestalt Journal Press.

Hycner, R. (2003). Für eine dialogische Gestalttherapie. Erste Überlegungen. In E. Doubrawa & F.-M. Staemmler (Eds.), *Heilende Beziehung. Dialogische Gestalttherapie*. Hammer.

Polster, E., & Polster, M. (1973). *Gestalt therapy integrated. Contours of theory and practice*. Brunner/Mazel.

Rogers, C. R. (1959). A theory of therapy, personality and interpersonal relationships, as developed in the client-centered framework. In S. Koch (Ed.), *Psychology: A study of science, Bd. 3: Formulations of the person and the social context* (pp. 184–256). McGraw-Hill.

Rogers, C. R. (2009). *Die klientenzentrierte Gesprächspsychotherapie. Client-Centered Therapy*. Fischer.

Sanders, P. (2015). *Person-centred counselling*. PCCS Books.

Staemmler, F.-M. (1993). *Therapeutische Beziehung und Diagnose. Gestalttherapeutische Antworten*. Pfeiffer.

Stein, R. (2005). *Einführung in die pädagogische Gestaltarbeit und die gestalttheoretische Sicht von Störungen*. Schneider-Verl. Hohengehren.

Yontef, G. M. (1993). *Awareness, dialogue and process. Essays on gestalt therapy*. The Gestalt Journal Press.

Chapter 11
Methodological Foundations

Gestalt therapeutic methods must follow the dialogical, existentialist and phenomenological basic principles that have been described. According to Naranjo, method is the spirit of technique, and the latter "must be used in the sense of the method, otherwise it loses its meaning" (Naranjo, 1993, pp. 28, 29). The Gestalt attitude is summarised by Naranjo (1993, p. 40) "as threefold—awareness, responsibility, and presence". All Gestalt therapeutic techniques originate from this essential attitude, and its experience and expression in the here and now facilitates the growth of consciousness and responsibility for one's own actions. Gestalt therapists use questions such as "What are you feeling?" or "What are you doing?" to direct the client's focus towards their inner experience. "The Gestalt therapist places more value on deeds than on words, on experiences than on thoughts" (Naranjo, 1993, p. 33).

Naranjo (1993) and Hartmann-Kottek (2004) describe various techniques, the most well-known and frequently used including identification with inner parts, working with polarities and empty chair work, as well as amplification of certain expressions (verbal or physical) through repetition and exaggeration. In our examples, the work with inner parts and polarities is particularly relevant. We should emphasise that we have focused almost exclusively in the role-plays on initial meetings with clients. Many Gestalt therapeutic techniques can only be used in a more established working relationship. At this stage, depending on the context and scope of the field, numerous creative media may be used, including art, ceramics or collage.

For the case role-plays presented in Part III, the concepts of *resonance*, *real fantasy*, and *cultivated uncertainty* were of particular technical relevance. These are presented below.

A. Schachameier et al., *Gestalt in Social Work*,
https://doi.org/10.1007/978-3-031-95528-0_11

Resonance

In Gestalt therapy, the therapist or counsellor may bring their own feelings into the dialogue in an intentional way. This is what is meant by congruence or authenticity; this technique involves the therapist being their 'own instrument'. This refers to the therapist's experience, or inner resonance. From a psychoanalytic perspective, this might be described as the countertransference processes. However, Staemmler (1993, p. 167) has described the way in which the term 'resonance'is more suitable within Gestalt therapy. This refers to two aspects: firstly, the initial, "immediate impression that the other person leaves in me in the given moment, and secondly, my emotional reaction to this impression" (ibid., 63). Staemmler criticises various psychoanalytic concepts of countertransference, pointing out in particular that transference and countertransference cannot be explained linearly, but rather represent an interactional event (ibid., 161, 162). He aligns himself with the psychoanalyst Heimann's (1950) perspective, agreeing that "*all* of the therapist's feelings count as countertransference, regardless of whether they are 'neurotic', reactive and unconscious or none of the above" (Staemmler, 1993, p. 162; emphasis in the original).

Staemmler (ibid., 167) sees no reason to include the term countertransference in Gestalt therapeutic vocabulary; "Even if the personal resonance which the therapist communicates to the client refers to an aspect of the client's behaviour that turns out, over the course of the dialogue, to belong to the client's transference, I find the term 'countertransference' unnecessary. For this case is no different in principle to any other in which the therapist feels a resonance and communicates this" (ibid., 167).

Grasping and articulating atmospheres and moods is an important aspect of consciousness work in humanistic-experiential approaches. There is much to be gained by the therapist using their own resonance as a therapeutic instrument.

Real Fantasy

In line with the concept of resonance and Buber's idea of "inclusion", a Gestalt therapist may also express what is known as a 'fantasy'. Staemmler speaks in this context of *real fantasy*, meaning the attempt to imagine the "subjective inner reality" of the other, in this context the client (Staemmler, 1993, p. 66). This "can of course always only be a more or less complete approximation of the subjective reality that the other experiences themselves. The more complete the approximation, the more real my real fantasy is" (ibid.). This intervention (i.e. the therapist communicating their real fantasy to the client), and the exploration which may arise from this, open up the possibility of dialogical encounter and fresh experiential exploration. The aim is to embody an I-Thou attitude, rather than in any way accusing the client of something, imposing anything on them, or making interpretations or projections; employing the technique of sharing real fantasy is not about pinning clients down, but rather about inviting them to explore additional subjective material which may have processual relevance.

Cultivated Uncertainty

Another touchstone of Gestalt therapy, *cultivated uncertainty*, "requires a willingness to entertain perpetual uncertainty in the current situation, which is certainly only possible on the basis of the stable security in oneself" (Staemmler, 1993, p. 80). For the counsellor, this is a prerequisite to adopting an attitude of cultivated uncertainty towards both the phenomena and the other person. For Staemmler (2003, p. 147), cultivating uncertainty means that as a therapist or counsellor, "I must remain aware that whenever I am uncertain in terms of which meanings I attach [to the current going on], I am dealing with a desirable, positive, welcome feeling [...] that indicates that I still have an at least partially clear grasp of interpersonal reality." Cultivated uncertainty can be used therapeutically, "by knowing and having to hand perspectives and practices which both allow [the counsellor] to regain a sense of orientation and support clients in their change process (ibid)."[1]

Staemmler proposes 'cultivating' uncertainty, rather than seeing it as something to be overcome; in other words, this means recognising it as pointing towards something important in the current process. This is why it can—paradoxically perhaps—provide a certain level of security to the practitioner, as it confirms that their experience is still grounded in the reality of not (yet) knowing, rather than being lost in assumptions. This signpost towards something new or surprising opens up the encounter with the client, inviting them back into the mutual process. The therapist's 'hypothesis' can thus be verified or modified by the client.

The second implication is that inhabiting uncertainty does not mean an inability to act: "I can remain uncertain without losing my orientation. And I can stand by my uncertainty with confidence and therefore lend confidence to my clients, so the uncertainty becomes productive on this level too" (ibid.).

Thus, the "expertise of the Gestalt therapist lies in their ability to dialogue, in their accurate perception, and in their capacity to support in a sensitive and differentiated way whichever process allows the emergence of new meaning and experiential possibilities for the client. They ask questions, share impressions, hunches, assumptions, even suspicions and fears, take in the client's reactions, listen for undertones, pay attention to facial expression and gestures, notice again and again what these impressions trigger inside them, and share this with the client, etc." (Staemmler, 1993, p. 80). The exploration of moment-to-moment experience on all levels—physical, emotional, and cognitive—is of central importance.

[1] In this context, reference should also be made to an article by Schachameier and Link (2021).

As mentioned, as a prerequisite to being able to adopt an attitude of cultivated uncertainty, the corresponding personal competencies must be held or gained by the therapist. Equally, in order to be able to work in different fields of social work in this way, it is necessary to develop the relevant competencies (see the section entitled "Personal Competencies in Social Work").

The theoretical and methodological background of the Gestalt approach as presented thus far lays the ground for the reflections which follow in the next section (Part III) of the book, as they refer to field-specific practice role-plays.

References

Hartmann-Kottek, L. (2004). *Gestalttherapie*. Springer.

Heimann, P. (1950). On counter-transference. *Int J Psycho-Analysis, 31*, 81–84.

Naranjo, C. (1993). Gestalt. In *Präsenz Gewahrsein Verantwortung. Grundhaltungen und Praxis einer lebendigen Therapie*. Arbor.

Schachameier, A., & Link, P.-C. (2021). Methoden der Suchtberatung aus humanistisch-experientieller Perspektive. *Sucht Aktuell, 2*(21), 20–27.

Staemmler, F.-M. (1993). *Therapeutische Beziehung und Diagnose. Gestalttherapeutische Antworten*. Pfeiffer.

Staemmler, F.-M. (2003). Kultivierte Unsicherheit. Gedanken zu einer gestalttherapeutischen Haltung: Doubrawa, E., Staemmler, F.-M. (Ed.). Heilende Beziehung. Dialogische Gestalttherapie. Peter Hammer Verlag.

Part III
Case Role-Plays

Chapter 12
Depression

The following case study is used in order to illustrate the topic of depression. It is about a case of severe recurrent depression that the client has been experiencing for many years. Over the course of our role-plays and exercises, we found that it made sense to deal separately with possible interventions in the case of suicidal thoughts. We will deal with this in the following chapter. In addition, at the end of this section, we use another example to illustrate the emergence of typical 'entanglements' that can cause the conversation to develop in a destructive direction.

Case Summary

Dave is 45 years old. After a divorce and various others strokes of fate in his career which he has not recovered from, he has become increasingly depressed over the last 15 years. He has already experienced several depressive episodes, and despite psychotherapy and medication, his complaints have worsened. For about a year now, he has been in a socio-therapeutic facility for people with mental health difficulties, as he was no longer able to cope with everyday life. According to the ICD-10 criteria, he suffers from a currently severe depressive episode without psychotic symptoms. In addition to the core symptoms of "depressed mood", "reduced drive" and "loss of interest or pleasure", Dave also complains about a negative and pessimistic perspective on the future, feelings of worthlessness, diminished self-esteem and self-confidence, disordered sleep, and a reduced ability to concentrate.

Please watch the video entitled "Depression" for more information (www.gestalt-socialwork.com).

A. Schachameier et al., *Gestalt in Social Work*,
https://doi.org/10.1007/978-3-031-95528-0_12

Experiences in the Client Role

Cognitive

Dave is very preoccupied with his thoughts and is brooding about whether he should go to occupational therapy or not. He knows that it has often done him good in the past. At the same time, given his current condition, he sees no point in attending.

In an internal dialogue, he puts pressure on himself with "I should" thoughts. He suspects that his condition will improve through occupational therapy.

On the other hand, he tends towards resignation, thinking that "it won't make a difference anyway". He attributes this internal resignation to his current state and sees it as proof that occupational therapy cannot save him from such states.

This internal conflict and the lack of ability to resolve it leads Dave to devalue himself with further thoughts and to put more pressure on himself, employing the typical pattern of "more of the same". This self-devaluation and the resulting internal pressure lead to a kind of vicious circle:

1) Dave is in a state of exhaustion.
2) His way of reacting to it is to put pressure on himself.
3) This leads to an increase in internal pressure and devaluation.
4) This increase in internal tension intensifies his exhaustion.

Since Dave doesn't know any other strategy for solution, his attempt to end the depressive state inevitably leads to a worsening of it.

Emotional

He feels depressed and desperate. The feeling of having failed in life is accompanied by a 'bottomless pit' of pain which is typical for people with depression. In order not to have to feel this in its depths, he distances himself internally, which leads to him feeling numb, as if he were sitting in a cloud, surrounded by fog. This does on the one hand reduce his experience of pain, but on the other hand also prevents him from having satisfying, authentic contact with others; in fact, in leads to him feeling alone.

Physical

Physically, Dave feels tired, heavy, and lacks energy; he has the feeling that he is being pulled down. Any "uprightness" in his body is perceived as strenuous.

Longing

Dave primarily longs for relief from this state of heaviness, despair, and exhaustion. He probably also wishes to be able to shape his life and everyday routine independently, as well as for satisfying interpersonal relationships and to be seen and accepted by someone for who he is. However, he is not really clear about what he longs for and what he would be willing to mobilise 'energy' for.

Action and Avoidance

By brooding, Dave withdraws into himself and avoids contact. His negative thoughts form a vortex that pulls him further and further down.

He is partially aware that he needs to take action to exit the depressive state. However, he does not understand that the way forward involves trying things out. Meaningfulness can only be experienced through living and doing, and less so through thinking.

Contact with the Outside World

He has withdrawn, is trapped in his world of thoughts, and feels helpless. Both intra- and interpsychically, the prevailing contact interruption is *deflection*, as contact with himself and the environment only take place in a weakened form. The inner pressure of "You should..." can be understood as an *introject*.

Identified Inner Parts

On the surface, Dave experiences destructive self-talk between the following inner parts.

A: "Depressive Experience": this part feels like a failure because a visit to occupational therapy does not seem possible. Dave "can't", and therefore devalues himself, feels ashamed, and is desperate and afraid. This is accompanied by the experience of meaninglessness, heaviness, and dissatisfaction.

B: "Pressure": this part puts pressure on Dave: he *should* go to occupational therapy.

C: "Longing": this part wants attention and understanding and longs for interpersonal closeness, normality, and someone to be with him and take care of him. This art wants to be seen and held with his pain.

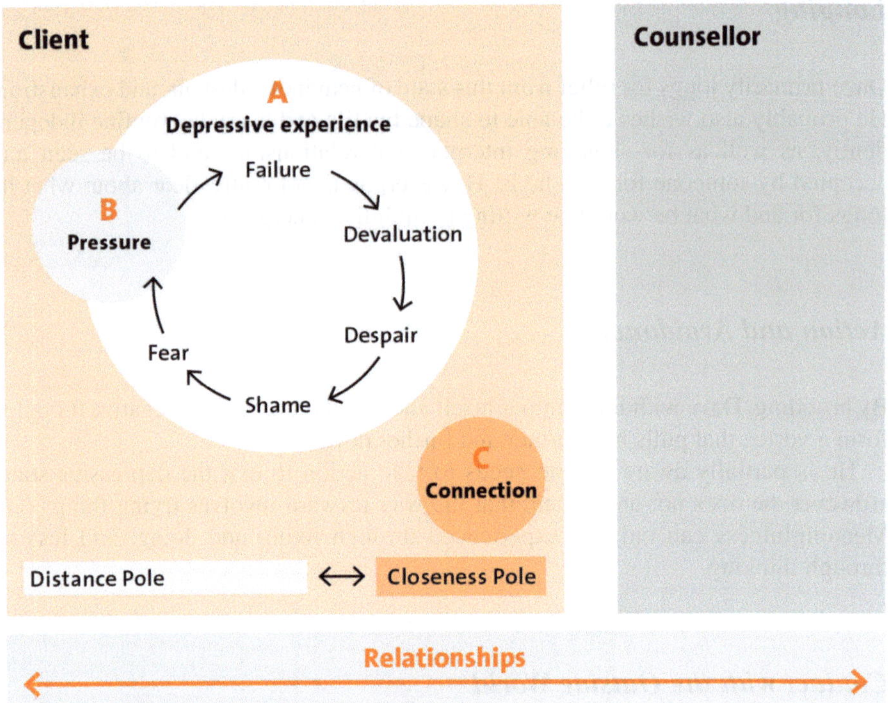

Fig. 12.1 "Depression"—identified inner parts

The inner dialogue could be depicted as shown in Fig. 12.1:

The focus here is on brooding, heaviness, and meaninglessness. The desire for attention and closeness is covered up by destructive self-talk. In destructive self-talk, there is usually one part which dominates (in this example part B) over the other (here, part A), the latter both suffering from this treatment and reacting defensively within its capacity. However, neither lead to a constructive solution, but rather to an avoidance of the actual longing.

On the one hand, there is pressure and devaluation, on the other hand, a feeling of meaninglessness and dissatisfaction. Only through an awareness of part C can contact with other people and the world be achieved (Staemmler, 1995, pp. 47–50).

Case Role-Play Transcript: Depression

Dave is sitting in his room and hasn't turned up for occupational therapy.

00:00:01

SW: Hello Dave. I just wanted to check on you because the occupational therapy group started quite a while ago and you haven't shown up. What's up?

00:00:12
C: I can't do it. It's just too much. I just can't do it.
00:00:24
SW: You just can't do it today.
00:00:26
C: No. Can't do it.
00:00:28
SW: Is it okay if I sit down with you for a moment?
00:00:30
C: Yes
00:00:34
SW: You say you can't do it. Can you describe a bit what's going on for you right now?
00:00:50
C: Got up early this morning and just realised, I don't have any energy.
00:00:57
SW: Mmm (affirming).
00:00:58
C: And then I tried, because I knew I had to go down to occupational therapy, but I just have no energy and then //.
00:01:10
SW: Mmm (affirming).
00:01:10
C: ...there's no point really, everything is so exhausting and //
00:01:18
SW: Mmm (affirming).
00:01:20
C: ...and it's been like this for so long and I'm just fed up of it.
00:01:23
SW: Mmm (affirming).
00:01:23
C: Fed up.
00:01:24
SW: Mmm (affirming).
00:01:26
C: It's just...
00:01:27
SW: It's exhausting.
00:01:28
C: Yes.
00:01:30
SW: And when you say no energy: is there a heaviness there, //.
00:01:36
C: Yes.
00:01:36

SW: ...that pulls you down?
00:01:38
C: Yes.
00:01:39
SW: Mmm (affirming).
00:01:39
C: It's just like... What's the point of it all? I'd just be sitting down there with no energy...and all I want to do is sleep.
00:01:52
SW: Mmm (affirming). So it feels pointless.
00:01:55
C: Mmm (affirming).
00:01:57
SW: And when you say you imagine yourself sitting down there, does that mean you're thinking about whether you should go down there after all?
00:02:11
C: Yeah, exactly. I know I should, I should go down, I should do something, I should be more active somehow...and I just can't do it.
00:02:24
SW: Mmm (affirming).
00:02:24
C: And so I stay here, but it's just the same. It doesn't make it any better.
00:02:30
SW: Yes.
00:02:31
C: I have the feeling it's getting worse.
00:02:34
SW: Mmm (affirming). And are you putting pressure on yourself? You should, you said.
00:02:42
C: Yeah... I should get better at some point, whenever that is. But it's... //.
00:02:49
SW: Mmm (affirming).
00:02:50
C: // pretty unbearable.
00:02:56
SW: Mmm, mmm (affirming). Yes, and it's not the first time you've had a phase like this, right? I've known you to have phases like this again and again.
00:03:09
C: Yes.

Effect on the client	Intervention and resonance
Dave feels understood, gets attention, the desire for contact is activated (Part C). Because the client feels understood, this strengthens the relationship with the counsellor. He feels valued as a human being.	Connecting with the client and exploring: What's going on? How is Dave doing? (**Dialogical attitude** and **Phenomenology**) First, the counsellor addresses Dave's state of mind. He is trying to understand what Dave is currently experiencing internally, which thoughts, feelings, and physical sensations are significant. Without judging, he accepts Dave's communications and tries to explore and understand his experiences through a dialogue, using mirroring, paraphrasing, and empathetic questioning. Through his general attitude as well as what he says, the counsellor signals that it's OK for Dave to be the way he currently is. It is important that the counsellor is not employing a technical approach, but offering a real encounter of two people (**Dialogical attitude**). It becomes clear how trapped Dave is in his sense of heaviness and lack of motivation, and how much he is struggling internally with himself and devaluing himself. **Counsellor's resonance:** The heaviness is clearly noticeable, both physically and emotionally, so much so that the counsellor feels a tendency towards being "pulled down" by it too. On the side of the "helper", a feeling of helplessness could arise, along with the urge to want to pull the client and oneself out of this unpleasant state. However, the Gestalt approach is more about beginning by simply allowing what is. This appreciation of the situation, the thoughts, the feelings, and also the person creates a tangible connection. The responsibility for change lies with the client (**Existentialism**). This knowledge helps the counsellor not to get entangled internally and to remain in an accepting attitude. He holds Dave in a fundamental respect as a human being (**Inclusion**, **Confirmation**).

00:03:09 T: And I really want to say: it's totally OK if you don't make it down to occupational therapy today. … How does it feel when I say that?

00:03:29 T: It *is* good...because I just can't do it. But at the same time, it's like... what next though? // How can things move forward?

00:03:44 T: So you're not really satisfied. On the one hand it feels like a relief, but it's not really satisfying?

00:03:54 T: Yeah.

This leads to relief on the one hand, but on the other hand, Dave is dissatisfied with the situation. An inner conflict becomes clear

The counsellor signalises that it's okay if Dave doesn't go to occupational therapy today. This interrupts the inner vicious circle to a certain degree (see Figure 12.1). The part that "can't" is accepted (**Stagnation**). The respectful exploration helps Dave to accept this part.

Resonance and **real fantasy**: both the heaviness and the relief are palpable, as is the dissatisfaction. The counsellor has the sense that Dave wants contact and that occupational therapy is too much for him today.

00:03:55

SW: Mmm (affirming). Well, Dave: I've been sitting here for a while now, and we've been having a chat. How do you feel about me being here, and having this conversation?

00:04:15

C: Yeah, it's alright.

00:04:18

SW: Mmm (affirming).

00:04:19

C: Wearing me out too.

00:04:22

SW: Mmm (affirming).

00:04:22

C: Yeah...I have the feeling that talking...that tires me out quite a bit.

Dave realises how much good it does him to be in contact with someone – the conversation, and that someone is there.

At the same time, he also notices that it is exhausting.

The counsellor tries to explore how Dave is experiencing the conversation with him, in the here and now. He asks about this directly (**Dialogical Attitude**).

00:04:29

SW: Mmm, Okay. So it's kind of good and exhausting at the same time. Mmm (affirming). And well... Dave, we know from experience that for example a short walk around the block has always done you good. How about taking a short walk with me? It'd be lovely if you...if you came along.

00:04:55

C: No, it's too.../ I can't manage it.

00:05:01

SW: Mmm (affirming).

00:05:01

C: Too exhausting.
00:05:03
SW: Mmm (affirming). Just can't do it today.
00:05:06
C: Uh-uh (shaking head).
00:05:07
SW: Yes. Mmm, that's a shame, I would have liked to walk around the block with you, but you say you just can't do it today, it's too much...then that's just the way it is. I'm going to go down again now, because I have some other things to do, but I'll come back and check on you again in about half an hour.

Dave clearly feels how nice it would be to go on a walk together, but is glad that the counsellor accepts that he just can't / doesn't want to right now.

Above all, he wants to continue to feel understood. Part C, the actual need, becomes clear.

In fact, Dave is isolating himself too much; he needs to develop in the direction of increased contact and connection. To do this, he must learn to perceive his need for contact and to act to ensure its satisfaction.

From experience, the counsellor knows that Dave has very little self-motivation in such phases. To communicate this, he makes Dave an open and sincere offer of contact. He suggests going on a walk together. This addresses part C. However, it's also fine for the counsellor if Dave doesn't agree to this. Through this intervention, the contractive pole (parts A and B) can become clearer.

The counsellor accepts that this is how it is today and shares his genuine disappointment. At the same time, he tells Dave that he can also understand it (**Existentialism**).

Note:

It is important to take into account that Dave and the counsellor have known each other for a long time. If it was their first meeting, the counsellor could use open questions to explore what might be good for Dave. Since the counsellor has experienced this situation before, he knows that Dave has few other interests but likes to walk.

00:05:30
C: Okay.
00:05:31
SW: Alright? I'll stop by again in a bit then.
00:05:34
C: Yes. Thank you.
00:05:35
SW: See you then.
00:05:36
C: Yeah.

Dave doesn't want the counsellor to leave. But he is very happy that he will come by again. Internally, he feels strengthened and has a bit more energy; in fact, he is on the verge of saying that he wants to come on the walk after all.

The relationship is thus maintained, because Dave is not sanctioned for his behaviour.

Farewell and further offer of contact:

the counsellor says he will stop by again in half an hour.

The most important thing is not to 'have an agenda', i.e. the professional should not have any expectations about the client's behaviour and leave the complete responsibility with the client. The goal is not to change the client or to motivate them to partake in an activity (**Existentialism** and **Dialogical Attitude**).

Value Squares

The value squares in Fig. 12.2 are designed to show directions of development for Dave. We wish to illuminate three levels. The first is the "intrapsychic" perspective, which refers to internal, cognitive-emotional processes of evaluation. The second, "interpersonal, relational", refers to internal dynamics that are important in dealing with other people. The third level, "behaviour", is ultimately the result of the preceding thoughts and feelings.

Such differentiation between the three categories is ultimately only possible to a limited extent, as the levels are mutually dependent. Nevertheless, we see the distinction between these perspectives as advantageous, as it allows us to recognise significant tendencies. The following development squares serve as suggestions, and were constructed through our exploration in the respective roles. These are intended to stimulate the formation of your own versions, as other similar perspectives and variations are certainly conceivable.

Discussion

We have repeatedly observed that when professionals adopt an inner attitude which views all responsibility for the client's actions as belonging to the client themselves (*Existentialism* and *Dialogical Attitude*), the professional is relieved of a burden, and more able to enter into an encounter between equals. For the client, this is a positive experience. The professional values them as they are, and does not demand change; they have no agenda. The client thus feels seen.

In social work, of course, there are situations which necessitate concrete practical assistance or suggestions for action. In many cases, however, it is of equal—or even primary—importance that the client's needs be understood. Humans long to be accepted and seen in their own subjective experience, in the way they are currently feeling. The dialogical exploration of their inner state creates a bond. Clients do not

DEPRESSION

Intrapsychic

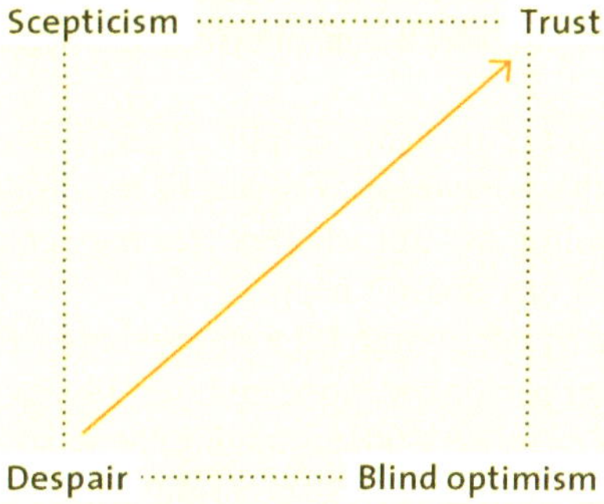

To interrupt the negative evaluation chains, the client must develop more trust. This involves a more positive assessment of the future, the person and the situation.

Interpersonal, relational

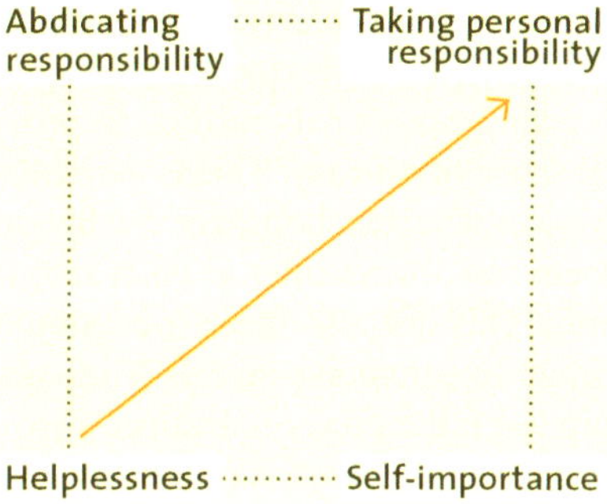

Here, development is linked to the client perceiving and acknowledging their need for contact and closeness. This is the prerequisite for taking responsibility and making conscious attempts at contact with others.

Behaviour

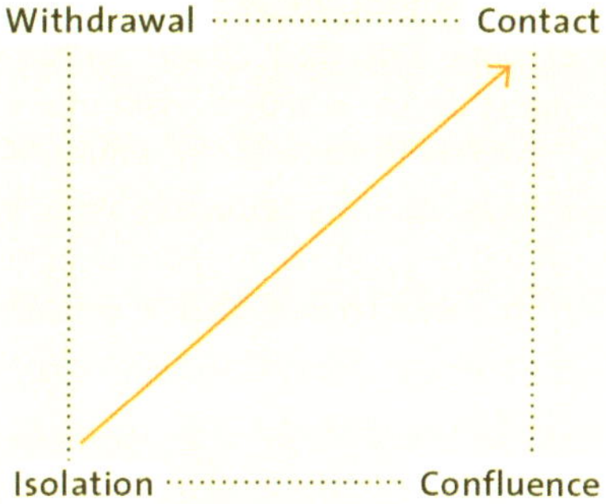

On the behavioural level, the goal is to acquire competencies to develop the client's capacity to interact with others.

Fig. 12.2 *Value squares for "Depression"*

necessarily want to receive advice. In the example above, Dave is pleased that the counsellor will come and see him again. Above all, he enjoys contact with a conversation partner who isn't pushing to bring about change or pressuring him to do something he doesn't feel up to. This allows him to trust the counsellor, and also serves as a model for the kind of inner dialogue which can interrupt the vicious circle of thought.

When clients feel seen and appreciated, a lot of pressure can lift. This is essential. It also opens up space for potential growth of openness to advice or the organic development of the client's own ideas as to solutions. But whether that happens or not is not the deciding factor—it's also okay if that doesn't happen.

The counsellor's relational independence is of central importance here. This means cultivating an attitude by which the other person owes one nothing. Just as we accept thoughts and feelings in a mindfulness exercise without judging them, so too must we listen to and understand clients. The counsellor is also permitted to be as they are. They are allowed to feel helpless, to not always have an immediate solution or strategy to hand. The Gestalt-informed helper is allowed to be helpless precisely because they don't see themselves as responsible for healing or helping on the "content level", but rather on the relational level. As a client, to receive recognition not only of one's own helplessness, but also of the general helplessness of the overall situation, can be very healing; much more so than professionals rushing to provide 'sticking plaster' solutions to protect their own sense of efficacy. This is particularly important when working with people who have lost relatives, homes or livelihoods.

In moments of "content helplessness", helpers can always offer to enter into dialogue together and to explore what is happening. This can also mean accepting that there are no 'simple' solutions. It is also important to communicate this. This can be relieving for clients, because on the relationship level, the power imbalance between seemingly competent helpers on the one hand and seemingly incompetent, needy clients on the other is reduced. It is no longer the case that the experts sit on one side with their solutions and the helpless clients sit on the other. The encounter thus takes place on a more equal footing, and the search for solutions can become a mutual team effort. When the pressure is removed in this way, it is also okay if there are setbacks or failures.

The task of the consulting professional is to work with their clients within the framework of their institutional mandate. They must decide whether crisis intervention and an increased level of care are necessary, possibly in a psychiatric clinic. They may offer one-off dialogues on a case-by-case basis, or—if compatible with their institutional mandate, their qualifications and their job description, may conduct more regular counselling sessions. In some cases, a psychotherapist may also be consulted.

Vicious Circle Dynamics

In some situations, destructive conversational dynamics can develop when the client feels forced to find a solution and change their current situation. In such a case, the client may feel relieved when the professional leaves, while the professional may feel frustrated and angry that the client is so resistant and uncooperative. While the professional will often feel some degree of incompetence, the client may well feel both incapable and misunderstood.

This dynamic is illustrated by Schulz von Thun with the graphic depicted in Fig. 12.3:

It is therefore crucial that all interventions are compatible with and affirm (rather than wanting to change) the inner experiential reality of the client. This is where the *dialogical attitude* (both in terms of the relationship and the encounter) as well as the focus on the client's moment-to-moment *phenomenological experience* are key. Systemic or other questioning techniques can be very helpful if they meet the client where they are. However, if the client is overwhelmed by the intervention and this is not picked up on, then this can lead to the vicious circle as described above. From the existentialist perspective of the Gestalt approach, with its focus on dialogical relationship and particular view on how change occurs, it is not necessary for a counsellor to develop activities and assistance to lead clients out of their current state. Instead, their role is much more about accepting what is. And if clients can't do anything right now, then that's alright.

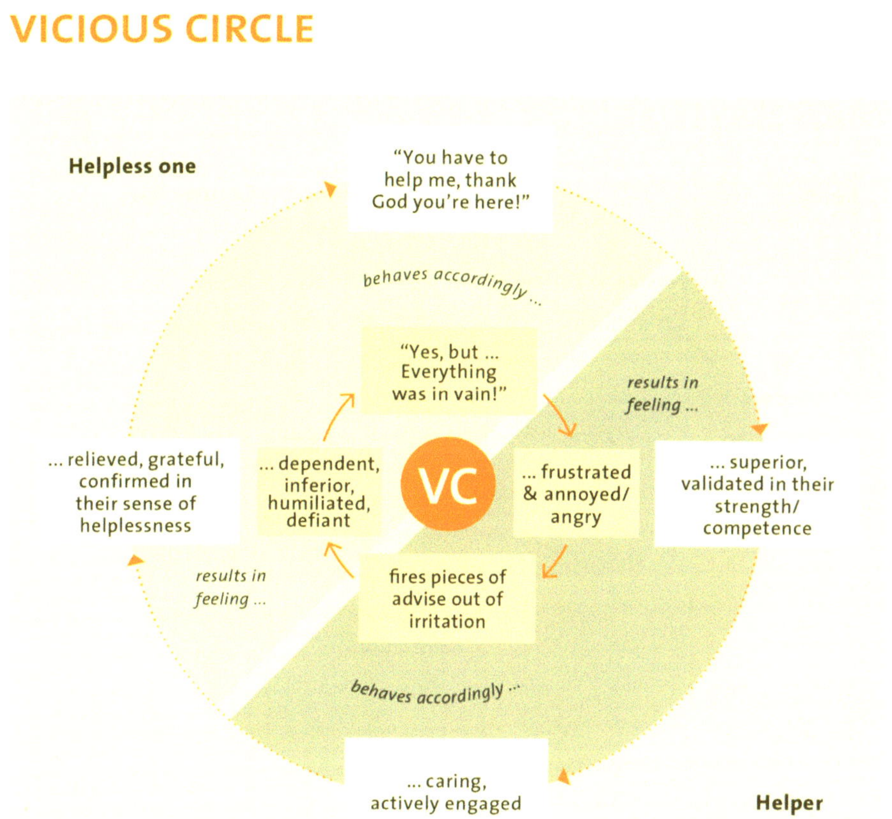

Fig. 12.3 *Vicious Circle* (Schulz von Thun 2006, p. 85)

Summary Graphic (Fig. 12.4): Client Experience and Key Interventions

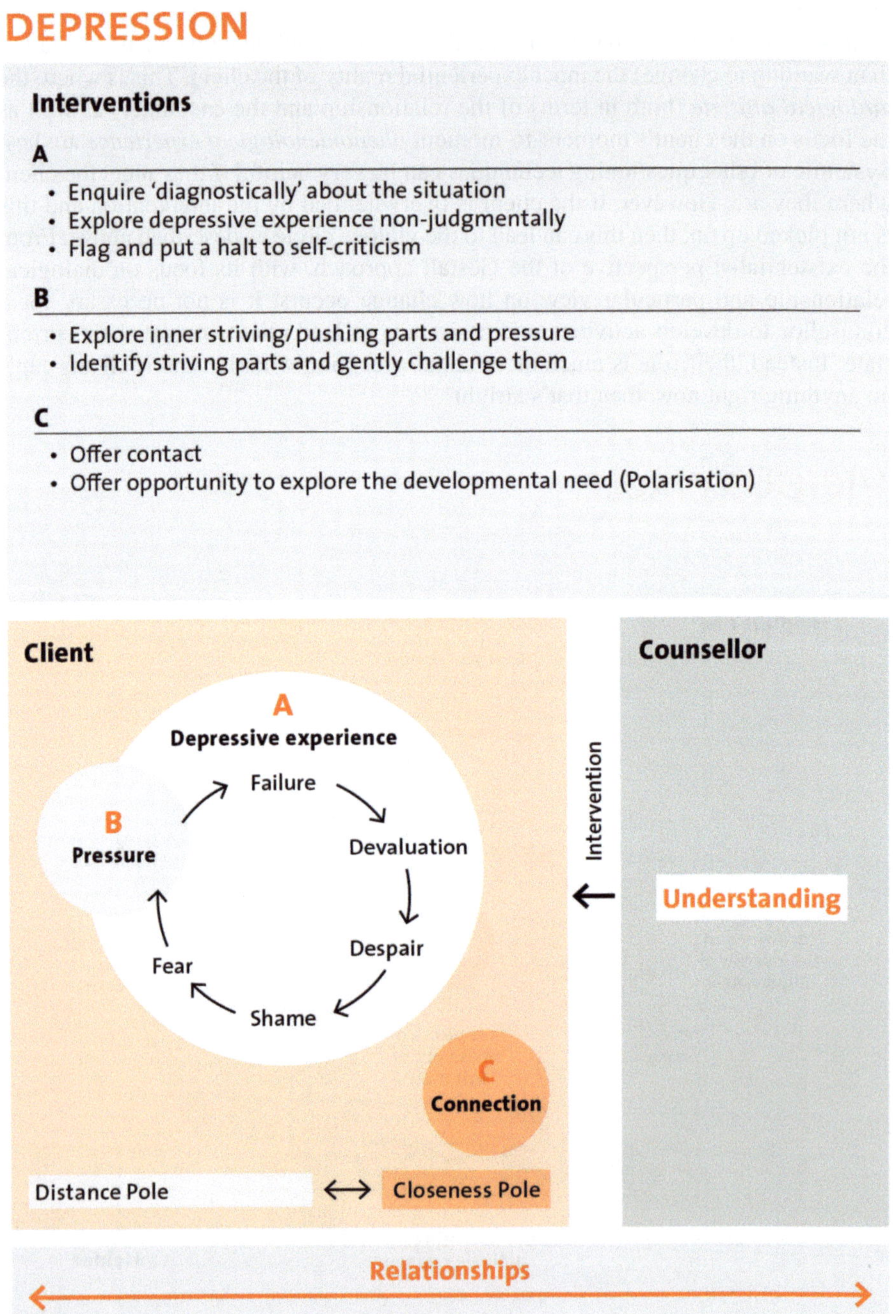

Fig. 12.4 "Depression"– summary graphic

References

Schulz von Thun, F. (2006). *Miteinander reden: 2. Stile, Werte und Persönlichkeits-entwicklung. Differentielle Psychologie der Kommunikation*. Rowohlt.

Staemmler, F.-M. (1995). *Der "leere Stuhl". Ein Beitrag zur Technik der Gestalttherapie*. Pfeiffer.

Chapter 13
Depression with Suicidal Thoughts

Case Summary

This role-play involves the same client with depression as previously discussed (see last chapter). Here however, suicidal thoughts are added to his symptoms.

Please watch the video entitled "Depression with Suicidal Thoughts"(www.gestalt-socialwork.com).

Experiences in the Client Role

The following summarises the role-player's experiences in the client role. To illustrate the differences between this case and the case of depressive experience without suicidal thoughts, we have juxtaposed both cases in Table 13.1. The right column contains the descriptions for the case that we want to focus on in this chapter.

Identified Inner Parts

A: "Depressive Experience": This part feels like a failure because He doesn't feel able to attend occupational therapy. Dave "can't", and therefore devalues himself, and feels ashamed, desperate and afraid. This is accompanied by the experience of pointlessness, heaviness, and dissatisfaction.

B: "Decision": This part broods over whether it would be better to take his own life and ponders on ways to carry this out.

C: "Longing": This part longs to be seen with its suffering and its (suicidal) thoughts and to have contact with others.

A. Schachameier et al., *Gestalt in Social Work*,
https://doi.org/10.1007/978-3-031-95528-0_13

Table 13.1 Comparison: Depression with and without suicidal thoughts

Without suicidal thoughts (see chapter "Depression")	With suicidal thoughts
Cognitive: Dave is preoccupied with his thoughts and is brooding about whether or not he should go to occupational therapy. It seems pointless to him. At the same time, he puts pressure on himself because he knows that it does him good. His thoughts are going round in circles	*Cognitive:* Everything is perceived as very strenuous and pointless. Resignation sets in, because "it's all just pointless." Dave's thoughts keep circling around the question and decision of whether he should take his own life Dave asks himself whether it would be better to commit suicide rather than constantly fighting and having little prospect of improvement
Emotional: He feels a heaviness that weighs him down. This makes him sad and depressed. He is feels desperate and numb, as if he were sitting in a cloud surrounded by fog. He experiences emotional pain	*Emotional:* The feeling of heaviness is predominant, a sort of spiral into a bottomless pit of despair and hopelessness that pulls him down, combined with an inner "paralysis". His decision is an existential one Dave feels shame about having failed and for having these thoughts in the first place. Hopelessness looms large
Physical: His body feels very heavy, he feels weighed down	*Physical:* He is experiencing a sense of heaviness and paralysis
Longing: Dave longs primarily for this state of heaviness, despair, and exhaustion to disappear. He also wishes to be able to shape his life independently, both in terms of the immediate everyday, and more broadly. Finally, he also longs for satisfying interpersonal relationships, and to be seen and accepted by another as he is	*Longing:* On the one hand, Dave longs for peace, or for the easing of his suffering and heaviness. At the same time, however, he has a quiet longing not to have to be alone, and to be seen
Action and avoidance: With his unconscious strategy ("everything's pointless"), he avoids getting the contact he actually wants. In order to fulfill his need, he would need to become more proactive and independently seek out interactions and activities in order to get out of his depressive state	*Action and avoidance:* Dave experiences a lot of shame and would actually like to hide his suicidal thoughts, even though he longs to be seen with them. He gets caught up in his fantasies and is increasingly withdrawing from the outside world
Contact with the outside world: Dave withdraws, and is trapped in his thoughts. Both in intra- and interpsychic terms, the predominant contact interruption is deflection	*Contact with the outside world:* Dave's loneliness is even greater; he is in the process of taking his leave from this life. He feels as if it has always been like this His perception has very much shifted inwards, and focuses primarily on his cognitive and emotional experience. The outside world and interpersonal relationships are becoming increasingly insignificant. The predominant contact interruption is a *deflection*

The inner dialogue could be depicted as shown in Fig. 13.1:

Case Transcript: Depression with Suicidal Thoughts

Dave is sitting in his room and hasn't turned up for occupational therapy.

00:00:01

SW: Dave, I just wanted to check on you. You know it's occupational therapy right now, don't you?

00:00:05

C: Mmm (affirming).

00:00:05

SW: Are you not able to join us today?

00:00:11

C: Can't do it today.

00:00:12

SW: Mmm (affirming).

00:00:12

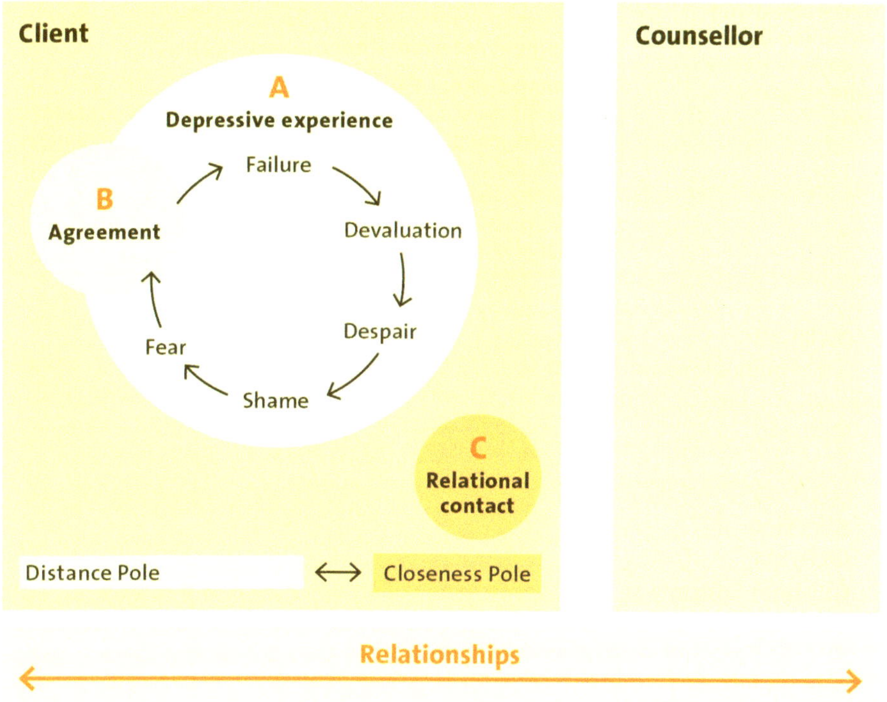

Fig. 13.1 "Depression with suicidal thoughts"—identified inner parts

C: I can't manage it.
00:00:12
SW: Mmm Okay. Dave, I'd like to sit down with you for a few minutes.
00:00:17
C: Mmm (affirming).
00:00:19
SW: I'll get a chair. Hmm. Can you describe to me briefly... What's going on when you say: "I can't do it today"?
00:00:37
C: Pfff, it's like a heaviness. It pulls me down into this chair and it's ... all just pointless. I mean, what's the point? I can't be bothered with it all anymore.
00:00:57
SW: Things seem very, very heavy today. You know this feeling, don't you? You sometimes seem to have a real heaviness on you. Today it seems to be even heavier than usual. Would you agree?
00:01:11
C: Yes, today's...even heavier than usual. Nothing makes sense anymore.

Effect on the client	Intervention and resonance
Dave feels understood and accepted because someone is there who responds to him.	Connecting and Exploring: What's going on for Dave? How is he doing right now? (**Dialogical Attitude, Phenomenology**) **Resonance/Real Fantasy:** The counsellor clearly feels the heaviness and despair 'in the room'. He suspects that Dave is having a particularly difficult day, and wonders if he is having suicidal thoughts. The counsellor asks directly if he is having thoughts about taking his own life. He slows down and pauses deliberately.

00:01:29
SW: Hmm, Dave, when you say, "Nothing makes sense anymore," I'm wondering: are you having thoughts about actually taking your own life?
00:01:40
C: Yeah.
00:01:40
SW: Yes?
00:01:44
C: Mmm (affirming), yeah, the thought comes up every now and then.
00:01:52
SW: Because it's so hard and so hopeless?
00:01:53
C: Yeah...it's almost unbearable. Pfff...I mean, if there were pills here right now, I would consider taking them.

Dave is relieved to be asked directly. This helps to overcome his shame. The pauses in conversation and the slowness do Dave good, as they allow him to clarify his thoughts.

Resonance:

In our experience, it is important to begin with to acknowledge these suicidal thoughts. The role-player's initial impulse was always just to sit with Dave and be silent together. This is because anything that he might say would be so "cognitive" that it would fail to meet the deep need for acknowledgment. This phase is all about showing that the counsellor is there. Genuine sympathy touches a primal and existential level that words and verbal exchange cannot convey. Here, understanding and acceptance of Dave's experience take place in silence.

00:02:11

SW: Mmm... I notice that really touches me. If I imagine I was to come into this room and you'd done something to yourself. And you were lying there, dead. That really...touches me.

00:02:30

C: Hmm. Well, it scares me a bit too when you...that image, when you say it like that. I wouldn't really want that either, but at the same time it's like: "What's the point? It doesn't make sense anymore."

00:02:54

SW: Mmm. I've known you for a while and know how you really struggle sometimes. How much you try. There are always phases where it really does feel hopeless. I can understand that ideas like that come up, so you don't have to bear it anymore.

00:03:13

C: Mmm.

Dave is startled by the image when it is reflected back to him so directly; he experiences the existential dimension of his thoughts and realises what this could mean for other people in his life.

Real fantasy: The counsellor expresses personal concern.
He describes his own image of what it would be like if Dave actually harmed himself and shares his concern.

Resonance: An image arises within the counsellor that triggers personal concern in him.

This personal concern represents an offer of relationship, as long as it is meant sincerely and not just 'professional talk'. However, it is helpful only if it does not subtly convey that it would not be okay if Dave took his own life, i.e., that it would make the counsellor feel bad.

00:03:22

SW: Dave, I get the impression that you're already a bit...out of it.

00:03:28

C: Mmm (affirming).
00:03:28
SW: Yes?
00:03:28
C: Yeah, I'm not quite all there anymore. It's almost like I've already started to say goodbye.

Dave feels accepted in his despair. The pause is good, as he can feel more clearly how he has indeed already started to take his leave. He is able to show up with his failure, his loss of face.

Inclusion and **Confirmation**

The counsellor makes it clear that he can understand Dave's thoughts and asks him if he has distanced himself from the world. This is witnessed and honoured through a longer pause.

Resonance: The counsellor senses that Dave is somehow far away.

00:03:55
SW: Mmm. Dave, I would really like to keep exploring this with you, to carry on looking at this together. And it's important to me to know how concrete these thoughts are. And in the sense that this is an institution, there are certain guidelines that I need to follow. I'd like to know if—if I can rely on you not to harm yourself in the next two days? Do you think you can promise me that?
00:04:34
C: I think so, yeah. I mean, the thoughts are still there and either I do it or I don't. But, no, not in the next 2 days.
00:04:49
SW: That sounds really good. I'm really glad to hear that, because I'd really value having some more time with you to look at this properly, at what's troubling you so very deeply. So I'm going to suggest that I briefly go and organise a few things which I need to take care of so that I have more time later. And then I'd like to come back in about an hour so that we can look at things bit by bit.
00:05:23
C: Yes.
00:05:31
SW: Yes? Is that okay for you?
00:05:31
C: Mmm (affirming).
00:05:36
SW: Good, Dave. See you soon.

We wish to point out that in such a case, this brief intervention is in no way sufficient. Further conversations must take place, and admission to a psychiatric clinic for crisis intervention may be necessary.

Client experience:

The no-suicide contract helps Dave to realise that his suicidal thoughts are not yet so strong that he will end his life within the next two days. He thus holds on to the opportunity to consider how his considerations and decisions may have an impact on other people.

Institutional level and further measures:

The counsellor is aware of the institutional obligation regarding documentation in the case of suicidal thoughts. He also decides to initiate a verbal no-suicide contract with Dave, and to hold further conversations with him. He informs Dave about the next steps. In addition to the organisational / institutional level, it is also important for the counsellor to gain clarity about Dave's intentions on a personal level.

Note:

The no-suicide contract is dealt with relatively quickly in the example. More time should be taken in practice.

Value Squares

The value squares in Fig. 13.2 are designed to show directions of development for Dave. We wish to illuminate three levels. The first is the "intrapsychic" perspective, which refers to internal, cognitive-emotional processes of evaluation. The second, "interpersonal, relational", refers to internal dynamics that are important in dealing with other people. The third level, "behaviour", is ultimately the result of the preceding thoughts and feelings.

Such differentiation between the three categories is ultimately only possible to a limited extent, as the levels are mutually dependent. Nevertheless, we see the distinction between these perspectives as advantageous, as it allows us to recognise significant tendencies. The following development squares serve as suggestions, and were constructed through our exploration in the respective roles. These are intended to stimulate the formation of your own versions, as other similar perspectives and variations are certainly conceivable.

Discussion

The specific phases of suicidality are described in the specialist literature, and are traditionally divided into deliberation, ambivalence, and decision phases (Pöldinger, 1968). However, the transitions are fluid and ultimately the individual's personal experience is decisive. Dave is probably in an advanced stage of the ambivalence phase. It should again be emphasised that further intervention and support would be necessary after this brief encounter.

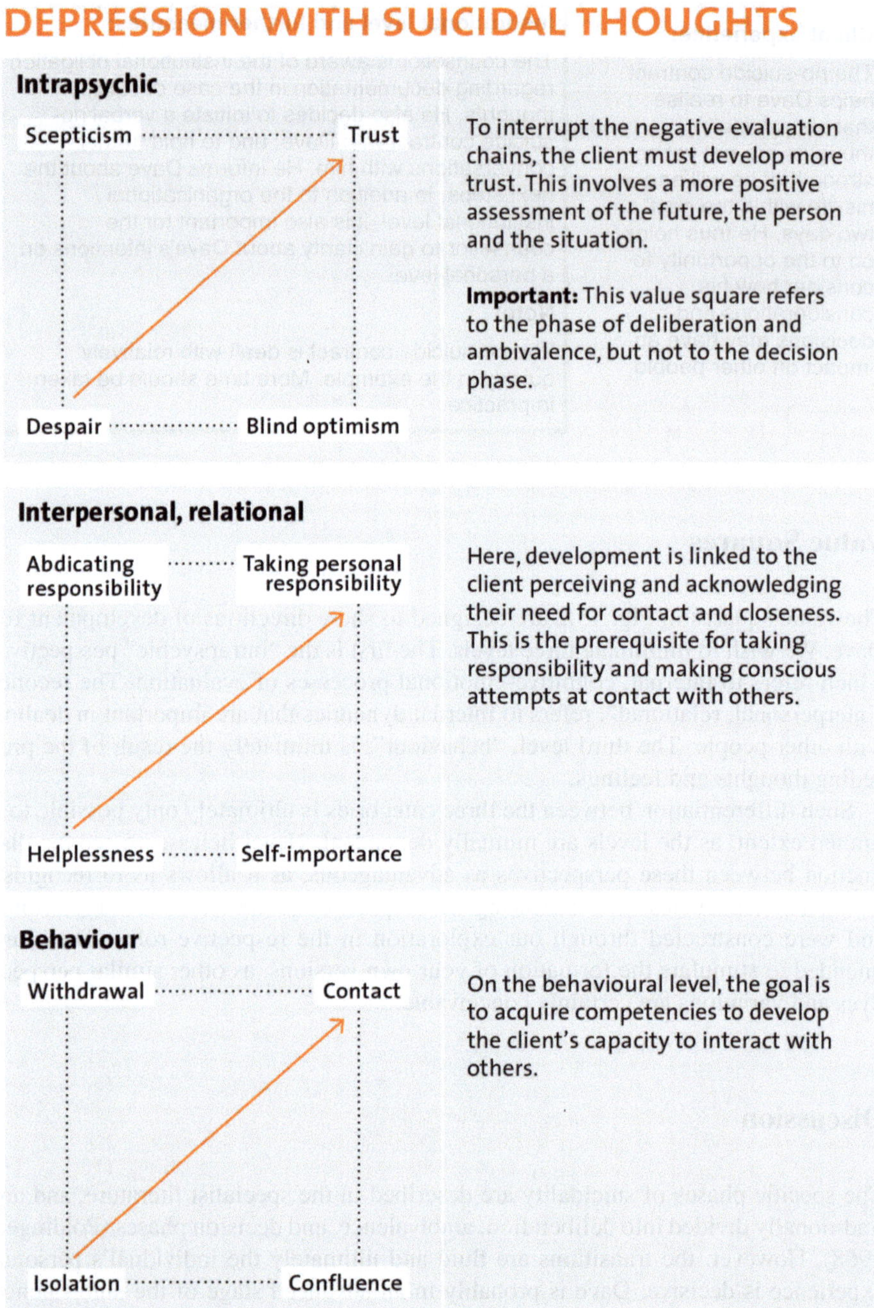

Fig. 13.2 Value squares for "Depression with suicidal thoughts"

In our reflective discussions, it was clear that an attitude that leaves the responsibility for action entirely with the client is incompatible with the legal requirements. German law (StGB BfJ, n.d.) stipulates that if there are any doubts about the person's ability to make a decision based on their own free will, then the position of guarantor must be assumed. In cases of mental illness, suicidality or profound impairment of consciousness, such as in severe depression, it is to be assumed that this ability is impaired. Professionals in the German context are thus obliged to act accordingly, and in cases of acute danger, involuntary admission of the client must be arranged (PsychKG §10 Abs. 1, 2 Justice-online, n.d.). We wish to point out that this legal norm is based on a medical understanding of illness. Indeed, clients can often distance themselves from their suicidal thoughts and impulses when they feel better at some point in the future. The purpose of the law is therefore one of existential protection in cases of acute self-endangerment, when it becomes necessary to temporarily suspend the individual's right to determine their place of residence as well as their right to free will.

Nonetheless, we are critical of the fact that suicidal thoughts and the desire not to go on living are declared a societal taboo on the basis of this constructed norm. Dave is also aware of this, and is ashamed about his supposed 'failure' and his suicidal thoughts. If a professional represents this understanding of normality and conveys to the client that it is not okay to have such thoughts and impulses, this is likely to intensify their sense of shame and inner withdrawal and make it more difficult to build a relationship. The message on the relational level would be: "You are not okay as you are". This is exactly what Dave is already experiencing. The corrective experience would be to receive an affirmation that he is okay as he is.

Seen from this perspective, the personal attitude which the professional brings into the encounter is of great importance. If they react with calm and acceptance, as in this example, and can ultimately also tolerate the possibility that the client *may* choose suicide, then they can offer a supportive relationship that allows *what is*. Of course, the institutional level also exists, based on the legal regulations. This must be made transparent to clients. But at the heart of the personal, dialogical encounter is the acceptance of all thoughts, impulses, and behaviours that arise in the client, regardless of their content (see summary graphic).

The intention to commit suicide can also be understood as aggressive behaviour against oneself. Verbalising the obvious increases the client's awareness of their own inner processes, in this case how Dave relates to himself. The phenomenological method (*Phenomenology*) is oriented towards subjective experience and creates space for what is. This includes the images and fantasies that describe what it would be like if Dave committed suicide. The chance to verbalise such thoughts and emotions means that the client can express these ideas to another, which may help free them from their own internal brooding. In this way, in the presence of another, there is more space for the client's inner experience, and therefore the opportunity to feel more clearly what suicide would mean. This can be frightening for both client and counsellor. At the same time, however, this clarity and distinctness can be very helpful. Above all, it opens up an experiential space with a 'witness'. Dave is understood and accepted in the depths of his experience. This stengthens the quality of relational connection.

An important relationship, an I-Thou encounter, is unfolding (*Dialogical Relationship*). This can act like an umbilical cord to the world, offering the opportunity to reestablish contact with other people. Of course, more time is needed beyond the short conversation in the transcript, in order to deliver the appropriate support. The foundations for such a relationship are nonetheless laid here.

In the course of our reflections, another image arose: what if Dave had lived in a small tribe or village. Imagine if it was customary there for everyone to come together when a member of that community was struggling in some way. Dave would therefore receive the full attention of the community, and would share his suicidal thoughts with them. Simply being seen can be very healing and represent a turning point, especially when communicating emotional experiences. This is in alignment with Gestalt therapy's understanding of how change occurs. However, it is also conceivable that Dave's wish to take his own life might remain, and that the community would support him in this process of ending his life. This would represent a different concept of normality, one which does not exist as such in our society. However, by naming this, we wish to draw attention to the potential diversity of viewpoints which exists; every professional must engage with the topic of 'voluntary death', death and dying in general on a personal level so that they are clear as to their own position and can discuss the topic authentically.

Regardless of the counsellor's personal standpoint, an I-Thou encounter can only arise if they can embody a fundamental attitude of acceptance (*Dialogical Attitude*). The legal norm corresponds to an I-It relationship, which complicates and may compromise the development of a truly healing relationship.

During our explorations, we also gained the impression that Dave has a desire to free himself from a strong sense of being determined by external forces in his life. If the wish for self-determination exists and cannot be realised in his life, this may explain why he might attempt to seek this through suicide. One might reflect on the fact that the institutional and legal procedures for compulsory admission contradict such a relational need. An offer of relationship which allows for open discussion without imposing a decision form the outside would be more aligned with this need.

In addition, we discussed how it might affect our assessment of the situation and ideas on intervention if Dave had agreed to the no-suicide contract but then went on to commit suicide once the counsellor had left the room. We believe that when working with adults, especially in this case, we can only truly encounter Dave when we see him as a self-responsible and self-determined human being. Gestalt therapy is based on an attitude of respect of our fellow humans and upon the recognition of each individual's personal responsibility. From such a perspective, we assume that each individual decides for themselves and is in turn responsible for how they act. As such, the counsellor places their trusts in the power of relationship, and leaves the room. Of course, he would experience a range of emotions if Dave didn't keep to the agreement. However, there is no absolute certainty that a client will adhere to such an agreement. What is crucial is the way in which agreements are made, and the professional's inner resonance as to the credibility of the client's promise. In any discussion on the topic of death and dying, it should become clear that there is no certainty, because life in this world can always present unforeseeable risks and developments against which a person may not be able to protect themselves. Dying is a part of life (*Existentialism*).

According to the Gestalt understanding of process, the suicidal pole, with the corresponding thoughts and emotions of wanting to take one's own life, needs space for exploration (*Polarisation*). According to our understanding, this will not increase the likelihood of suicide. The fear that giving space to suicidal thoughts makes actual suicide more likely is unjustified. In fact, we maintain that inhibiting honest confrontation with the suicidal pole actually hinders the development of the pole which wishes to live, the true force of which cannot unfold in this way. Indeed, Dave experiences relief when his thoughts can be openly addressed and verbalised, because this breaks the taboo of not being allowed to talk about it. Only when the suicidal pole is thoroughly explored and described is it possible for the opposite pole, the part that wants to continue living, to come into expression. Once the dilemma of the contradiction between the two poles and the resulting stagnation becomes tangible, a process of holistic change may be set into motion, seeing the emergence of corresponding solutions.

As a final point, when in the client role, we noticed a high sensitivity towards that which separates. It is for this reason, too, that the experience of being met with acceptance for what is carried so much meaning, because it builds connection and relationship. We suspect that many people ultimately leave this life, or commit suicide, because they are not seen, and are left alone, in their inner experiences. It is therefore so important to have a space to talk about it and for another to 'reach out their hand' on a relational level.

Summary Graphic (Fig. 13.3): Client Experience and Key Interventions

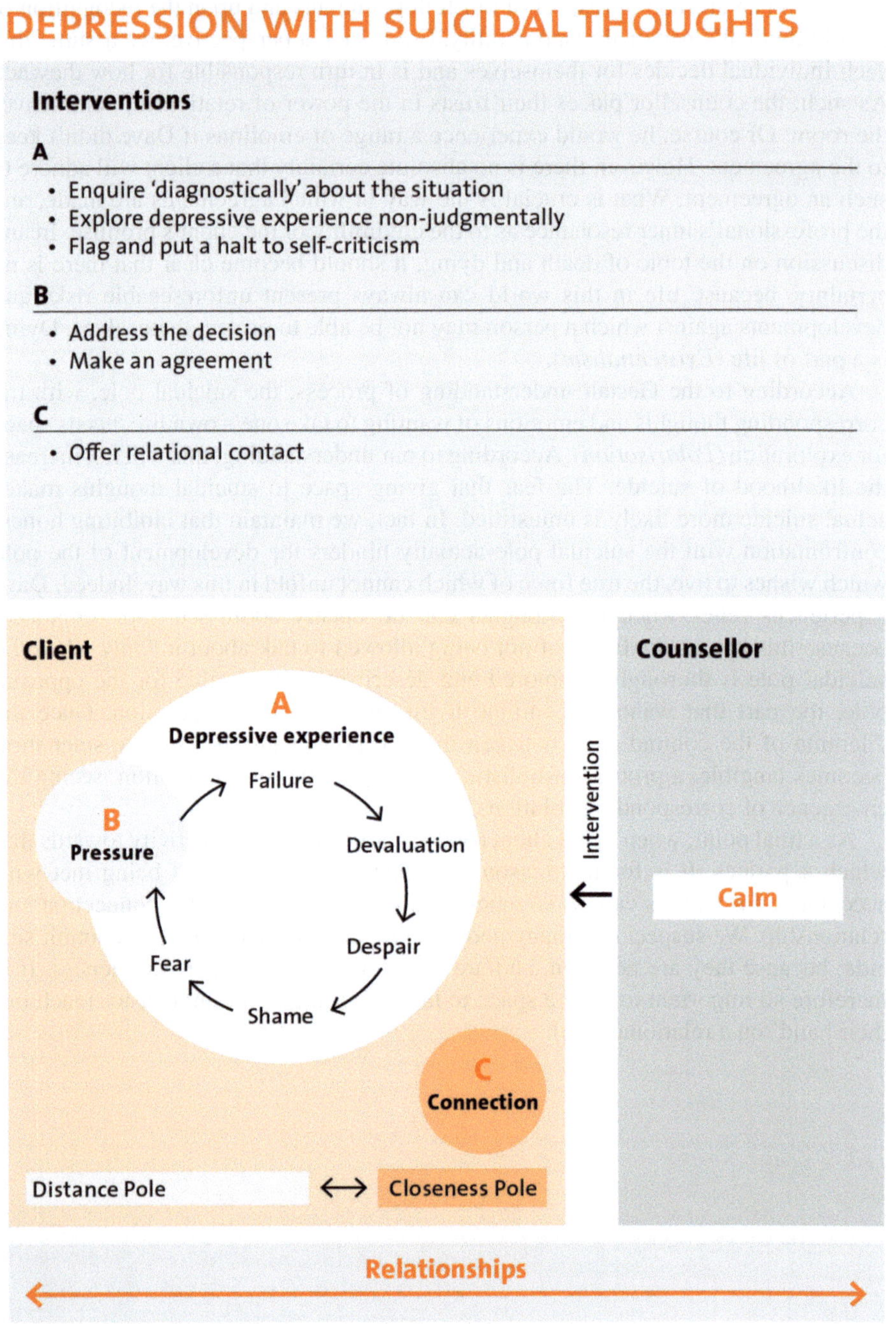

Fig. 13.3 "Depression with suicidal thoughts"—summary graphic

References

BfJ (o. J.). Strafgesetzbuch (StGB). (n.d.). *§ 20 Schuldunfähigkeit wegen seelischer Störungen.* https://www.gesetze-im-internet.de/stgb/__20.html (Stand 24.08.2022).

Justiz-online. *Justizportal Nordrhein-Westfalen (o. J.).* (n.d.). *Gesetz über Hilfen und Schutzmaßnahmen bei psychischen Krankheiten (PsychKG).* https://www.lexsoft.de/cgi-bin/lexsoft/justizportal_nrw.cgi?templateID=document&xid=146892,11,20170101&task=chose_fliesstext (Stand: 24.08.2022).

Pöldinger, W. (1968). *Die Abschätzung der Suizidalität.* Huber.

Chapter 14
Substance Dependence

Case Summary

In this example, Paul (client) is 45 years old. He is married and has two children (10 and 12 years old). He lives with his family in their own house in a small village. He works as a scaffolder in a small company. A fixed aspect of his life are his visits to the village pub three times a week, as well as going for a morning pint on Sundays. He generally drinks at least three litres of beer per evening, and there are sometimes several rounds of spirits too. In addition, he also drinks on birthdays or other festive occasions. Paul's boss still tolerates his behavioural abnormalities, but problems in the form of lateness and unreliability are increasing. He regularly argues with his wife when he comes home very drunk. His GP has found abnormal values in a liver function test, and has suggested an association with Paul's alcohol consumption. She has recommended that he seeks addiction counselling.

Diagnostically, according to the ICD-11 criteria, Paul displays an alcohol dependence syndrome:

> Alcohol dependence is a disorder of regulation of alcohol use arising from repeated or continuous use of alcohol. The characteristic feature is a strong internal drive to use alcohol, which is manifested by impaired ability to control use, increasing priority given to use over other activities and persistence of use despite harm or negative consequences. These experiences are often accompanied by a subjective sensation of urge or craving to use alcohol. Physiological features of dependence may also be present, including tolerance to the effects of alcohol, withdrawal symptoms following cessation or reduction in use of alcohol, or repeated use of alcohol or pharmacologically similar substances to prevent or alleviate withdrawal symptoms. The features of dependence are usually evident over a period of at least 12 months but the diagnosis may be made if alcohol use is continuous (daily or almost daily) for at least 3 months. (ICD-11, 2024)

See the video entitled "Substance Dependence" for more information (www.gestalt-socialwork.com).

A. Schachameier et al., *Gestalt in Social Work*,
https://doi.org/10.1007/978-3-031-95528-0_14

Experiences in the Client Role

Cognitive

Paul is somewhat worried about his health. He finds the doctor's message and her recommendation that he visit an addiction counselling centre very disturbing. This is primarily because he wishes to continue his life as he has led it for the last 20 years. He hopes that the addiction counsellor will not see his lifestyle as problematic. On a conscious level, he has no motivation to change, as he is not taking the situation seriously. On a more unconscious level, he realises that his alcohol consumption is harming him and that both professional problems and marital conflicts are increasing.

Note: In the video sequence, the counsellor only addresses Paul's health difficulties, as he has been sent by his doctor due to abnormal liver values. In further conversations, his work and social environments should also be discussed.

Emotional

Paul is shocked by the news from his doctor. He is concerned enough to visit the addiction counselling centre, but at the same time, he maintains a great inner distance to the problem and doesn't really want to acknowledge it. Internally, he faces the situation with a certain numbness. In addition, he harbours an inner resentment and is annoyed because he feels that his lifestyle is threatened. He has little access to his feelings. However, visiting the counselling center is associated with shame and the fear that it might be more serious than he thought.

Physical

He has little access to his body sensations, and especially lacks any sense of his physical condition. He has an inner distance to himself. He follows a 'pattern', i.e. a weekly schedule with fixed slots for drinking and ignores his physical condition.

Longing

Paul doesn't want to change his lifestyle and wishes to continue living as before. He hopes that an expert will confirm that everything is okay. At the same time, Paul also wants to live a healthy and self-determined life. He sometimes notices that his consumption is harming his health, and is worried because his uncle had liver cancer.

Action and Avoidance

He is looking for a simple solution and wants to avoid real change. He is ashamed to talk about the negative effects of consumption and doesn't wish to be associated with the topic of alcoholism.

Contact with the Outside World

He trivialises the early warning signals which are already present and is deceiving both himself and his environment about the actual problem. He is on high alert to avoid acknowledging potential consequences and to maintain the status quo. Above all, he does not want to be labelled and stigmatised as an alcoholic. The prevailing contact interruption is deflection.

Identified Inner Parts

A: "Consumption behaviour": "I want to maintain my lifestyle, live a self-determined life and continue to consume."

B: "Conflicts": "The doctor says I drink too much. There are conflicts with my wife about the drinking."

C: "Denial": "I have no problems."

D: "Longing" for recognition and self-determination

The inner dialogue could be depicted as shown in Fig. 14.1:

Case Transcript: Substance Dependence

00:00:01
SW: Hello, Paul. Good to see you. You made an appointment with me. What brings you here?

00:00:08
C: My GP. She said I should come by.

00:00:11
SW: Mmm (affirming).

00:00:12
C: Yeah, I had an examination. There was something up with the liver values, and she thought it could have to do with my alcohol consumption.

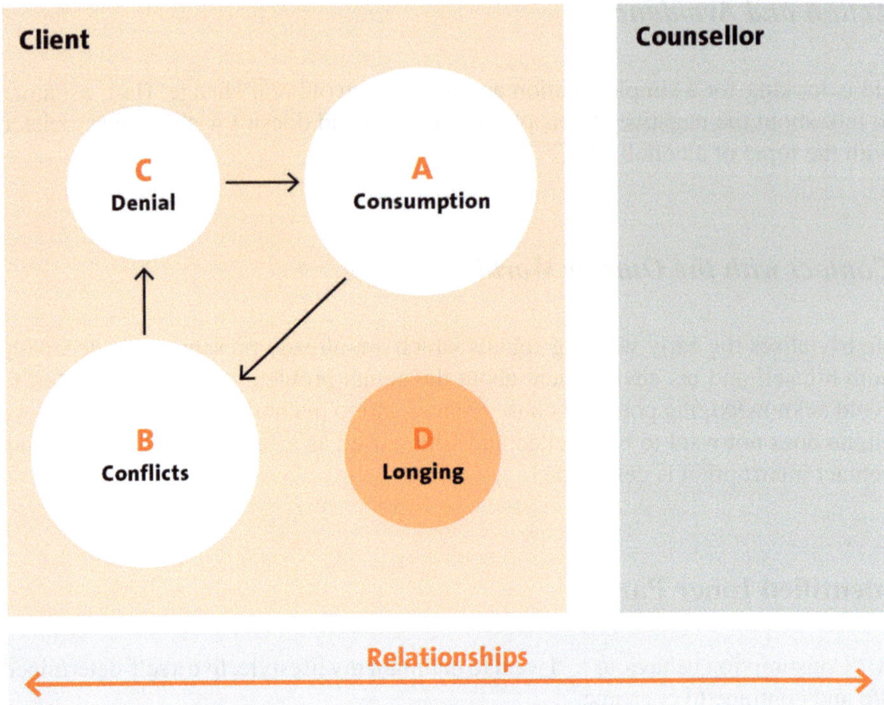

Fig. 14.1 "Substance dependence"—identified inner parts

00:00:19
SW: Oh, okay.

00:00:20
C: I don't reckon it's that, but…yeah, that's why I'm here.

00:00:22
SW: So you can't imagine there being a connection between your liver values and your life?

Effect on the client	Intervention and resonance
Paul feels understood. This intervention resonates with this inner experience and he feels seen in his concern.	The counsellor meets Paul where he is, namely in his scepticism that the liver function values could be connected to his consumption of alcohol, and clarifies the concern with which Paul has come to counselling. (**Dialogical Attitude, Phenomenology**)

00:00:26
C: Well, I mean, I drink a normal amount.

00:00:29
SW: Mmm (affirming). You drink a normal amount, you say. And it sounds to me like you just want to hear what I think about it.

00:00:38
C: Yeah, uh-huh.

00:00:38
SW: A second opinion from me.

00:00:40
C: Mmm, I mean…she said that my liver isn't working properly, but…I don't think it's that, it must be something else.

00:00:43
SW: Mmm.

00:00:43
C: I mean, because it still works. But yes…I guess that's why I'm here.

00:00:48
SW: Mmm. Okay. So… I need to ask you a bit more specifically, so that I can get a feel for how much you *are* drinking. When you say "normal": What is normal? I mean…how much would you say you drink in a week?

00:00:56
C: Well…just like everyone else I know. I mean—we have a group of regulars, we meet three times a week usually.

00:01:04
SW: Uh-huh.

00:01:04
C: So.

00:01:04
SW: Mmm (listening).

00:01:04
C: In the pub.

00:01:07
SW: Mmm (listening).

00:01:07
C: Exactly. Sometimes there's a morning pint on Sunday too. I'd usually be there for that too.

00:01:15
SW: Yes.

00:01:15
C: It's a good crowd.

00:01:15
SW: And how much do you drink there? Mmm…and what do you drink there? Beer, spirits?

00:01:19
C: Mostly beer.

00:01:20
SW: Beer.

00:01:20
C: Yeah. I drink my five, six beers…or…if it's a very long evening sometimes seven, eight beers maybe.

00:01:25
SW: Uh-huh.

00:01:25
C: Yep. And sometimes there's rounds, whiskey mostly.

00:01:30
SW: Mmm. What does a round of whiskey mean? Like one or two shots, or…?

00:01:33
C: Yeah. So usually there are one, two rounds of whiskey, it'd be rare that there'd be more. You know, like on birthdays or when there's a home game or something. When there's something to celebrate. But no, normally it'd just be four, five, six beers and one, two shots to go with it.

00:01:48
SW: Okay.

00:01:49
C: That's basically it, yeah.

00:01:49
SW: Okay, so that's about four fixed days in the week,

00:01:51
C: Yeah.

00:01:51
SW: Where you drink let's say…five beers on average, plus shots—sometimes a little more, sometimes a little less?

00:01:56
C: Yeah.

00:01:57
SW: And how about the other days?

00:02:00
C: I mostly just sit at home and I'd have one, maybe two after-work beers, nothing more.

00:02:03
SW: Uh-huh, and nothing during the day?

00:02:04
C: No, no, no…

00:02:05
SW: Uh-huh.

00:02:06
C: Only after work, in the evening.

00:02:07
SW: Ah, because you're at work before that. What is it that you do?

00:02:09
C: Scaffolding.

00:02:09
SW: Scaffolding… Uh-huh, so you're in construction, okay. And how long have you been living like this? I mean, drinking like this. A couple of years, or…?

00:02:18
C: Well, I guess probably since my apprenticeship. When I was 17.

00:02:20
SW: Mmm.

00:02:20
C: Now I'm 45. It was just what everyone did. Back then when I started…the boys at work took me along.

00:02:29
SW: Mmm. So it's been over 20 years that you've been drinking like this, more or less…

00:02:31
C: Yeah.

00:02:31
SW: Consuming this amount of alcohol.

00:02:34
C: Yeah.

Paul tries to portray the amount he consumes as unproblematic. From his point of view, it is normal to live and consume this way. As such, he trivialises his drinking behaviour.

The counsellor asks Paul about the amount he consumes and how long he has been consuming in this way. He collects information for an initial diagnostic assessment.

00:02:35
SW: Okay. So… You told me you'd like my opinion. And it was important to get a bit more information… But you came here wanting an assessment from me. And—it might be a bit challenging to hear this—but I can tell you relatively clearly that your drinking *will* be having a harmful impact on your health. At that level. You're drinking much more than the body can handle. The probability that your health will be damaged is very high.

00:03:06
C: You reckon? No, I don't think so.

00:03:06
SW: Yes. And I would even go as far as to use the word alcoholism.

00:03:12
C: Nah, I wouldn't—no. I manage my life, I'm on top of things. I'm not an alcoholic. I drink beer, and sometimes a shot—and suddenly I'm an alcoholic? No.

Paul doesn't want to accept this opinion. That would feel disastrous for him. He feels distressed, ashamed and angry.

At the same time, he is confused because he can't fit the "diagnosis" together with his previous self-image.

Part A comes to the fore.

The counsellor gives Paul his expert assessment. He points out the danger of increasing damage to Paul's health with this level of drinking and classifies his consumption as a form of alcoholism.

He thus addresses part B. By so doing, a process of polarisation is initiated (**Stagnation** and **Polarization**)

00:03:23
SW: Does it make you angry to hear that?

00:03:25
C: Yeah, for sure!

00:03:26
SW: Mmm.

00:03:26
C: Yeah, so…

00:03:27
SW: Because you see it completely differently.

00:03:28
C: Yeah—those are the people who hang around at the bus stop, the alcoholics. The ones who are drunk at ten in the morning and then pee in the corner! No way. I'm not an alcoholic. I manage my life. I have a house, I have kids, a wife, I go to work. *I'm* an alcoholic?

Paul expresses his anger and his perspective and tries to distance himself internally from the problem. Part A remains active.

The counsellor supports him in his experience of anger through acknowledging and making space for his subjective experience (**Phenomenology**).

00:03:43
SW: Mmm. And—that doesn't change the fact that I can tell you with a high degree of certainty that your liver will continue to be damaged if you keep drinking like this.

00:03:53
C: (Sighs) (Silence)

00:03:57
SW: What's it like—to hear that?

00:03:59
C: Yeah, it's shit. My uncle had liver cancer. He didn't look great, I don't want to go there. So, I don't like what you're saying.

00:04:08
SW: So it's hard for you to accept what I'm saying?

00:04:11
C: Yeah, well, sure. I mean, I don't believe the bit about being an alcoholic. But that my liver is getting damaged. That's shit. I don't want that, no.

00:04:18
SW: Yeah. So…your health is important to you?

00:04:20
C: Yeah, I mean—liver cancer isn't really…what anyone wants. So yeah.

00:04:25
SW: Mmm (agreeing). Because you have a family, and want to carry on being able to work.

00:04:30
C: Yeah.

00:04:33
SW: Mmm.

00:04:33
C: Uh-huh.

00:04:33
SW: So, your health is important to you?

00:04:35
C: Yeah.

00:04:36
SW: Mmm.

00:04:36
C: Yeah, I want to be fit. I don't want any of that shit.

Paul clearly feels that he wants to maintain his health. He thus becomes very aware of Part B.

At the same time, he is struggling internally. An inner conflict between parts A and B arises.

The counsellor recognises the denial inherent in Paul's attempt to distance himself and once again draws attention to possible health damage; in other words, he confronts Paul again explicitly with part B. This intensifies the inner polarisation and allows Paul to express more from this side.

The counsellor acknowledges and allows space for this state (**Dialogical attitude**).

00:04:40
SW: And at the same time, I'm assuming, you actually like living the way you live. The drinking buddies, the pub nights and so on.

00:04:49
C: Yeah, that's the perk I guess…

00:04:50
SW: Yeah.

00:04:53
C: I feel good there. There's no stress.

00:04:54
SW: Yeah.

00:04:54
C: I don't have to achieve anything, I can just relax.

00:04:55
SW: Yeah

00:04:56
C: It's just nice…you have a good time there.

00:05:00
SW: Mmm (understanding). What's it like to imagine changing something? I mean like…I don't know, perhaps going to the pub and drinking less or not drinking at all?

00:05:09
C: Nah, that's not gonna happen. Everyone's buying rounds of beer, and I just order a lemonade or what? I'd never hear the end of it. Nope, not gonna work.

00:05:16
SW: That wouldn't be possible at all?

00:05:17
C: Well no—a round's a round.

00:05:17
SW: Uh-huh.

00:05:19
C: (Shrugs). Yeah.

00:05:20
SW: Mmm. I can imagine this is difficult for you right now.

00:05:26
C: (sighs)

Paul becomes aware of how satisfied he is with his life, especially in terms of his social drinking. A change in his consumption seems impossible.

The counsellor is now allowing Paul to explore part A by sharing a **real fantasy**. In particular, he asks how this part would react to a change in consumption.

00:05:26
SW: Because on the one hand, it's clear that your health is important to you. And you've just heard me saying that if you carry on like this, your health will be damaged. And at the same time, you don't want to make any changes to your life, either.
(Silence 00:05:36–00:05:40).

00:05:42
C: Pffff, yes. I don't know what to say right now.

00:05:45
SW: It's a lot to take right now, isn't it?

00:05:49
C: Mmm yeah, yeah.

00:05:52
SW: It's overwhelming right now, isn't it?

00:05:56
C: Yeah. I don't like it.

00:05:58
SW: You don't like it.

00:05:58
C: No, I don't like it at all. No.

00:06:00
SW: Yeah.

00:06:00
C: No, no. I don't want to change anything, not at all. But, liver cancer. I don't want that either. It's crap.

00:06:06
SW: It's a dilemma, isn't it?

00:06:08
C: Yeah. It's shit!

00:06:09
SW: And it's hard, right now.

00:06:13
C: Yeah. I can't believe it.

00:06:14
SW: Yeah. You can't believe it at all.

00:06:15
C: Yup.

00:06:16
SW: Mmm. And I have the impression you can't even form a clear thought right now. As if everything's kind of spinning.

Paul is desperate and overwhelmed because he can't see a way out. He can't think clearly anymore and is relieved to be seen in that.

The counsellor creates a framework for exploration by naming both parts and tries to make space for Paul's current state from moment to moment.

The aim is to further explore this polarisation. The responsibility and decision for / against any further steps towards reducing or abstaining from consumption remain with Paul (**Stagnation and Polarisation).**

00:06:27
C: Yeah, yeah.

00:06:27
SW: Mmm (affirming). Paul, it's often like that at this point. Yeah? In my experience, when someone hears an expert opinion like this, and finds out their drinking is harmful to their health, then it's hard to digest at first. And it takes time. Mmm. It's not something you can sort out just like that. And that's exactly what I can offer you. So that—if you want, right?—you can come back, and we can carry on here where we left off, and have a think about what you can do. And take time to digest the whole thing.

00:07:02
C: Yeah. Uh-huh (pondering).

00:07:05
SW: How does that sound? My offer?

00:07:09
C: Yeah, pff…yeah. I mean…I think that would make sense.

00:07:11
SW: Yeah.

00:07:11
C: I don't have a better idea right now.

00:07:15
SW: Because in my experience, it's good to talk to someone about it and not just to go it alone.

00:07:21
C: Pfff, yeah. Uh-huh.

Paul is aware that he can't deal with this topic on his own and can imagine returning and accepting further help.

The counsellor doesn't put pressure on Paul, instead giving him time to digest what he has heard. This is because he notices that Paul is struggling with himself and is not able to process any further information at the moment.
He suggests meeting again to return to this topic where they are leaving it.

00:07:22
SW: Yes? Shall we leave it at that for now? And meet up again?

00:07:27
C: Yeah. Yeah.

00:07:28
SW: You make another appointment and then we'll carry on where we left off, and have a think. And you can let this settle a bit.

00:07:35
C: (sighs)

00:07:35
SW: And then we'll see where you stand. When you come back.

00:07:39
C: Yeah. Yeah, okay, thank you.

Value Squares

The value squares in Fig. 14.2 are designed to show directions of development for Paul. We wish to illuminate three levels. The first is the “intrapsychic” perspective, which refers to internal, cognitive-emotional processes of evaluation. The second, “interpersonal, relational”, refers to internal dynamics that are important in dealing with other people. The third level, “behaviour”, is ultimately the result of the preceding thoughts and feelings.

Such differentiation between the three categories is ultimately only possible to a limited extent, as the levels are mutually dependent. Nevertheless, we see the distinction between these perspectives as advantageous, as it allows us to recognise significant tendencies. The following development squares serve as suggestions, and were constructed through our exploration in the respective roles. These are intended to stimulate the formation of your own versions, as other similar perspectives and variations are certainly conceivable.

Discussion

In the role-play, it was above all the clear naming of the alcohol problem that got through to the client. Attempts to convey this message gently, or to relativise or trivialise it, lead Paul to distance himself further from the problem internally. We assume that he only really feels seen and taken seriously when the counsellor names what is being denied. This confrontation creates a relationship. Initiating and supporting the client to really experience the polarity between change and resistance is an important part of motivational work, and this experience must be allowed rather than passed over too quickly. It is essential for the process that the counsellor follows the client on a moment-by-moment basis, rather than asking more questions or discussing further steps too early.

In working with people with addiction disorders, the “motivational interview” (Miller & Rollnick, 2009) is significant. This is an evidence-based tool (see for example Rumpf et al., 2015) for developing motivation for abstinence. Client-centred and systemic methods and techniques are fundamental. To bring about motivation for change, an attempt is made to create internal dissonance in clients, such as by contrasting arguments for and against consumption. Simply put, clients are encouraged to reflect in order to develop a goal for change (Prochaska et al., 1997). This idea stems from the transtheoretical model, which describes change processes as passing through various states of change, from pre-contemplation (where there is no intention of changing behaviour) through contemplation and preparation, to active modification of behaviour and the maintenance needed to sustain this change (ibid., 61).

This bears certain similarities to Gestalt therapy’s model of change, but Staemmler and Bock’s theory of change (1998, **Holistic Change Processes**) puts a much stronger emphasis on the holistic experience—in other words, insisting that the dialogue takes place on more than just a cognitive level. In the example discussed above, the difference becomes clear in that it is Paul’s holistic experience

SUBSTANCE DEPENDENCE

Intrapsychic

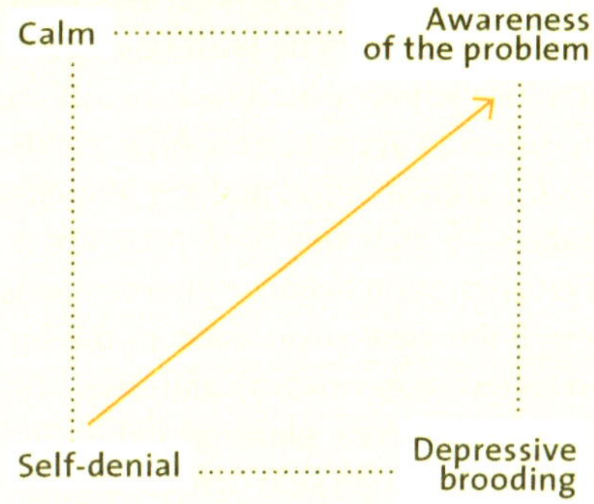

An important developmental step for Paul is to be more honest with himself, and to develop an awareness of the problem rather than trivialising it.

Interpersonal, relational

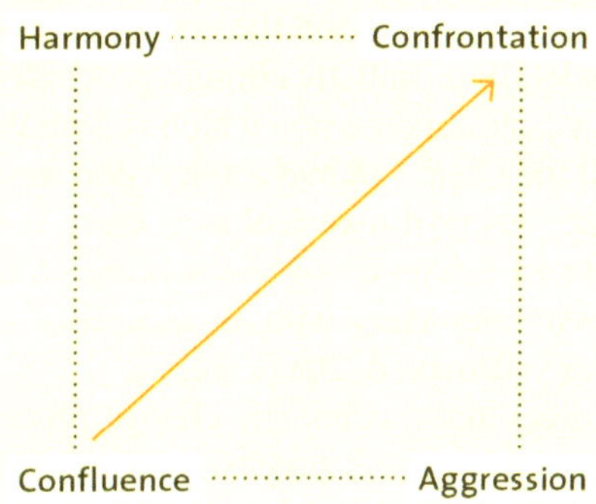

In contact with others, it is about engaging in necessary conflicts and dealing constructively with difficulties.

Behaviour

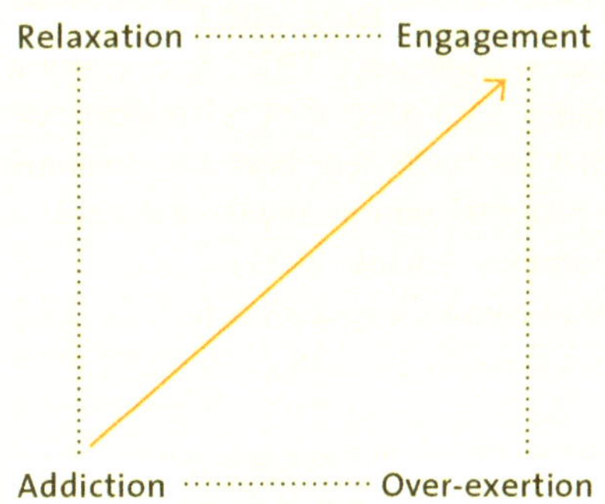

On the behavioural level, an important developmental step is to become more active, to tackle important professional and private tasks and not to pursue the addictive behavior.

Fig. 14.2 Value squares for "substance dependence"

that is attended to. While the cognitive level is involved, the counsellor aims to support Paul's awareness of his emotional and physical sensations, as far as this is possible in an initial conversation like this.

Further into the consultation or treatment process, the relevant inner parts could be physically represented in the room and brought into dialogue with one another: for example, the part which enjoys consumption or the part which is aware of various social conflicts. This dialogical, experience-oriented approach enables clients to develop an awareness of their inner motivation for consumption and the associated patterns of thought and behaviour. The resistance—which stands in opposition to the need—wants to maintain the status quo of consumption because pleasant sensations are associated with it, for example. Through the clear expression of the inner movement and the inner reactions to this movement (e.g. towards and away from consumption), an increasing awareness of emotional motives, patterns and attitudes of the two parts emerges. Clarity can also arise as to how one side 'tricks' the other, how this might be counteracted, and what the client's experience was in phases when less or nothing was consumed.

When a change process runs an 'ideal' course, according to Staemmler and Bock (1998), the solution for the conflict does not arise primarily on the cognitive level. The fundamental principle is that of **self-actualisation** (**holistic change processes**). Here, the counsellor does not push the client in a certain direction which is desirable from their point of view, but rather waits until the client can make a decision themselves. Space is made for the 'impasse' phase, where it may feel as if there is no solution; the polarity is held and explored "in its fullness," "while waiting on the shift that can occur when the client, having sat completely with all aspects of the ambivalence, chooses one figure over the other" (Brownell, 2012, 38).

In practice, however, it is unrealistic to expect that this holistic change process will run its ideal course at the beginning of a therapeutic process or within the framework of a counselling process. Instead, we suggest that elements of organismic self-regulation can be experienced, or aimed towards, and can effect change themselves. This can mean allowing enough time for noticing feelings and sensations, and accepting the client's pace and capacity, empathising with their constructions of reality, and entering into the encounter with respect. Of course, caution is also required in this regard, as in practice, clients often need a lot of support due to multiple challenges. A careful distinction must be made here between reasonable and productive 'letting go' and 'trusting the process' on one hand, and necessary supportive interventions on the other (Schachameier & Link, 2021).

Social workers who are employed in addiction counselling centres usually hold an additional therapeutic qualification. This makes it possible to carry out outpatient rehabilitation and to work therapeutically. Addiction is often co-morbid with other forms of mental illness, and it can may be fruitful or necessary to involve or cooperate with other psychiatric or psychotherapeutic professionals during the course of treatment.

In terms of the case featured in this chapter, continuing the consultation in the context of an outpatient rehabilitation service would be one of several possibilities, while admission to a specialist clinic would also be conceivable. Attention should also be drawn to options such as participating in self-help or other group settings, and the possible necessity for rehabilitation therapy communicated.

Summary Graphic (Figs. 14.3 and 14.4): Client Experience and Key Interventions

Step 1: Exploring

SUBSTANCE DEPENDENCE – STEP 1

Interventions

A

- Enquire 'diagnostically' about the addictive behaviour
- Explore emotional aspects of addictive behaviour non-judgmentally

B

- Ask about external conflicts (health, social problems, finances)
- Explore internal emotional conflicts non-judgmentally

C

- Raise awareness of and flag any denial or trivialisation of conflicts

D

- Be on the look-out for possible longings (health, self-determination, social relaxation)

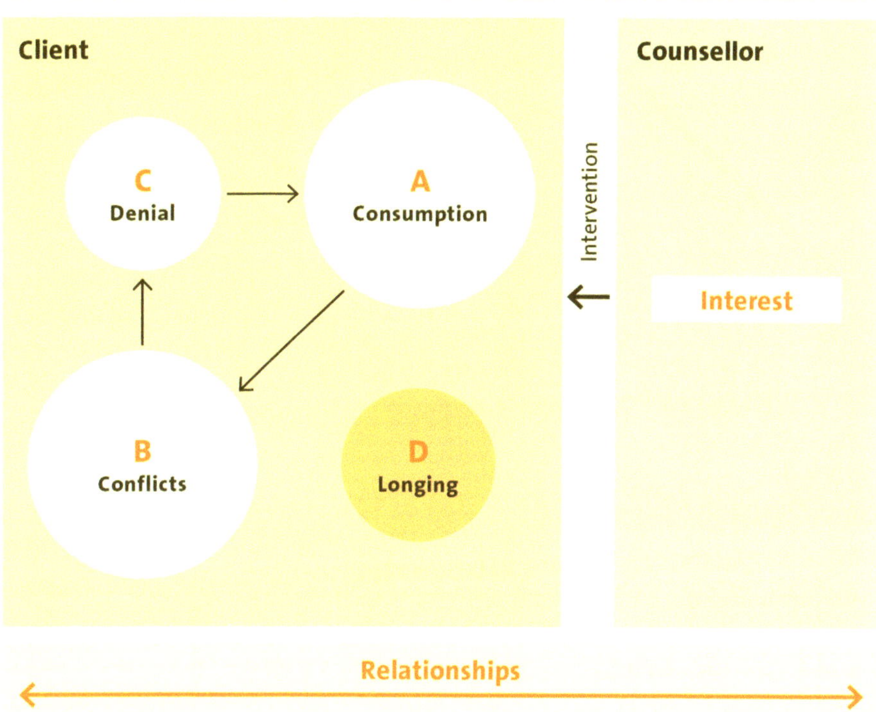

Fig. 14.3 "Substance dependence/exploration"—summary graphic

Step 2: Confronting

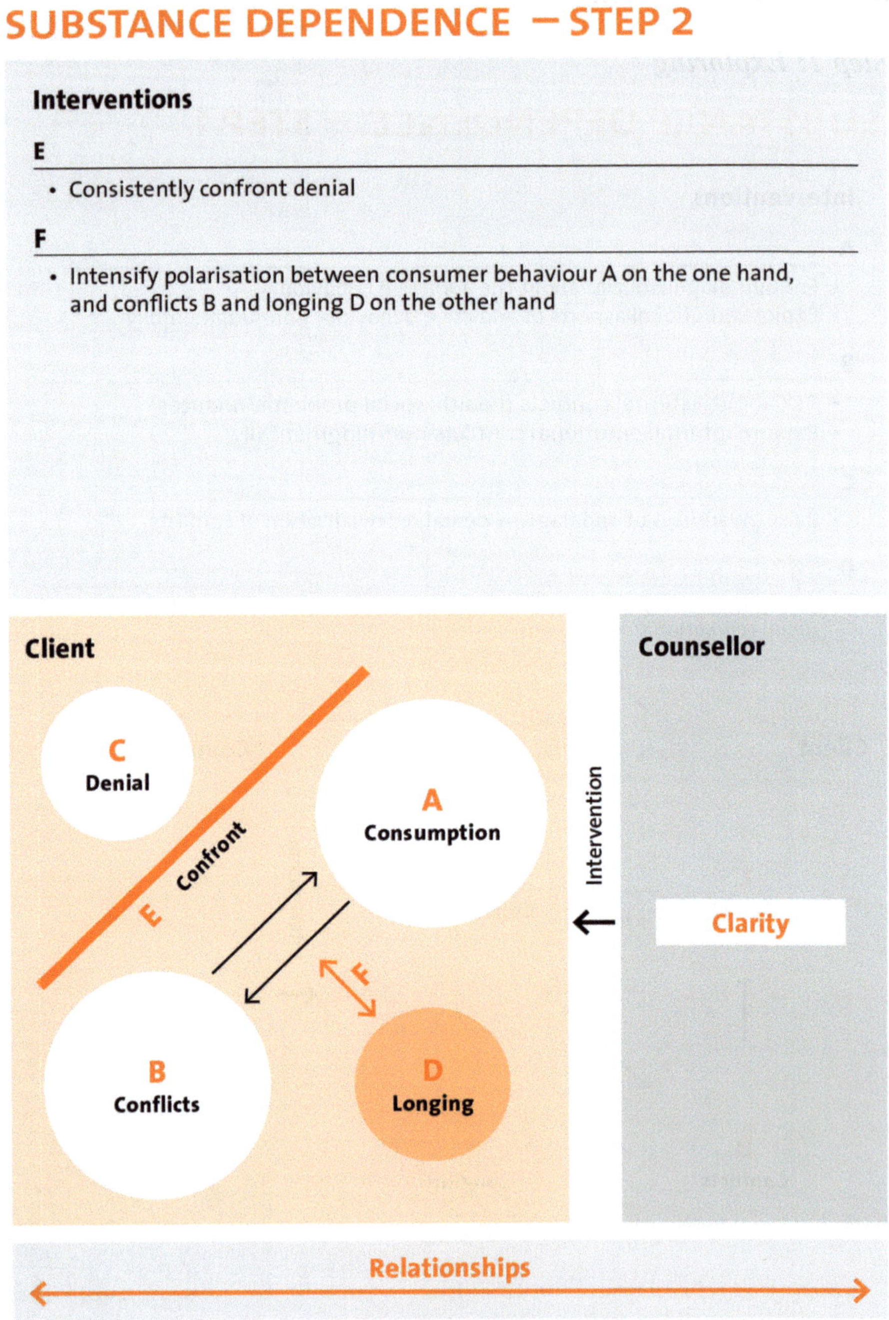

Fig. 14.4 "Substance dependence/confrontation"—summary graphic

References

Brownell, P. (2012). *Gestalt therapy for addictive and self-medicating behaviors*. Springer.

ICD-11. (2024). 6C40.2 Alcohol dependence. In: *International classification of diseases 11th revision*. Retrieved January 13, 2025, from https://icd.who.int/browse/2024-01/mms/en#1580466198

Miller, W. R., & Rollnick, S. (2009). *Motivierende Gesprächsführung*. Lambertus-Verlag.

Prochaska, J. O., Norcross, J. C., & DiClemente, C. C. (1997). *Jetzt fange ich neu an*. Droemersche Verlagsanstalt.

Rumpf, H.-J., Bischof, G., Demmel, R., Freyer-Adam, J., Kremer, G., & Neumann, T. (2015, February 23). Behandlung von schädlichem und abhängigem Alkoholgebrauch. In Arbeitsgemeinschaft der Wissenschaftlichen Medizinischen Fachgesellschaften (Ed.), *S3-Leitlinie "Screening, Diagnose und Behandlung alkoholbezogener Störungen"*. AWMF Online.

Schachameier, A., & Link, P.-C. (2021). Methoden der Suchtberatung aus humanistisch-experientieller Perspektive. *Sucht Aktuell, 2*(21), 20–27.

Staemmler, F.-M., & Bock, W. (1998). *Ganzheitliche Veränderung in der Gestalttherapie*. Peter Hammer Verlag.

Chapter 15
Substance Dependence in a Mandatory Counselling Context

Case Summary

Jack (client) is 17 years old in this example. He still lives with his parents, has a high school diploma and is in the second year of training to become an electronics technician. He has been consuming cannabis regularly for about two years and smokes several bongs (water pipes) per day. His social life consists exclusively of meeting friends with similar habits of consumption; he does not engage in any other leisure activities. To help finance his addiction, he has started selling marijuana. He was recently caught by the police with about 100 g and received a juvenile sentence which requires him to complete 30 hours of community service and to take 7 hours of addiction counselling.

Diagnostically, according to the ICD-11 criteria, a cannabis dependence syndrome is present:

> Cannabis dependence is a disorder of regulation of cannabis use arising from repeated or continuous use of cannabis. The characteristic feature is a strong internal drive to use cannabis, which is manifested by impaired ability to control use, increasing priority given to use over other activities and persistence of use despite harm or negative consequences. These experiences are often accompanied by a subjective sensation of urge or craving to use cannabis. Physiological features of dependence may also be present, including tolerance to the effects of cannabis, withdrawal symptoms following cessation or reduction in use of cannabis, or repeated use of cannabis or pharmacologically similar substances to prevent or alleviate withdrawal symptoms. The features of dependence are usually evident over a period of at least 12 months but the diagnosis may be made if cannabis use is continuous (daily or almost daily) for at least 3 months. (ICD-11, 2024)

Please watch the video entitled "Substance dependence in a mandatory counselling context", for more information (www.gestalt-socialwork.com).

A. Schachameier et al., *Gestalt in Social Work*,
https://doi.org/10.1007/978-3-031-95528-0_15

Experiences in the Client Role

Cognitive

Jack has not come to counselling voluntarily, but has rather been forced to by an external authority. He defends his lifestyle, including his cannabis use, and has no conscious intention of changing. Above all, he finds it very unfair that there are no comparable penalties for alcohol consumption. He is very critical of the existing legal norms and society at large. However, according to the current law where he lives, his behaviour constitutes a crime—a fact of which he is aware. His top priority is not to have any more 'stress' with the authorities. He has experienced the various confrontations with the police, the court, and his parents as a great burden. He is afraid of the addiction counsellor sending a negative assessment to the court, which could lead to his case being retried.

Emotional

Jack is somewhat anxious and cautious because he does not know what to expect. He knows that he is dependent on the assessment made by the addiction counsellor. This represents a threat to him, and therefore another initially stressful event. Internally, he is closed off in the attempt to avoid conflict.

Physical

Jack tries to appear 'unobtrusive' on the outside, but is tense internally.

Longing

On the one hand, Jack wants to avoid getting into further trouble and somehow sit out these compulsory hours, aiming to get through them so that he can continue living as before. At the same time, however, the overall situation and in particular the stress with his parents are weighing on him. Self-determination is also important to him. But there is a deeper longing that he is unaware or only partially aware of. In contact with other people, he is actually very insecure and shy. Deep down, he longs for more inner stability, self-assurance and confidence. He also wishes he had someone he could talk openly to about himself and his life, because he does sometimes notice that his consumption has got out of hand.

Action and Avoidance and Contact with the Outside World

The immediate danger for Jack lies in a negative assessment by the addiction counsellor and the consequences thereof, namely a further court trial. He is therefore strategic, and avoids authentic contact. He is very careful and controlled about what he reveals about himself.

Deflection is the predominant contact interruption.

Identified Inner Parts

A: "Consumption": "I believe in, and defend, my lifestyle. Smoking weed is part of my life, as is the whole culture associated with it."

B: "Conflicts": "I have stress with the court and my parents."

C: "Denial": "I don't see any problem with my consumption and lifestyle."

D: "Longing": "I want to get rid of the stress and live a self-determined life. Actually, I am an insecure person, and would like to interact more confidently with people."

The inner dialogue could be represented as depicted in Fig. 15.1:

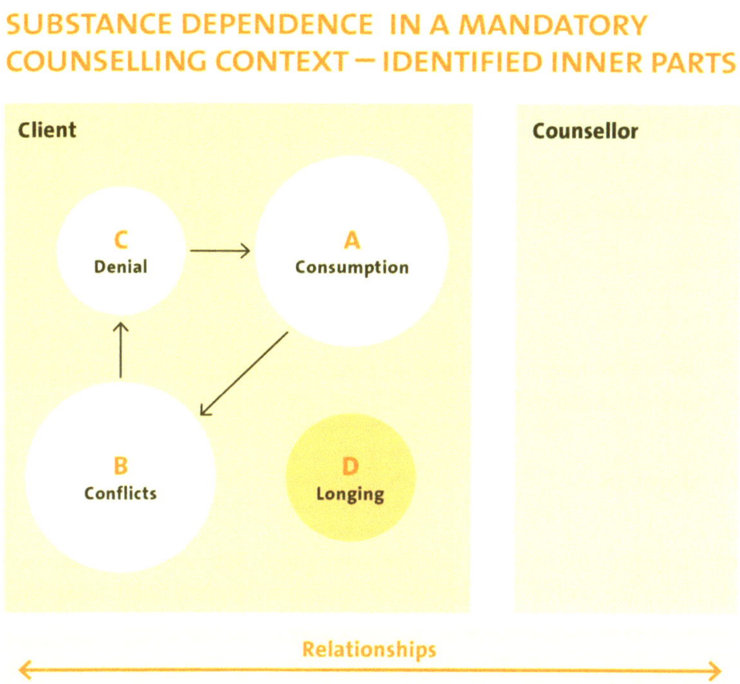

Fig. 15.1 "Substance dependence in a mandatory counselling context"—identified inner parts

Case Transcript: Substance Dependance in a Mandatory Counselling Context

00:00:00
SW: Hello, Jack.

00:00:00
C: Hello.

00:00:01
SW: Good to see you here.

00:00:03
C: Mmm (affirmative).

00:00:03
SW: You made an appointment, and handed in some paperwork, which I've had a look through. But tell me in your own words: why are you here?

00:00:09
C: Yeah. Well… Just like it says in the paperwork. I got caught with weed and the court said I have to do seven hours of addiction counselling. That's why I'm here.

00:00:28
SW: Uh-huh (affirmative). It wasn't clear from the paperwork, but judging by the sentence, I'm assuming you had quite a bit of weed on you? How much was it?

00:00:36
C: Well, about 100 grams.

00:00:40
SW: Mmm (affirmative). That's quite a substantial amount.

00:00:44
C: Yeah.

00:00:44
SW: And now you're here, and you're not here because you're choosing to be here, but because you have to be.

00:00:49
C: Mmm (affirmative).

00:00:51
SW: That probably doesn't feel particularly good. My sense is that you're a bit guarded because you're not sure what's going to happen here, what you can say and what you can't.

00:01:02
C: Mmm (undecided). Yeah, yeah, I don't want anything to happen here…where I get done again, or where the sentence gets changed or something. I'm not up for that, okay, so…

Effect on the client
Part C is addressed. Jack feels understood, but at the same time is surprised and sceptical about this understanding, wondering if it comes with an unspoken expectation, or is a 'trick'. Nevertheless, the intervention gives him space to express his biggest concerns.

Intervention and resonance
The counsellor addresses the involuntary nature of the situation at the beginning. He tries to put himself in the client's shoes, and expresses a **real fantasy**. He suspects that Jack is cautious and might not know what he can safely say. The counsellor is applying the principle of naming the immediate, here-and-now aspects of their relationship.

00:01:15
SW: That's completely understandable. Let's have a bit of a look at what this thing means, that you've been sentenced to, and that you've turned up here for. I think that might be helpful so that you have more orientation. So, what the court requires is that you come here seven times. Today is a kind of introductory or orientation session so we can discuss your consumption.

00:01:36
C: Mmm (affirmative).

00:01:36
SW: It's not about you telling me that you're not going to smoke weed anymore. That would probably be a lie, because you're not here voluntarily. So it's about when and why you consume cannabis, and how you feel about your cannabis consumption.

00:01:53
C: Mmm (affirmative).

00:01:53
SW: And—I have to provide the court with a short report at the end of today's appointment, but only stating whether you attended and whether you engaged in the discussion. I'm not going to report on the content. So everything you say here will be treated confidentially and won't be used against you in a negative light.

00:02:11
C: Okay, so no one can do anything, you mean?

00:02:16
SW: No, if you…

00:02:17
C: Unless I don't show up.

00:02:17
SW: Exactly, unless you don't show up or you refuse to talk here and act as if the whole thing has nothing to do with you.

00:02:26
C: Okay, so I *do* have to talk to you?

00:02:27
SW: Yes, that's the point.

00:02:32
C: Mmm (affirmative).

This puts Jack at ease and gives him orientation. In particular, it addresses part A, i.e. he is not put under pressure to change his consumption behaviour. The requirement is merely that he discusses his consumption behaviour with the counsellor.

The counsellor is transparent about the framework within which the counselling is taking place, with respect to the external court order, the remit of the counsellor, and the form that the work must take. He also clarifies which information is passed on to the court (**Dialogical attitude**). Here, transparency means authenticity.

00:02:33
SW: And you implied earlier that you have no interest in making things more complicated than they already are, right?

00:02:37
C: Mmm (affirmative).

00:02:38
SW: Has it been a challenging time?

00:02:40
C: Yeah. A whole lot of stress has come out of it.

00:02:45
SW: Mmm (affirmative). What's been most stressful about it? When you say it was stressful…what in particular?

00:02:49
C: Yeah, well mainly the parents. I still live with my parents, even though I'm in the second year of my apprenticeship, and they gave me a whole lot of stress. And then there's the community service I've got to do too. I'm done with all this! (laughs).

00:03:07
SW: Mmm (affirmative). And it's challenging, this tension between living at home and managing your own life? And now your parents are on your case because there's a court ruling?

00:03:15
C: Yeah, yeah, it's not easy. So… //

00:03:19
SW: Mmm (affirmative) and that's one possible topic we could use the time here to talk about—what makes things difficult at home; which areas there are where you see or deal with life differently than your parents, and where these differences bring up stress. And how you deal with it. That could be a topic we could discuss.

00:03:36
C: Okay, so we could talk about that kind of stuff?

Part B is addressed here. This arouses Jack's interest, because the stress with his parents in particular has been substantial. He realises that it would do him good to be able to speak about that.

Again, the counsellor tries to put himself in Jack's shoes (**Real fantasy**) and asks him about the stress he has been experiencing. He offers him the opportunity to talk about this, and explains which topics might be covered by the counselling sessions. The expectations Jack obviously has about the experience serve as a yardstick here (**Phenomenology**) and are discussed during the conversation (**Dialogue**).

00:03:39
SW: Exactly. If you had 100 grams of weed on you, I'm assuming you also like to smoke yourself?

00:03:47
C: Yeah.

00:03:47
SW: Uh-huh? How often and how much, as a rough orientation?

00:03:53
C: Well, everyday really…

00:03:56
SW: Mmm (affirmative).

00:03:57
C: Well mainly hanging out with mates in the evenings. We meet up.
00:04:05 SW: And you seem to get a lot from it? You seem to enjoy it? Is that the case?

00:04:10 C: Yeah, I do enjoy it. I mean, hanging out together, I like that.

Jack describes the amount he consumes rather vaguely, due to his ongoing scepticism and tendency to trivialise the problem.

Part A ("consumption behaviour") feels seen. This creates more openness towards the counsellor.

The counsellor addresses the consumption behaviour and expresses his assumption that Jack experiences his lifestyle as positive and has no interest in changing it.

00:04:20
SW: I'm assuming if you didn't have to be here, you wouldn't be here at all?

00:04:24
C: Here with you?

00:04:24
SW: Yes.

00:04:25
C: No (laughs)

00:04:27
SW: That's completely legitimate and at least you're honest about it! And in my experience, there are people who have to come here, and at the end they say it was actually good to have someone to talk to about some of this stuff. They might not have had the feeling before they came in that they needed anything, but it did them good anyway. To have a chat and maybe even realise that there are moments sometimes when it might be more relaxed to smoke a bit less on the odd evening, or even not to smoke at all sometimes. And if so, how might that look, how could you go about that? Does that sound interesting to you at all? It might not. But that could be a personal advantage of these conversations here.

00:05:08
C: Okay.

00:05:09
SW: Time will tell, right?

00:05:10
C: Yeah, okay.

00:05:10
SW: Mmm (affirmative).

00:05:14
C: Yes. Mmm (affirmative).

This somewhat addresses part D. The longing for an authentic relationship where there is space to talk about himself is hardly conscious to him, but the counsellor's short description of others' experiences of counselling generates a positive emotional response.

Jack has a positive feeling overall and is happy to come back.

The counsellor speaks from his experience and tells Jack about some of the feedback from former clients who have had positive experiences reflecting on their consumption (**Inclusion**).

00:05:15
SW: Right? So now you have an idea of what these sessions are about. Next time we'll talk more about your life, your consumption habits. Today is more about orientation.

00:05:30
C: Yeah, good, okay then.

00:05:32
SW: Do you have any more questions?

00:05:33
C: No, that's fine.

00:05:35
SW: That's fine?

00:05:36
C: Mmm (affirmative).

00:05:37
SW: Okay Jack, so if you get yourself another appointment at the front desk, then we'll see each other next time.

00:05:43
C: Alright. Okay.

00:05:43
SW: Great. See you then, then. Bye.

00:05:46
C: Bye.

Value Squares

The value squares in Fig. 15.2 are designed to show directions of development for Jack. We wish to illuminate three levels. The first is the "intrapsychic" perspective, which refers to internal, cognitive-emotional processes of evaluation. The second,

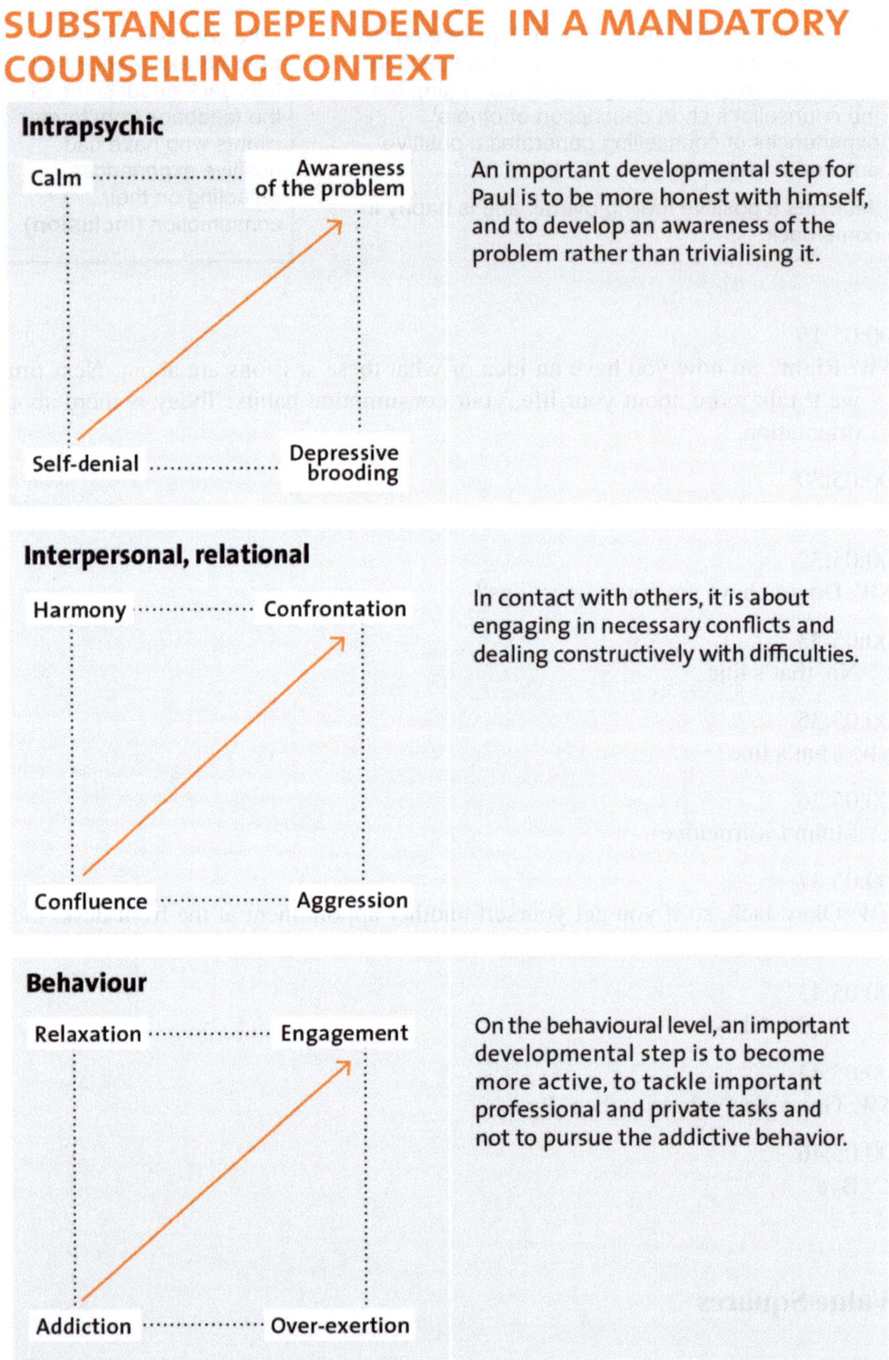

Fig. 15.2 Value squares for "Substance dependence in a mandatory counselling context"

"interpersonal, relational", refers to internal dynamics that are important in dealing with other people. The third level, "behaviour", is ultimately the result of the preceding thoughts and feelings.

Such differentiation between the three categories is ultimately only possible to a limited extent, as the levels are mutually dependent. Nevertheless, we see the distinction between these perspectives as advantageous, as it allows us to recognise significant tendencies. The following development squares serve as suggestions, and were constructed through our exploration in the respective roles. These are intended to stimulate the formation of your own versions, as other similar perspectives and variations are certainly conceivable.

Discussion

In our view, this initial conversation addresses all of Jack's relevant internal parts. The main focus is on building a sustainable working relationship. A polarisation, as described by the **holistic change model**, is not yet recognisable or possible in this phase; at most, it is subtly detectable between parts A (consumption behaviour) and B (conflicts) versus C (denial). During further sessions, the counsellor could attempt to uncover any internal motivation which might exist for reducing consumption. Such work would focus on activating both this motivation, and part D (Jack's longing). As these come into the foreground, the polarisation (experience of internal tension between the endeavor to reduce consumption on the one hand, and resistance towards this on the other) would increase in strength. Out of this internal dissonance, the motivation for change can arise.

Another point we want to address briefly here is the obligation to "report" to the court. Depending on the offense, court order and objectives of the institutions involved, information about the content and progress of the counselling sessions may be passed on. This naturally necessitates the signing of a data protection declaration or confidentiality release form by both parties. In the case described here, the court needs to ensure that the relevant number of hours of counselling hours have taken place, and have included reflection on the consumption behaviour. Whether consumption was actually reduced or changed as a result is not decisive. In residential settings, when clients have chosen to undergo therapy instead of a prison sentence, information on abstinence is required by the court and must therefore be detailed in reports. This influences the collaboration between counsellor and client, and the establishment of a supportive working relationship; the stricter the conditions, the more cautious the client is likely to be. We therefore believe that it is important to be as transparent as possible about the legal framework in a mandatory context. Similar advice can be found in the literature (e.g., Kähler, 2005, 97).

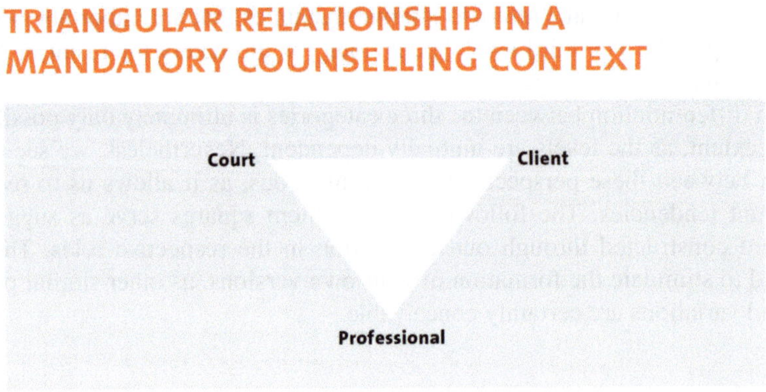

Fig. 15.3 The triangular relationship in a mandatory counselling context (Conen & Cecchin, 2018, 85)

The dynamics of diverging mandates and objectives can be depicted as a triangular relationship (see Fig. 15.3).

The court imposes certain conditions on the client, with which the client does not usually agree. The obligation to attend the addiction counselling centre and come to their appointments stands at odds with the fact that they may hold little or no motivation for change. The professional is also under a mandate, and is obliged to report to the court. At the same time, the counsellor must establish a relationship with the client. These are the tensions that commonly exist within the context of mandatory counselling (Conen & Cecchin, 2018, 85).

Summary Graphic (Fig. 15.4): Client Experience and Key Interventions

SUBSTANCE DEPENDENCE IN A MANDATORY COUNSELLING CONTEXT

Interventions

A

- Enquire 'diagnostically' about consumption behaviour
- Explore emotional aspects of consumption behaviour non-judgmentally

B

- Ask about external conflicts (health, social problems, finances)
- Explore internal emotional conflicts non-judgmentally

C

- Raise awareness of and flag any downplaying of conflicts

D

- Be on the look-out for possible longings (health, self-determination, social relaxation)

E

- Confront denial consistently

F

- Intensify polarisation between consumption behaviour A on the one hand, and conflicts B and longing D on the other hand

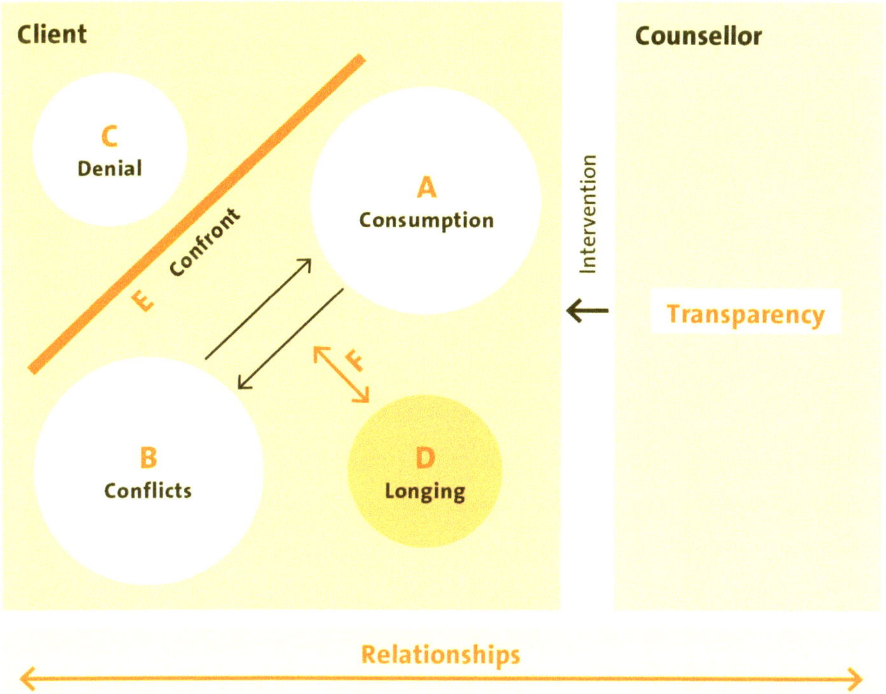

Fig. 15.4 "Substance dependence in a mandatory counselling context"—summary graphic

References

Conen, M.-L., & Cecchin, G. (2018). *Wie kann ich Ihnen helfen, mich wieder loszuwerden? Therapie und Beratung mit unmotivierten Klienten und in Zwangskontexten*. Carl-Auer.

ICD-11. (2024). 6C41.2 Cannabis dependence. In: *International classification of diseases 11th revision*. Retrieved January 13, 2025, from https://icd.who.int/browse/2024-01/mms/en#1129015467

Kähler, H. (2005). *Soziale Arbeit im Zwangskontext. Wie unerwünschte Hilfe erfolgreich sein kann*. Reinhardt.

Chapter 16
Excursus: Help and Control from a Gestalt-Theoretical Perspective

In the practice scenes we have role-played, the counsellor is confronted with a variety of different remits or mandates. For example, one client comes to addiction counselling through a court order, as he was caught dealing cannabis. The counselling process therefore takes place within a certain framework, with societal and legal norms impacting the support process. In such a context, the professional must try to build a relationship with the client while simultaneously having to operate within the legal framework of the court order. These two perspectives can be understood as internal parts of the counsellor and can be referred to as the poles of help and control. Gaining knowledge of and experience in dealing with such conflicts can greatly enhance the working relationship.

Concrete advice on this topic can be found in the literature, for example, in Kähler (2005) and Conen and Cecchin (2018). According to Heiner's (2004) competence-oriented approach, mediating between help and control is a core task in social work. Böhnisch and Lösch (1973) refer to this as a dual mandate. Accordingly, professionals are obliged on the one hand to help the individual, but at the same time, they also fulfill a mission which stems from the state or society. We do not aim to delve deeper into the mandate discussion here, but rather to present our Gestalt-theoretical perspective, both in practical and theoretical terms.

However, before so doing, we wish to mention briefly the idea of the triple mandate, which has established itself in social work and stems from the work of Staub-Bernasconi (2019, 111 ff.). The latter sees social work as a human rights profession with a state-independent, ethical frame of reference which goes beyond the dual mandate. In simplified terms, we understand the third mandate perspective as one which sees the polarity between help and control in a critical light, and strives to protect clients' human rights.

In the broadest sense, social legislation must also be constantly reflected on from this perspective. This sometimes plays a role in our day-to-day contact with the clients. For example, in the context of "emergency care cases", parents are usually informed by youth welfare officers of their right to object (Schone, 2019, 146 ff.).

A. Schachameier et al., *Gestalt in Social Work*,
https://doi.org/10.1007/978-3-031-95528-0_16

This could be seen as belonging to the category of the third mandate. However, it could be critically countered that this legal aspect simply belongs to the 'help pole', and that the perspective of the third mandate has no significance here. Nevertheless, there are practical cases in which the third mandate plays a crucial role (Staub-Bernasconi, 2019, 111 ff.; Borchert & Fritzsche, 2020, 220 ff.).

In contact with clients, the relaying of help and control is usually the focus. For this reason, we focus our attention on building relationships within this context where tension is classically experienced. We are concerned with the question of how the client's emotional experience can be adequately supported despite the mandatory context. Fundamental to our understanding is the idea that counselling sessions are always embedded in a real-life context with its own respective societal, cultural, and economic peculiarities. Both clients and social workers bring into the encounter their own subjective view of the world, of other people, and of themselves, which they have acquired through socialisation and by interacting with their respective environment. Every person internalises their biographical experiences in some way or other, and these are always connected with certain values and norms from their living environment.

From a Gestalt-theoretical perspective, this process is described by the contact cycle, which leads to the formation of personality functions. This part of the self forms the background, or 'ground', for further interactions (Dreitzel, 2004, 41; Gremmler-Fuhr, 2001, 388). The idea of an internal representation of societal norms and values can also be found in the social sciences with other well-known authors. For example, Sigmund Freud refers to this part as the "super-ego" (Freud, 1923). In sociology or social psychology, Mead (1934, 180 and 217 ff.) describes the "I" and the "Me". The latter is used to describe taking a perspective on oneself through the lens of others and the associated norms of the living environment. In the sociology of knowledge, Schütz and Luckmann (2017, 109) speak of an intersubjective "we-relationship", of "shared experiences", which are continuously confirmed. This creates a bank of knowledge that serves as a reference for the respective interpretations of the world (ibid., 33). Figure 16.1 shows the inner parts of the counsellor in the context of help and control.

In practice, this means that the counselling professional develops an internalised understanding of help and control, represented by inner parts, and brings these into their encounters with clients; in turn, the latter have their own internalised understanding of their world and its norms. Deviations from society's accepted norms can lead to problems, and it is often in such cases that social workers are required to perform their work. This might for example involve a violation of the Narcotics Act, whereupon the person is forced to seek addiction counselling; another example could be acute psychosis (see chapter "Psychosis"), where the person's self-concept may be in strong contradiction to the accepted norm. Child protection cases are based on fundamental rules around the child's right to safety. As a rule, the relevant law is a reflection of societal norms and values.

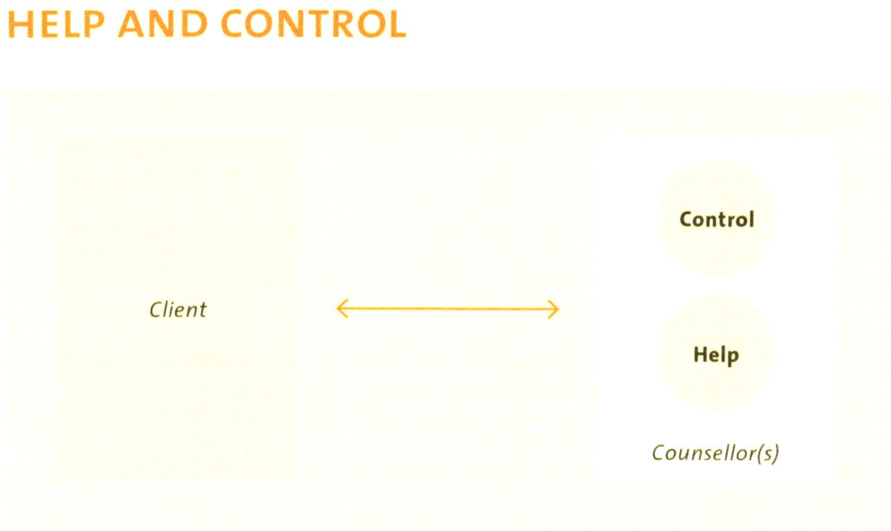

Fig. 16.1 Help and Control

In encounters with clients in social work contexts, the counsellor has the task of building a relationship with them within the framework of the existing norms and societal or state mandates that result from them. We have tried to illustrate what this work of meditating between the two can look like from a Gestalt perspective in the corresponding video examples. Furthermore, as we reflected on this polarity between help and control in the role-plays, we realised that the same polarity often occurs in a similar way within the Gestalt-based trainings and workshops we offer in other contexts. There, the control pole corresponds to the rules and framework of the workshops. These are agreed on by the group at the beginning, and include, for example, punctuality and abstinence from drugs and alcohol. If someone acts in a way which 'deviates' from these rules, a conversation must be held in which the participant is confronted with the rules. In this dialogue, as in other fields of social work, the control component must be clearly named and advocated for. In such a case, the inner attitude of the facilitator, and the way in which they themselves understand and relate to the rules, is of decisive importance. The more convincingly they are advocated for, the more authentic the encounter.

In our experience, it makes sense to structure such a conversation as follows: first, the professional should describe the behaviour and name the 'violation' of the rule. Next, they should ask the protagonist their perspective and seek to understand their reaction. Subsequently, the consequences of this violation must be communicated (control pole), whilst simultaneously offering support and contact (help pole).

References

Böhnisch, L., & Lösch, H. (1973). Das Handlungsverständnis des Sozialarbeiters und seine institutionelle Determination. In H.-U. Otto & S. Schneider (Eds.), *Gesellschaftliche Perspektiven der Sozialarbeit*. Luchterhand.

Borchert, A., & Fritzsche, K. (2020). Menschrechtsprofession. In P. U. Wendt (Ed.), *Soziale Arbeit in Schlüsselbegriffen* (pp. 220–224). Beltz Juventa.

Conen, M.-L., & Cecchin, G. (2018). *Wie kann ich Ihnen helfen, mich wieder loszuwerden? Therapie und Beratung mit unmotivierten Klienten und in Zwangskontexten*. Carl-Auer.

Dreitzel, H. P. (2004). *Gestalt und Prozess. Eine psychotherapeutische Diagnostik oder: Der gesunde Mensch hat wenig Charakter*. EHP.

Freud, S. (1923). *Das Ich und das Es. GW XIII*. Fischer.

Gremmler-Fuhr, M. (2001). Grundkonzepte und Modelle der Gestalttherapie. In R. Fuhr, M. Sreckovic, & M. Gremmler-Fuhr (Eds.), *Handbuch der Gestalttherapie*. Hogrefe.

Heiner, M. (2004). *Professionalität in der Sozialen Arbeit. Theoretische Konzepte, Modelle, und empirische Perspektiven*. Kohlhammer.

Kähler, H. (2005). *Soziale Arbeit im Zwangskontext. Wie unerwünschte Hilfe erfolgreich sein kann*. Reinhardt.

Mead, G. H. (1934). *Mind, self and society. From the standpoint of a social behaviorist*. University of Chicago Press.

Schone, R. (2019). Zwischen Hilfe und Kontrolle – der ASD im Spannungsfeld zwischen Dienstleistung und Schutzauftrag bei Kindeswohlgefährdung. In Merchel (Ed.), *Handbuch Allgemeiner Sozialer Dienst (ASD)* (pp. 146–158). Ernst Reinhardt.

Schütz, A., & Luckmann, T. (2017). *Strukturen der Lebenswelt*. UVK Verlagsgesellschaft mbH.

Staub-Bernasconi, S. (2019). Vom beruflichen Doppel- zum professionellen Triplemandat – Eckstein der Entwicklung der Sozialen Arbeit als Disziplin und Kritische Profession. In S. Staub-Bernasconi (Ed.), *Menschenwürde – Menschenrechte – Soziale Arbeit. Die Menschenrechte vom Kopf auf die Füße stellen* (pp. 111–124). Barbara Budrich.

Chapter 17
Co-Dependency

Case Summary

Ben is 45 years old, married and has two children (6 and 8 years old). He works as a care worker in a facility for people with special educational needs. His wife works part-time in the accounting department of a large company. Over the last two years, her alcohol consumption has increased significantly. As a result, she is increasingly unable to take proper care of their children. She forgets important appointments or to pick up the children from school. She is doing less and less of her share of the housework and has been threatened with dismissal from her work if any further issues occur. Ben tries to help her by being considerate and taking on a lot of the management of family life, very often stepping in to 'take up the slack'.

The classic ICD and DSM diagnostic systems do not define "co-dependency". In Flassbeck's (2010) attempt to determine diagnostic criteria, he describes a "co-dependent entanglement" as follows: "In contact with, or in a relationship with an addict, the other person experiences typical patterns in terms of their experience and behaviour which are referred to as co-dependently entangled. These patterns of experience and behaviour are initially to be classified as normal, healthy and helpful, but they carry a risk and can become problematic for the person. A problematic co-dependent entanglement can lead to a psychological disorder, the central symptoms of which are being preoccupied with the desire to help the addict and a strong complex of shame and guilt."

Flassbeck speaks of a co-dependency syndrome, which can be conceptualised and classified as a form of behavioural addiction (Flassbeck, 2010, 29).

Please watch the video entitled "Co-Dependency", for more information (www.gestalt-socialwork.com).

A. Schachameier et al., *Gestalt in Social Work*,
https://doi.org/10.1007/978-3-031-95528-0_17

Experiences in the Client Role

Cognitive

Ben has been trying to help his wife for several years now. He is fixated on helping and wants to know how he can help his wife to stop drinking alcohol. He is convinced that without his actions, the family will fall apart. He derives much of his self-worth from his helping role.

Emotional

He is restless, nervous, and tense. He has little contact with his feelings. He is aware of his exhaustion on a cognitive level, hardly on an emotional level. He is proud of himself for being able to 'hold' so much.

Physical

Due to the general overload, he is very tense. This mainly manifests as neck and back pain. His increasingly high blood pressure is causing him trouble.

Longing

He longs for a solution. His greatest wish is for his wife to stop drinking and thus for normality to return to family life. He longs for a behavioural change in his wife.

Action and Avoidance and Contact with the Outside World

He avoids or trivialises his exhaustion. Due to his focus on his wife's behaviour, he avoids authentic contact with himself as well as with the addiction counsellor. Only during the course of the conversation does he become aware of an internal conflict between a part that needs recovery, and a part that wants to continue as before. The prevailing contact interruptions are on the one hand **Introjection**, because he has internalised a very strong ideal around helping, as well as **Confluence**, because he cannot set boundaries.

Identified Inner Parts

A: "Helper": "This is not about me, it's my wife who needs help."

B: "Conflicts": "I am exhausted, I feel frustrated because my efforts aren't leading to the desired result."

C: "Denial": "I am trapped in my helper role, I barely perceive my own needs and don't question my actions."

D: "Longing": Being able to feel my own needs and live a self-determined life.

The inner dialogue could be depicted as shown in Fig. 17.1:

Case Transcript: Co-Dependency

00:00:01

SW: Ben—good to meet you. We spoke briefly on the phone. Tell me again what brings you here.

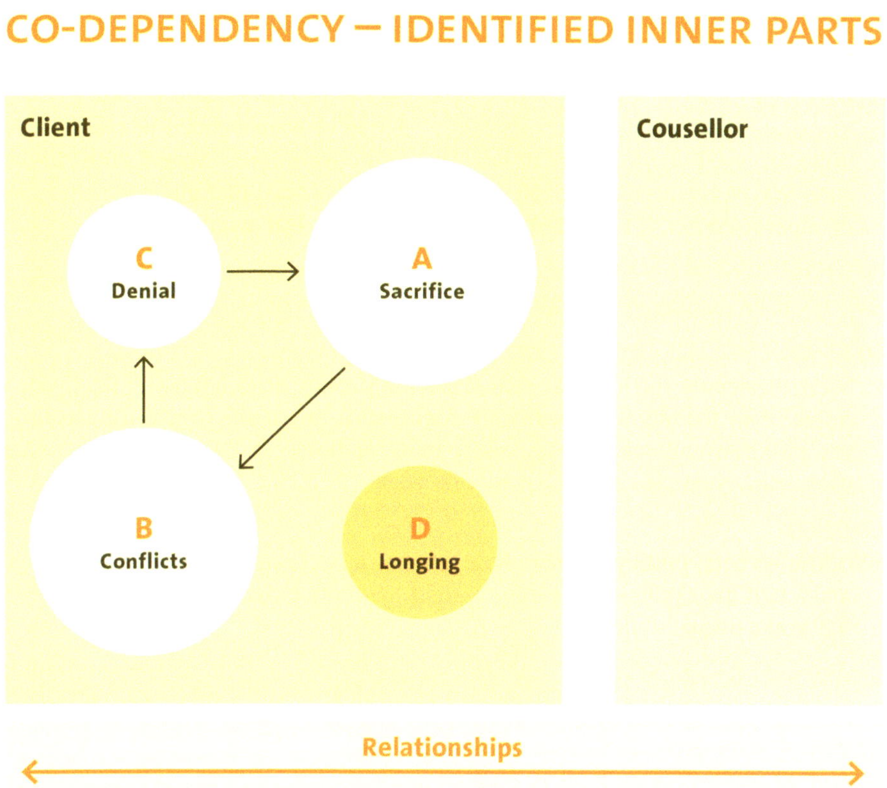

Fig. 17.1 "Co-Dependency"—identified inner parts

00:00:09

C: Yeah…how should I put it? Well, my wife, she drinks…she drinks so much now that it's just… (exhales sharply) …it's been escalating…for the last sixth months or so now. So she sometimes gets up at night and drinks more, and then she can't get out of bed in the morning, and then she doesn't go to work and I have to take care of the kids… I work full time, then I come home, and…sometimes I come home, and she's lying somewhere in the living room asleep because she's so drunk. Then it gets better for a few days. I like a pint too, or on special occasions, but…and it actually used to be quite good, or…well, how should I say it? It just felt normal. But now, over the last year and a half, maybe even two, it's been getting worse and worse with her—and yeah, it's hard for the kids. I try to…

00:01:01

SW: So it's been a year and a half already, two years, you say?

00:01:05

C: Yes, it's been…it's been a long time already but…/It's just been so gradual. I can't even say exactly, but it's…//

00:01:11

SW: We're talking about a *long* period of time, just to make sure I understand correctly.

00:01:14

C: Yes, and it's like, I've tried everything… There've been fights, I've taken everything off her, I've taken care of her. Then there were times when I said, "I don't care, maybe she needs it". Then there were times when I thought, maybe if I kind of supervised her, if I was just there and whatever. But somehow//

00:01:39

SW: It's been escalating for one-and-a-half to two years?

00:01:41

C: Well, especially the last half year. That she's really drinking out in the open, at home. And for me at work/I can't concentrate anymore. I mean (mumbling), my children call me and say she's lying at home in her own vomit, whatever…so…yeah, it's really…madness, yeah.

00:02:00

SW: You've been putting an incredible amount in to keep things going. For a year and a half, two years. If I heard you right, with the kids, at work, with your wife while she drinks so heavily.

00:02:11
C: (Exhales) Yeah, what else can I do? Course, it's my/It's like//

00:02:17
SW: You keep trying so that things can keep going and maybe get better?

00:02:21
C: Get better? I try and stop things from getting even worse. I try…and keep the show still on the road somehow.

00:02:31
SW: Mmm, but you're really doing a lot.

Effect on the client	Intervention and resonance
It feels good to Ben when the effort he puts into looking after the family and his struggles are recognised (Part A). This makes him feel appreciated, understood, and he can open up. At the same time, the inner part B, "exhaustion", becomes more noticeable. He then names this.	The counsellor begins by listening to Ben and appreciating the effort he is putting in. He helps Ben become aware of how much he is investing, how hard he is working (**Dialogical Attitude** and **Phenomenology**).

00:02:37
C: Yeah, I mean…if I don't do it, there's just no one else there./I mean I do care about her, I'm just hoping she'll come out the other side.

00:02:55
SW: Yes, I really hear that, you're taking responsibility.

00:02:58
C: Yeah, of course.

00:02:58
SW: A lot of responsibility.

00:02:59
C: Of course. It's also for my children. So it's for the whole/

The client realises how much responsibility he is taking for the family (Part A).	The counsellor helps the client to realise how much loyalty he shows towards his wife and how much responsibility he takes on.

00:03:10
SW: Yes, of course. Of course. Ben, if you had a wish, or an aim, for these conversations, this session, what would it be? Can you try and put that into words?

00:03:22
C: Yes, I…/Well, I'd just like… if you could just give me some advice on what I can do…well, so that my wife doesn't drink so much. You're competent in these sorts of things, I reckon, you probably get these kinds of situations quite often. I want to know what I can do. Because I sometimes think I must be doing something wrong. You know? I feel like I've tried everything…

00:03:46
SW: You'd like more tips on how to make it less, or make it stop?

00:03:53
C: Uh-huh, yeah, exactly. Yes (sighs).

The client states that he wants support to help his wife (rather than himself).

The counsellor inquires about Ben's motivation for seeking help, and goes along with the statements he makes (**Dialogical Attitude** and **Phenomenology**).

00:03:54
SW: Okay. (Exhales). Take a deep breath for a moment. Ben, I'm also wondering how *you're* doing, when I hear that you've been doing so much over the last eighteen months, even two years?

00:04:08
C: (Exhales). Me? Mmm, honestly, I'm exhausted. I'm really tired. I notice it at work with my concentration. I keep making mistakes, or forgetting things. That never used to happen to me, sometimes I don't sleep well either, I feel it physically. It's really… I've also got issues with my heart, high blood pressure…I mean, I've always had that a bit, but/.

00:04:33
SW: So you're actually already a bit over your limit in terms of what you're putting in.

00:04:38
C: Well, I wouldn't be surprised if I collapsed at some point. I mean…I can't go on like this anymore. I…I can't carry on like this, but…

00:04:52
SW: (interrupting) It takes a *lot* to keep firing yourself up internally, but it's like you have to.

00:04:55
C: Yeah, of course.

00:04:59
SW: Yes.

00:04:59
C: But if I collapse…

00:05:01
SW: Then nothing will work anymore.

00:05:02
C: Then the whole system collapses, and…I mean, the kids, everything else, what happens then? If I did collapse—if I had to lie there in a hospital bed for a few weeks, for example…

00:05:10
SW: Then you wouldn't be able to do anything. Ben, honestly…it's amazing how much you've given, over such a long period of time, without breaking down. And apparently, thank God, you have a constitution that's allowed you to do it. For your children, for your wife, for yourself.

00:05:30
C: I do really care, you know?

Ben reveals his sense of overload (Part B), and at the same time, a part becomes visible that 'has to' continue because it feels responsible for the whole family system.

The counsellor now inquires how *Ben* is doing with the situation, thus directing his attention to the exhaustion (Part A).

00:05:31
SW: Mmm (agreeing). And your wish is that we look together at how you can support your wife.

00:05:38
C: That would be my wish, yeah, that things get better.

00:05:41
SW: Ben, to use a metaphor: there's a fire burning here, isn't there? Your wife has been displaying behaviour that is highly destructive; it's destroying her, weighing down your family, it feels like it's breaking you. And you've already spent a lot of time trying to put out the fire. You're constantly at it, watching out, pouring your energy into the situation in all sorts of ways. And I hear you saying you've already tried a lot, and that your wish would be to get more tips on how you can extinguish the fire?

00:06:14
C: Yes.

00:06:14
SW: Yes. So I have a very frank question for you, Ben: what's it like to imagine carrying on trying to put out this fire that's already been burning for two years now? You've tried everything. If you really imagine for a moment that we sat here together and came up with more ways of investing your time and energy to extinguish this fire.

00:06:39
C: Well, if it *can* be extinguished, then I'd do anything.

00:06:41
SW: Do anything.

00:06:42
C: Yeah.

00:06:43
SW: Mmm (affirming). If we could come up with some ways of putting out this fire.

00:06:47
C: Yes.

This addresses the helper part (part A). It would carry on, regardless of Ben's exhaustion. As such, he is entering more and more into an inner conflict (between parts A and B).

The counsellor honours Ben's efforts again, and refers to the desire to help his wife. He uses a metaphor to increase Ben's awareness of the situation. He asks Ben what it's like to imagine continuing with the same helping behaviour, if there was a solution.

00:06:51
SW: And imagine, Ben: how would it honestly feel if it took another year, maybe two more years, to extinguish the fire? Try and imagine that—take a moment to really imagine yourself carrying on firefighting for another year.

00:07:15
C: (sighs) Mmm, well, it's like…

00:07:19
SW: When you say you're at your limit already… And when you say you can't go on anymore?

00:07:26
C: At the same time, um//

00:07:26
SW: What's it like to imagine that?

00:07:26
C: I don't know, maybe/Well…if I knew that it would be extinguished in a year's time, I think I'd…

00:07:33
SW: …keep going, right?

00:07:34
C: I'd try again. I think I'd just see if I could…
00:07:37 SW: Although you're already running on the last drop, the tank's empty…

00:07:40
C: Yeah.

00:07:42
SW: Mmm. There's something that you see as *your* task.

00:07:45
C: Yeah, of course. There's no one else there.

00:07:48
SW: Yes, and the fire has to be put out. It won't go out by itself.

00:07:51
C: Uh-huh.

The inner conflict or dilemma becomes clearer: on the one hand Ben feels as though he *has* to help, because no one else is there (part A, "helper"), and on the other hand, he can't, has run out of energy (part B, "conflicts") **(Stagnation)**.

The counsellor intensifies the imagined scenario. What would it be like if another year passed in the same way even though Ben has run out of energy already?

00:07:56
SW: Ben. Honestly, I don't know if there's anything that can stop this fire from burning. I really don't know if there's anything that can stop your wife's drinking. And the question is, how much energy do you have left to keep trying and trying? I'm impressed by your loyalty, your idealism, the way you say you'll keep going until the end.

00:08:27
C: Mmm.

00:08:29
SW: You want to keep going till the end. Even if you drive yourself into the ground in the process. You'd rather go to the dogs knowing you've tried everything than not try everything?

00:08:57
C: Mmm, I think so, sometimes…yes. When I look at it like that. And yes, I am a bit…

00:09:04
SW: You're a bit…? Exhausted, no?

00:09:07
C: (sighs) I'm exhausted.

00:09:10
SW: And you're at a loss about what to do.

00:09:11
C: Yeah…I just don't know…

00:09:27
SW: Mmm. Exhausted and at a loss.

00:09:30
C: Yes.

The inner conflict becomes ever clearer and the tension between the poles increases. Ben becomes aware of his exhaustion and is at more and more of a loss, and confused. The denial begins to break down.

The counsellor confronts Ben. He questions whether it is actually possible to stop his wife drinking, and asks Ben how much more energy he has to continue along these lines. At the same time, he reflects back to Ben how loyal he is, how willing to try everything, until the very last (**Polarisation**).

00:09:33
SW: What I can offer you here is to support you during this incredibly difficult time. Maybe we will find a tip or two that can help you shift your perspective on this fire, or to contain it a little. I don't think I can give you any tips on extinguishing the fire. You've already tried so much to that end, and I think it's really important that *you* get support so that you don't break down. And I say that for you, and I also say it for your children, *and* for your wife, who you're so loyal to. Which doesn't mean that you have to put up with everything she does.

00:10:15
C: Pff… (exhales)

00:10:15
SW: It's not what you came here for, *and* I think it's really important that *you* get some support.

00:10:26
C: (exhales) I can't describe it right now, but it's a bit like.../I feel like it needs to sink in first.

00:10:33
SW: Yes, and I think that's also the exhaustion speaking...

00:10:36
C: Yes.

00:10:37
SW: The hopelessness.

00:10:39
C: Mmm, and it's like this... It's like... It can't go on like this. That's what I'm noticing right now: I can't go on like this.

00:10:52
SW: Yes. That's becoming really clear.

Ben needs some time to digest and process. He describes how he is feeling.

The counsellor gives Ben time to feel his exhaustion and helplessness. He offers him further dialogue with the focus on supporting him. This represents a new motivation or goal, a new potential contract for their work together.

00:10:56
C: Yeah. And I know...I feel like I've *got* to carry on, like I've *got* to find a way somehow. And...I'm at a loss right now, with everything, and... I think it needs to sink in right now.

00:11:09
SW: Yes. Give it a bit of time to sink in, Ben, and then please do feel free to get back in touch so you can get some support here, so we can see what's possible.

00:11:19
C: Yes. Good. Thank you.

Value Squares

The value squares in Fig. 17.2 are designed to show directions of development for Ben. We wish to illuminate three levels. The first is the "intrapsychic" perspective, which refers to internal, cognitive-emotional processes of evaluation. The second,

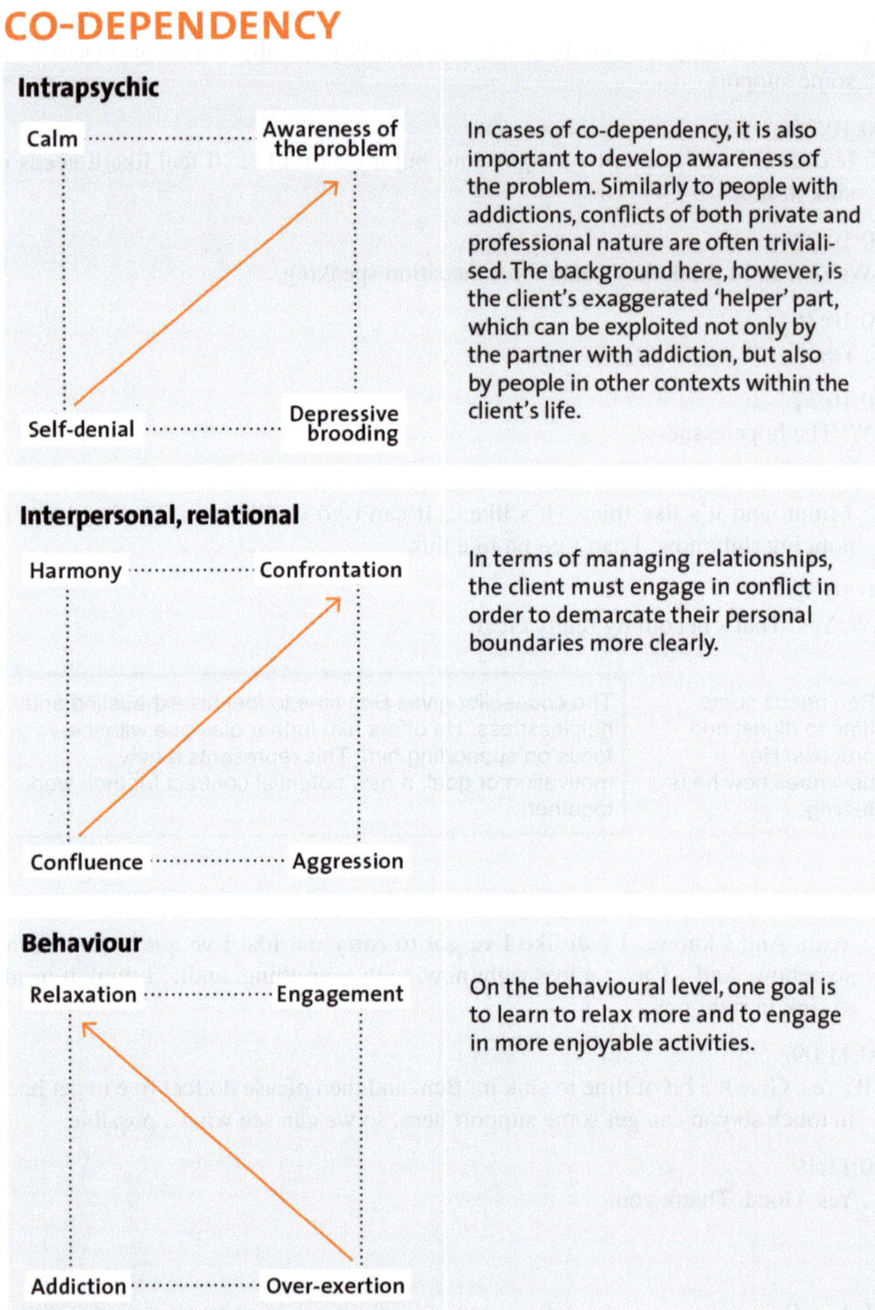

Fig. 17.2 Value Squares for "Co-Dependency"

"interpersonal, relational", refers to internal dynamics that are important in dealing with other people. The third level, "behaviour", is ultimately the result of the preceding thoughts and feelings.

Such differentiation between the three categories is ultimately only possible to a limited extent, as the levels are mutually dependent. Nevertheless, we see the distinction between these perspectives as advantageous, as it allows us to recognise significant tendencies. The following development squares serve as suggestions, and were constructed through our exploration in the respective roles. These are intended to stimulate the formation of your own versions, as other similar perspectives and variations are certainly conceivable.

The first two value squares are identical to those in the two previous chapters (see Fig. 17.2). The behaviour is different, however, because instead of experiencing a substance dependence, the client is in a way addicted to helping, which leads to over-exertion.

Discussion

This support process is centred around Ben handing back the responsibility he has taken on for his wife's drinking behaviour. The responsibility and decision for (or against) sobriety lie with the drinker. Relatives are often so focused on helping that such a goal initially seems strange. Psychoeducation around basic family dynamics and co-dependent entanglements is very helpful in this regard. However, the example shows that at the beginning especially, the client may be able to absorb only a very limited amount of information, as such a perspective calls previous behavioural strategies into question and therefore must be defended against. In this respect, the example represents the beginning of a process of growing awareness.

As such a process went on, repeated emphasis would be necessary on the fact that the responsibility for a change in his wife's alcohol consumption cannot lie with Ben himself. This is fundamental, even when working with a modularised group process such as the CRAFT model (Smith & Meyers, 2013), an approach that aims to develop strategies for the non-consuming person to motivate the consuming person to seek treatment. In addition, self-help groups for relatives are highly recommended, as they promote awareness around appropriate boundaries and can contribute to corresponding behavioural change.

Furthermore, the issue of time should be taken into account. If the addiction or the helper's problems are already chronic, clinically classifiable diseases may manifest. We must assume that the healing process or path towards developing more appropriate coping strategies takes time. Relatives with co-dependent disorders

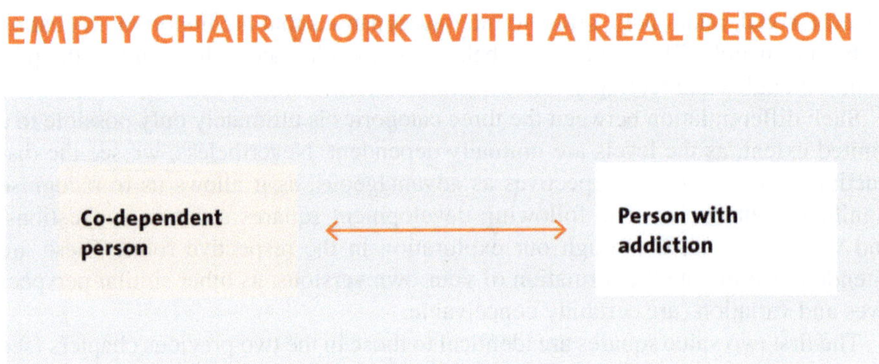

Fig. 17.3 'Empty chair work' with a real person

often suffer from other mental illnesses such as depression, anxiety disorders, psychosomatic syndrome, trauma-related disorders or their own addictions (Flassbeck, 2010, 29–30).

Over the course of counselling or therapy, one aim is to 'shake up' the clients so that they regain access to their healthy instincts; to feel angry, take action, overcome their sense of helplessness, feel the joy of life again, focus on their own life again, scream, cry and laugh out loud (ibid., 21–22). This means noticing and acknowledging all that's going on emotionally, physically and cognitively, exploring what is there beyond the rigid helper patterns. Gestalt therapeutic methods can be used for this, for example by using empty chair work with a 'real' counterpart. This involves the addicted person being placed symbolically on an empty chair so that the client can express how they feel towards them, how their bodies react and above all, how they themselves deal with these sensations, how they react to them mentally and physically. This might, for example, bring anger and grief into the foreground, along with an awareness of the self-sacrificing nature of their efforts to help the person with addiction.

This is essential, as clients in co-dependent entanglements often behave confluently (**Confluence**) to avoid having to perceive differences, conflicts and limitations. Being connected to others and empathising with them is fundamentally an important capacity in order to be able to form relationships (Dreitzel, 2004, 64; Stein, 2005, 70). However, it becomes problematic when the feelings of another are given so much priority that one's own feelings and needs are no longer clearly perceived and one is therefore also unable to articulate them (ibid.). Figure 17.3 shows the idea of empty chair work with a real person.

Summary Graphic (Figs. 17.4 and 17.5): Client Experience and Key Interventions

Step 1

CO-DEPENDENCY – STEP 1

Interventions

A

- Enquire 'diagnostcally' about the helping role
- Help explore emotional aspects of helper role non-judgmentally

B

- Enquire about conflicts
- Explore emotional conflicts (exhaustion) non-judgmentally

C

- Raise awareness of and flag denial or downplaying of conflicts/failure

D

- Be on the look-out for possible longings

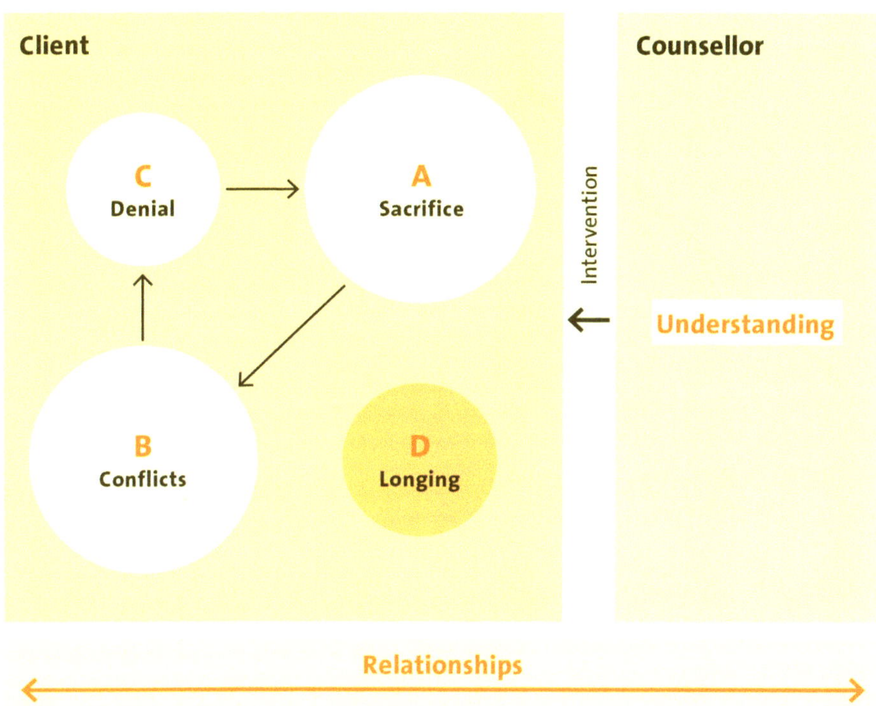

Fig. 17.4 "Co-dependency/Step 1"—summary graphic

Step 2

CO-DEPENDENCY – STEP 2

Interventions

E

- Consistently confront the denial

F

- Intensify the polarisation between consumption behaviour A on the one hand and conflicts B and longing D on the other hand

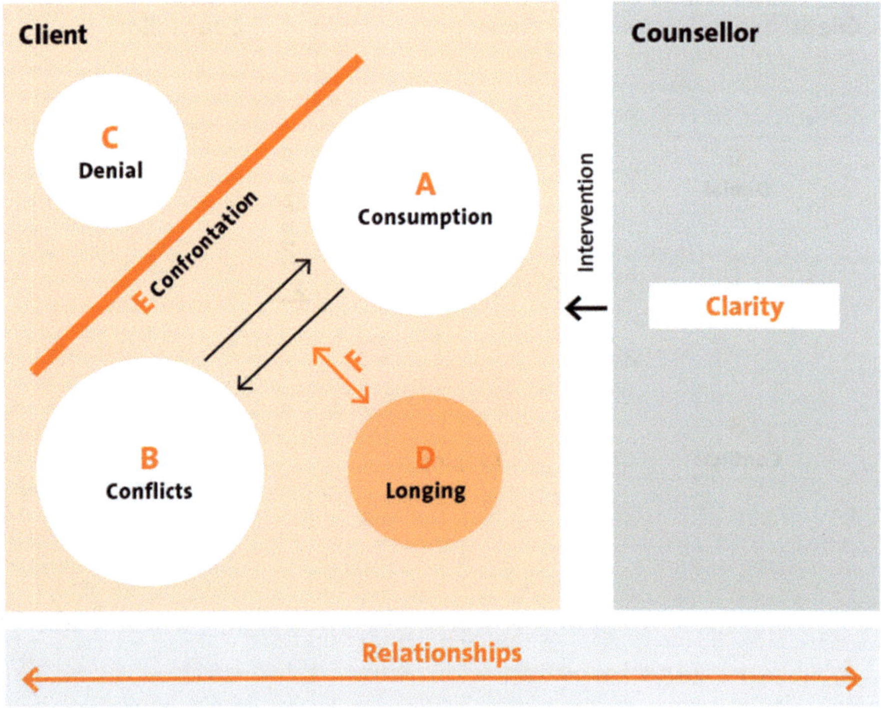

Fig. 17.5 “Co-dependency/Step 2”—summary graphic

References

Dreitzel, H. P. (2004). *Gestalt und Prozess. Eine psychotherapeutische Diagnostik oder: Der gesunde Mensch hat wenig Charakter*. EHP.

Flassbeck, J. (2010). *Co-Abhängigkeit. Diagnose, Ursachen und Therapie für Angehörige von Suchtkranken*. Klett-Cotta.

Smith, J. E., & Meyers, R. J. (2013). *Mit Suchtfamilien arbeiten – CRAFT: Ein neuer Ansatz in der Angehörigenarbeit*. Psychiatrie Verlag.

Stein, R. (2005). *Einführung in die pädagogische Gestaltarbeit und die gestalttheoretische Sicht von Störungen*. Schneider Verlag Hohengehren.

Chapter 18
Chronic Psychosis

This chapter focuses on a situation that could occur in a socio-therapeutic facility for people with chronic psychoses.

The underlying diagnosis is F20.0 "paranoid schizophrenia" according to ICD-10 (BfArM, 2022), which describes "relatively stable, often paranoid, delusions, usually accompanied by hallucinations, particularly of the auditory variety, and perceptual disturbances. Disturbances of affect, volition, and speech, and catatonic symptoms, are not prominent."

Case Summary

Bill has been suffering from mental illness for many years. He repeatedly goes through psychotic phases, during which he suffers from delusions. At these times, he hears voices giving him commands and suspects that his thoughts are being intercepted.

Despite medication, his symptoms are so debilitating that he can no longer work, nor cope with everyday life without professional help. He therefore decided to seek admission into a residential facility for people with mental illness.

He has been living in this facility for several months now. A social worker, the counsellor in this dialogue, is his contact person. The scene takes place during a phase in which he is hearing voices more frequently again, and seeks out the counsellor.

Please watch the video entitled "Chronic Psychosis", for more information (www.gestalt-socialwork.com).

A. Schachameier et al., *Gestalt in Social Work*,
https://doi.org/10.1007/978-3-031-95528-0_18

Experiences in the Client Role

Cognitive

Bill is preoccupied by imperative voices which are commanding him to drive to Hamburg. He is confused and doesn't know what to do. He also fears that he is being pursued by the secret service. Even the counsellor could pose a threat.

Emotional

The voices put him under pressure and trigger strong feelings of fear in him.

Physical

The fear is noticeable as a stress reaction in the body. His pulse is elevated, his breathing is shallow, and his hands are sweaty.

Longing

He longs to experience inner peace and security. He also longs to be in contact with others in a way which feels safe.

Action and Avoidance

He initially follows the urging of the voices, hoping that this will lead to a solution and inner peace.

Contact with the Outside World

He displays his inner suffering and is open to conversation, but at the same time, is very suspicious. He projects his mistrust onto the people around him, whom he thinks might be from the secret service and want to spy on him (**Projection**).

Identified Inner Parts

A: "Psychotic experience": The psychotic experience is characterised by imperative voices, instilling in him the sense that "I have to drive to Hamburg". This causes pressure, fear, and helplessness.

B: "Intrapersonal longing": "I need inner peace and security."

C: "Interpersonal, relational longing": "I need contact with other people, I want to feel safe and held."

The inner dialogue could be represented as depicted in Fig. 18.1:

Case Transcript: Chronic Psychosis

00:00:00
C: Okay. Erm, Phil?

00:00:07
SW: Yes, Bill?

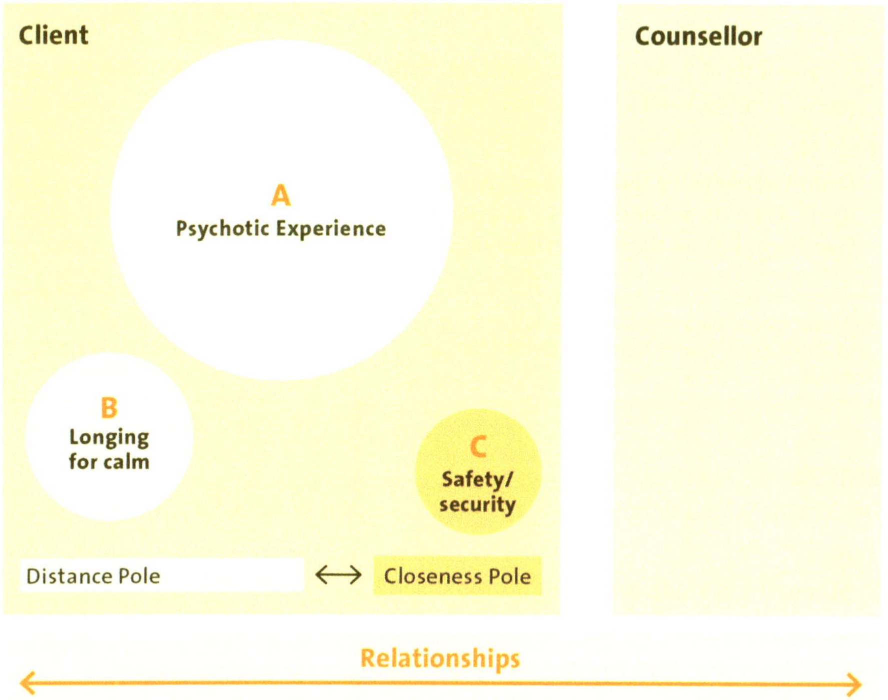

Fig. 18.1 "Chronic psychosis"—identified inner parts

00:00:08

C: I think I need to go to Hamburg. I don't feel right here. Mmm, I need to go and check something. I think I'm being spied on here.

00:00:22

SW: Oh, okay. I'm afraid I don't have long right now because I've got a meeting in a moment. But it sounds important, so I can give you five minutes. Let's see what I can do for you in that time, okay? So, you're saying there are voices, you're hearing voices? They're saying you need to go to Hamburg?

Effect on the client	Intervention and resonance
Bill understands that the counsellor only has five minutes, but is glad that he can talk to him.	The counsellor takes Bill's concern seriously and sets a time frame for the conversation (**Dialogical attitude** and **Phenomenology**).

00:00:46

C: Yes, they're giving me orders, I have to go to Hamburg and check, because I don't know if they're sending things into my head when I'm here… And I'm not sure… I think there might be cameras or transmitters or something in here.

00:01:07

SW: So you think you're being spied on. Who by? Or can you describe that a bit more? Is it the voices saying that?

00:01:18

C: I don't know if it's the secret service or who it is, I don't know. But I can tell it's there. Then the voices come…and they're the ones I can maybe find out about in Hamburg. I think they're in Hamburg.

Bill describes his symptoms: he is hearing voices and is afraid of being followed by the secret service.	The counsellor inquires about what exactly is going on.

00:01:34

SW: Mmm. What I definitely notice is that you seem to be under a lot of pressure.

00:01:41

C: Mmm, it's not safe here. And it's too much.

00:01:45

SW: It's too much. And you feel like you need to get out of here quickly.

00:01:49
C: Yeah, I don't know if I can stand it much longer with the voices.

00:01:54
SW: Mmm.

Bill feels seen and describes his condition in more detail (uncertainty, effort).

The counsellor does not address the content, but rather refers to the pressure he perceives in the client.

00:01:55
SW: Does that scare you too?

00:01:58
C: Yeah, I don't even know what I can say here. I don't even know if you might be one of them.

00:02:10
SW: Ah, okay. So you're not sure if you can trust me, in case I'm one of them.

00:02:19
C: I don't know. You might be.

Bill feels understood.

The counsellor tries to put himself in Bill's shoes. He shares his impression (**Real fantasy**). In particular, he addresses Bill's fear.

00:02:23
SW: You think I might be. Well… I want to assure you that I'm not one of them, okay? I'm a social worker, and I work here, running your group. It's my job to help you, support you. That's what I'm interested in. And at the same time, I understand of course, or I *hear* you saying you're suspicious of me, and I can accept that.

00:02:53
C: Mmm.

00:02:56
SW: What's it like when I say that to you?

00:03:00
C: Mmm, it's okay, it's quite good… Feels like it's getting a bit calmer.

00:03:10
SW: Aha.

This does Bill good, he's getting a bit calmer. He's also getting a bit closer to his actual longing (Part C).

The counsellor directly addresses this mistrust and addresses the relational level in the here and now.

He gives an authentic answer that contradicts Bill's perception. However, he also understands his distrust, which is Bill's perception (**Dialogical Attitude**).

00:03:11
C: Even though I obviously don't know 100 percent, do I? But just then it was somehow… It was… I mean, you feel safe here, right? You don't have the feeling that there's something here?

00:03:23
SW: No, no, I don't. I've actually been working here for ten years and I do feel safe here, I feel pretty comfortable here most of the time. That's how I perceive it, and it's clear that you have a different perception right now. It doesn't feel safe to you.

00:03:42
C: Mmm.

00:03:43
SW: That's how it is right now, and that's okay!

00:03:50
C: I guess, but what should I do then?

00:03:53
SW: Hmm. Do you mean that you're not sure anymore if you still want to go to Hamburg right now?

00:04:03
C: I don't know. No, I'm not so sure anymore. Right now I'm a bit/

Bill feels calmer, and is now unsure about whether he really should go to Hamburg. He is confused. He can no longer trust his idea of having to go to Hamburg.

The counsellor makes it clear that they both have different perceptions and that this is okay (**Dialogical Attitude**). He conveys through his language and attitude that there is no danger here.

00:04:16
SW: A bit…?

00:04:21
C: Mmm, I'm thinking maybe there's something wrong with me. You know, you just said that everything's fine here, so maybe it's just that there's something strange going on inside *me*, you know? I mean…it was pretty strong, just then, but now it's not so strong.

00:04:39
SW: Okay, so it's not so strong right now. And you're worried about whether there's something wrong with you. You know…I have quite a lot of experience of things like this. And people do sometimes have phases when they hear voices like that, and… I mean, I have the feeling that when you ask whether you should go to Hamburg or not, my sense is that right now, it's more about staying here and seeing how you might be able to relax, what might help you stay here and relax in there a bit.

00:05:20
C: Yeah, that would be good. Although…maybe I won't be able to relax until I've figured it out. I'm not sure right now.

00:05:27
SW: Mmm, so you're still a bit unsure. It's okay not to know, yeah.

00:05:33
C: Mmm.

Bill is feeling increasingly calm.

The counsellor describes his own perspective, namely that the important thing right now is to find out how Bill can stay here in a more relaxed way (**real fantasy**). He addresses part C ("Longing") and takes the lead in the conversation.

00:05:33
SW: And is there something that might help right now? Something you might enjoy doing? Anything that relaxes you a bit?

00:05:43
C: Mmm, I think I need a smoke now.

00:05:44
SW: Yeah.

00:05:47
C: I think I need a cigarette.

00:05:50
SW: Go for it, okay? Go out, have a smoke.

00:05:54
C: Okay, yeah—going outside is a good idea, cause when I'm…/I think I need to get outside.

00:05:59
SW: Yeah.

00:06:00
C: Yeah, I think going outside is a good idea. I think I'll go outside and have a smoke out there.

00:06:04
SW: And some fresh air. Mmm, and as I said, I have to go to that meeting now. So…if you need anything, you can always just ask the other staff members, okay? And I'll be back in an hour. You're welcome to come back and find me later if you need to.

00:06:22
C: Yeah, okay. Right, I'll go and have a smoke now then.

00:06:29
SW: Okay. Go for it.

Bill wants to go outside and have a cigarette.	The counsellor acknowledges Bill's uncertainty, asks about he might be able to support himself, and offers further support later on if needed.

Value Squares

The value squares in Fig. 18.2 are designed to show directions of development for Bill. We wish to illuminate three levels. The first is the "intrapsychic" perspective, which refers to internal, cognitive-emotional processes of evaluation. The second, "interpersonal, relational", refers to internal dynamics that are important in dealing with other people. The third level, "behaviour", is ultimately the result of the preceding thoughts and feelings.

Such differentiation between the three categories is ultimately only possible to a limited extent, as the levels are mutually dependent. Nevertheless, we see the distinction between these perspectives as advantageous, as it allows us to recognise significant tendencies. The following development squares serve as suggestions, and were constructed through our exploration in the respective roles. These are intended to stimulate the formation of your own versions, as other similar perspectives and variations are certainly conceivable.

CHRONIC PSYCHOSIS

Intrapersonal

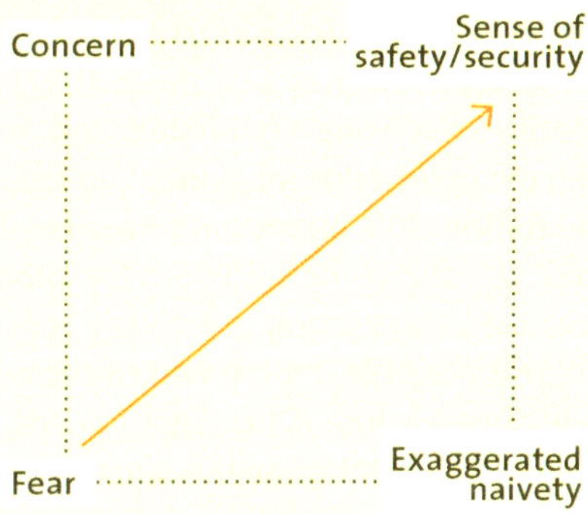

An important developmental step is to develop a greater sense of safety/ security.

Interpersonal, relational

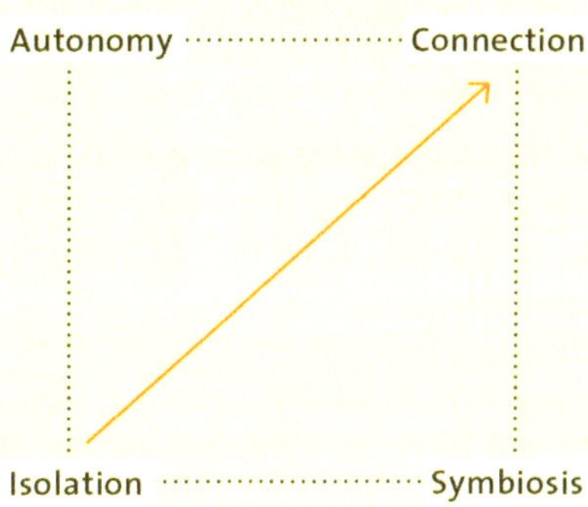

A central goal on the interpersonal level is that the client begins to seek out more contact with others, thus re-emerging from social isolation.

Behaviour

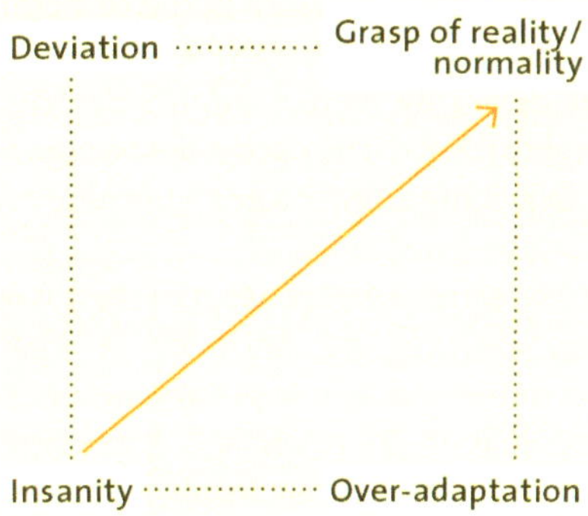

On the behavioural level, a significant step is to develop a stronger reference to reality and normality.

Fig. 18.2 Value squares for "chronic psychosis"

Discussion

At the beginning of this encounter, it is crucial for the counsellor to name and accept their differing perceptions. This, along with the opportunity for Bill to verbalise his mistrust in contact with the counsellor and be understood, has a calming effect on Bill. When a client feels insecure, it is helpful to activate stabilising and self-soothing parts (resource activation). To do this, the counsellor must take the lead in the conversation in order to give the client orientation. It is important to realise that the counsellor often represents both a threat and the solution or a way out for clients.

Even over the course of this short sequence, the conversation moves towards an I-Thou contact (**dialogical attitude**); this makes it possible, by the end of the conversation, for the counsellor to communicate his impression of the situation and its inherent safety. Through offering his assessment, he addresses and activates Bill's longing for safety and security.

The professional literature also emphasises the usefulness of a dialogical approach in this context (Bock, 2013, 99 ff.). The counsellor is advised to adopt a respectful attitude towards clients and their psychotic experiences. When dealing with delusions in particular, the client's perception should be acknowledged and regarded as their subjective truth (Bock, 2013, 127 ff.).

When clients are suspicious, it is also recommended that the professional reveals a little more about themselves (Lincoln & Heibach, 2017, 86). It can also be helpful to change the setting and take a walk together or ask the clients to look around the room to see if there are indeed any cameras or similar.

Amador (2015, 110) works with the "Listen-Empathise-Agree-Partner" (LEAP) method. Of particular importance in this concept is reflective listening. Among other things, this includes conveying security and respectfully encountering what has been heard, as well as trying to go along with the client's inner world and let one's own counselling goals stay in the background.

People with psychoses often suffer from formal thought disorders and neurocognitive deficits (Lincoln & Heibach, 2017, 88). They may therefore find it difficult to maintain concentration during conversations or to answer precisely. Another reason for this, however, can be that people are distracted by hallucinations, delusional thoughts, fears, and also self-deprecating thoughts (ibid.). The pace must be adjusted accordingly and repetition may be necessary. In a counselling context, keeping calm is essential.

The task of the counsellor is dependent on the institutional concept of their workplace as well as their own qualifications. In any situation, they must decide whether a short intervention is sufficient or whether a more intensive level of care or even admission to a psychiatric clinic for crisis intervention are necessary. According to their qualification, they may be able to offer individual sessions themselves, or—if available—refer the client to a specialist in psychotherapy.

Summary Graphic (Fig. 18.3): Client Experience and Key Interventions

CHRONIC PSYCHOSIS

Interventions

A

- Accept psychotic events (pressure, fear, helplessness)
- Radiate calm
- Present a different perspective
- Lead calmly and clearly

B

- Detect the longing for calm and relaxation

C

- Offer contact: safety and security through relationship

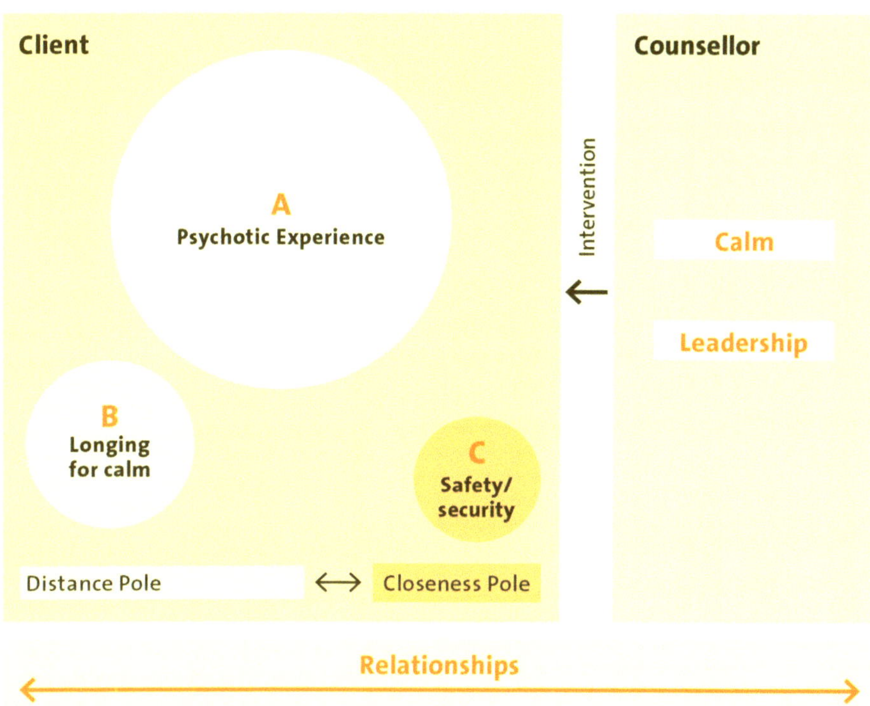

Fig. 18.3 "Chronic psychosis"—summary graphic

References

Amador, X. F. (2015). *Lass mich – mir fehlt nichts! Ins Gespräch kommen mit psychisch Kranken.* Georg Thieme Verlag.

BfArM (Ed.) (2022). *ICD-10-GM: F20-F29 Schizophrenie, schizotype und wahnhafte Störungen.* Retrieved October 04, 2023, from https://www.icd-code.de/icd/code/F20.0.html

Bock, T. (2013). *Basiswissen: Umgang mit psychotischen Patienten.* Psychiatrie Verlag.

Lincoln, T., & Heibach, E. (2017). *Psychosen.* Hogrefe.

Chapter 19
Acute Psychosis

This chapter deals with a client in an acute psychotic state. The underlying diagnosis is F20.0 "paranoid schizophrenia" according to ICD-10 (BfArM, 2022), which describes "relatively stable, often paranoid, delusions, usually accompanied by hallucinations, particularly of the auditory variety, and perceptual disturbances. Disturbances of affect, volition, and speech, and catatonic symptoms, are not prominent."

Case Summary

Matt is 40 years old and lives with his wife and their daughter (12 years old) in a small city apartment.

Social Services have been in contact with the family because of parenting difficulties, and have offered them the support of a family support worker for a few hours per week. After the initial introductory talks, the family helper received a call from Matt's wife, who was very worried because her husband's health had deteriorated significantly. She reported that he was suffering from severe paranoia and thought that the secret service was after him. He had built a cave out of blankets under the desk and was spending most of his time hiding there. He was also neglecting his personal hygiene and was afraid that his food and drink were poisoned. He was therefore hardly drinking anything, and his physical condition was very poor.

Based on the available information, the family support team conducted a risk analysis and decided that the family's support worker would carry out a home visit with a colleague. This scene is the moment when the family support worker goes into Matt's room and tries to talk to him.

Please watch the video entitled "Acute Psychosis", for more information (www.gestalt-socialwork.com).

A. Schachameier et al., *Gestalt in Social Work*,
https://doi.org/10.1007/978-3-031-95528-0_19

Experiences in the Client Role

Cognitive

Matt's thoughts revolve around possible surveillance and intrusion into his own thoughts, e.g. by the secret service. He is focused on needing to be vigilant and fending off possible attacks. He suspects that his food and drink are poisoned. He feels safest in his room. His thought processes are erratic.

Emotional

Access to his own emotions is obscured. At the centre of his experience is mistrust, accompanied by fear, which can hardly be verbalised because he is preoccupied with thoughts of persecution at a cognitive level. When we identified with the client role during the role-play, our experience was that he felt very distant internally and could only hear or understand a fraction of what the family support worker said on the content level.

Physical

Matt is physically very tense, nervous, restless and agitated.

Longing

Matt longs for security, peace, and clarity.

Action and Avoidance

He is preoccupied—internally, and to some extent externally—with warding off potential dangers. It is difficult for him to make contact with the family support worker.

Contact with the Outside World

Out of fear, and to try and protect himself, he has withdrawn very far from his surrounding environment. He is distant from the outside world.

Identified Inner Parts

A: "Psychotic experience": "I am being pursued, I need to be careful". This triggers fear, pressure and helplessness. He is also increasingly confused.

B: "Intrapersonal Longing": "I need inner peace and security."

C: "Interpersonal, relational Longing": "I need contact with other people, I want to feel secure."

The inner dialogue could be depicted as shown in Fig. 19.1:

The inner dialogue could be depicted as follows:

Case Transcript: Acute Psychosis

00:00:11
SW: Hello Matt. I'm Phil, I'm from the Family Support Team. Do you remember me?

00:00:19
C: Yeah? What…? What are you doing here?

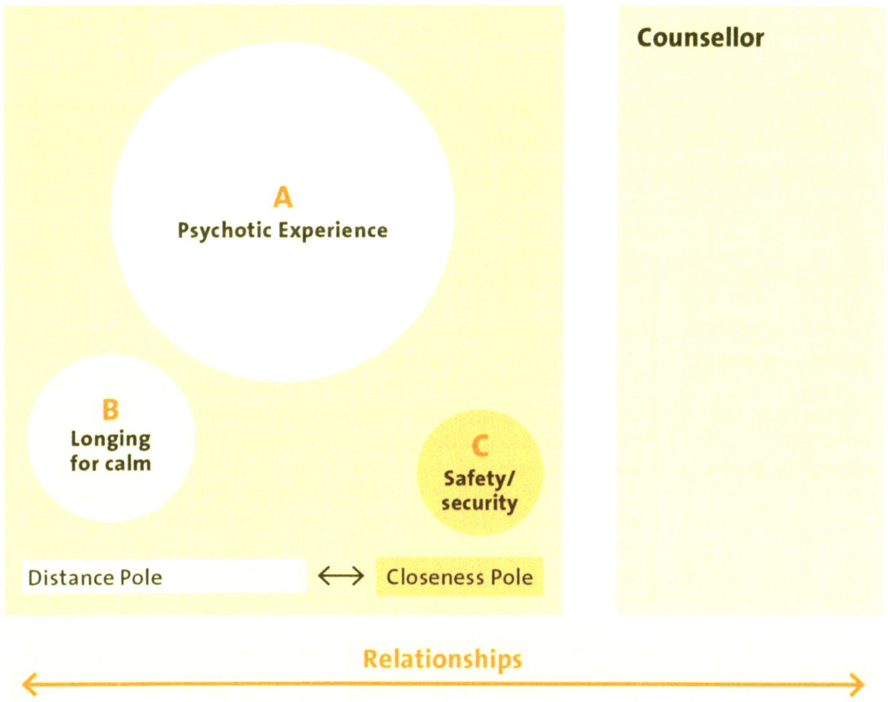

Fig. 19.1 "Acute psychosis"—identified inner parts

00:00:22
SW: I'm Phil, from the Family Support Team. I've been here before. I'm going to sit down for a moment. Your wife contacted me, she said I should check on you, see how you're doing, because you're hardly eating or drinking anymore. That's why I'm here. How are you doing?

00:00:51
C: Are you one of them?

00:00:54
SW: One of who…who do you mean?

00:00:54
SW: (Silence 00:00:56–00:00:59)

00:00:59
C: The ones that are poisoning me.

00:01:01
SW: Ah, someone wants to poison you? Who's trying to poison you?

00:01:04
SW: (Silence 00:01:04–00:01:09)

00:01:10
C: Maybe… Maybe you're one of them. Or/

00:01:20
SW: Okay, you think I might be one of them. One of the people who want to poison you? I seem a bit suspicious to you. But I can promise you, I'm from the family support team. I'm here because I'd like to help you. I notice you're looking around…?

Effect on the client	Intervention and resonance
Matt is somewhat calmed by this intervention. He feels safe enough to share more.	The family support worker tries cautiously to establish contact with Matt. He asks open-ended questions to understand what Matt is feeling. He then mirrors the mistrust he perceives and thereby acknowledges Matt's perception and experience. At the same time, he answers Mr. Matt's question and offers his own perception of reality (**Dialogical attitude**, **Phenomenology**). The family support worker takes the lead in the conversation, conveys calm and gives orientation, so that Matt can relax and feel a little safer.

00:01:40
C: I've got to be careful.

00:01:44
SW: Ah. What do you have to be careful of?

00:01:47
C: (Silence 00:01:49–00:01:52)

00:01:52
C: They want to get into my head.

00:01:54
SW: Into your head?

00:01:56
C: Thoughts.

00:01:56
SW: Ah. They're putting thoughts into your head?

00:02:05
C: Yeah. You too, maybe.

00:02:07
SW: You think that I might be too?

00:02:09
C: I don't know.

00:02:11
SW: You're not sure, you don't know? Now you're looking down... (...) And the blanket, you're holding the blanket. (...) Now you're looking at me.

Matt feels increasingly calmer through this intervention.

The family support worker's verbalisation of his behaviour helps him to be in the here and now, giving him orientation; this interrupts the delusions.

The family support worker reflects what Matt is saying again and names how he is behaving (where he is looking, how he is holding the blanket) (**Dialogical attitude, Phenomenology**).

He thus guides the contact between them and maintains the connection to Matt.

00:02:33
C: What are you doing here? Now? What are you..? Why are you here? What do you want from me?

00:02:38
SW: Matt, I'm here to help you. We're worried about you. Your wife, the family support team. Are you thirsty?

00:02:46

C: I can't drink anything. It's all been poisoned. There's poison in it. All the drinks are poisoned.

00:02:56
SW: Or do you want to eat something? Are you hungry?

00:03:00
C: That's poisoned too.

00:03:01
SW: The food's poisoned as well?

00:03:02
C: They're poisoning everything. Even my thoughts, they're poisoned too.

00:03:06
SW: Okay. Matt, if you don't drink or eat, that's very dangerous. And you might die. That's why we'd like to take you to a clinic.

Matt is convinced that his food is poisoned due to his delusions.

The family support worker checks for signs of self-endangering behaviour (as required by German law) by asking the client about intake. Special attention is given here to the refusal to drink.

00:03:23
C: (Silence 00:03:25–00:03:31)

00:03:32
C: Do you hear that, do you hear that?

00:03:32
SW: You hear something?

00:03:33
C: Yeah.

00:03:33
SW: What can you hear?

00:03:34
C: There's something there. You know what it is?

00:03:38
SW: What are you listening to exactly? You can hear something there.

00:03:47
C: So it doesn't go into my head.

00:03:50
SW: You need to watch out…?

00:03:52
C: Yeah.

00:03:52
SW: Matt, we want to help you. We want to take you to the clinic, to the psychiatric ward. So you can eat and drink again.

00:04:06
C: I'm staying here.

He doesn't want to go, he's scared and tries to maintain control. His nervousness and tension are increasing.

The family support worker offers to help Matt by taking him to the clinic.

00:04:06
SW: Ah, you're staying here?

00:04:09
C: I'm staying here.

00:04:10
SW: You're staying here?

00:04:10
C: I'm not going anywhere.

00:04:11
SW: You're not going anywhere. You know, at the clinic, they can help you. So you can feel better again and eat and drink.

00:04:24
C: They might poison me too.

00:04:26
SW: Are you worried that *they're* like that too?

00:04:30
C: Did they send you?

00:04:36
SW: No. We know them. You don't have to worry. They'll help you. Just like us.

00:04:40
SW: (Silence 00:04:43–00:04:49)

00:04:49
SW: Are you looking around again?

00:04:49
C: I'm staying here.

00:04:52
SW: You're staying? What's different here?

00:04:58
C: It's…it's better, better.

00:05:00
SW: Matt, I'd like to take you to the clinic. Will you come with me? Now?

00:05:08
C: (Silence)

00:05:11
SW: No? If you won't come with me, then I *will* have to notify the police. And then the police will take you there. (…) Now you're looking at me. (…) Now you're looking away again.

00:05:26
SW: (Silence 00:05:29–00:05:40)

00:05:40
SW: If you don't want the police to take you there, then come with me. Shall we go there now, together? To the clinic.

Matt doesn't want to go to the clinic. He feels safer in his room.

When the police are mentioned, he is somewhat startled. He is unsure and doesn't know what to do.

He feels helpless and longs for someone to guide him.

The family support worker repeatedly offers to help Matt and take him to the clinic.

He confronts him with the possible consequence of police involvement if the client is not willing to agree to go with him to the clinic.

00:05:49
SW: (Silence 00:05:52–00:05:53)

00:05:53
SW: Ah, okay, that's another one of those sounds… One of those sounds. You're listening carefully?

00:06:02
C: Yeah.

00:06:03
SW: You're being careful! You're making sure that nothing gets into your head. Matt?

00:06:13
C: Yeah?

00:06:13
SW: I'm going to stand up now.

00:06:14
C: (coughs).

00:06:21
SW: Now I'm standing here. You're sitting there. You're looking at me. Stand up too Matt. We're going now.

Matt is relieved on the one hand that the family support worker is leading him, but on the other hand, still doesn't want to leave the room.

The family support worker increasingly takes the lead by verbally mirroring Matt's behaviour. The family support worker proceeds very incrementally to avoid unsettling him.

The interactions can still be understood as offers of support, as the family support worker maintains an inner attitude whereby these offers can still be rejected (**Dialogical attitude**). The family support worker stays very close as he leads Matt and focuses on here-and-now experience in external reality. This prevents Matt from getting lost again in his delusions.

00:06:32
SW: (Silence 00:06:35–00:06:37)

00:06:37
SW: Now you're looking around again.

00:06:41
C: I can't do it.

00:06:41
SW: It's hard to get up? You're looking around. Looking at yourself. Come on, let's stand up. Are you going to stand up? The blanket, you have a blanket in your hand, don't you? You can put that away. Put the blanket away, just on the chair. And then stand up. Exactly. Stand up…there you go, it's not easy, you've been sitting here for a long time. Up you go. Now you're standing up. Here I am, standing here. And you're standing there.

00:07:34
C: But why?

00:07:35
SW: We're going to the clinic now, both of us.

00:07:40
C: I'm not coming, I'm staying here!

00:07:42
SW: You stay here and we'll go one step. We'll go one step. That's it, just take one step. Another step. Look at me again. Have a look around.

On the one hand, Matt is relieved that someone is helping him and providing security, but at the same time he wants to stay in his familiar environment because he is afraid.

The family support worker mirrors and names what Matt is obviously doing and establishes a contextual connection to his feelings. In this way, he addresses the part that wants to stay at the same time as leading him out of the room (**Phenomenology**).

The family support worker 'speaks Matt's language' and chooses words that he will understand.

00:07:58
C: Erm, I have to stay here.

00:07:59
SW: You have to stay here?

00:08:00
C: Yeah, I have to stay here, I have to stay here.

00:08:04
SW: And we keep going. We keep going step by step. Let's get out of this room. Exactly.

Value Squares

The value squares in Fig. 19.2 are designed to show directions of development for Matt. We wish to illuminate three levels. The first is the "intrapsychic" perspective, which refers to internal, cognitive-emotional processes of evaluation. The second, "interpersonal, relational", refers to internal dynamics that are important in dealing with other people. The third level, "behaviour", is ultimately the result of the preceding thoughts and feelings.

Such differentiation between the three categories is ultimately only possible to a limited extent, as the levels are mutually dependent. Nevertheless, we see the distinction between these perspectives as advantageous, as it allows us to recognise significant tendencies. The following development squares serve as suggestions, and were constructed through our exploration in the respective roles. These are intended to stimulate the formation of your own versions, as other similar perspectives and variations are certainly conceivable.

The value squares are identical to those in the chapter on "Chronic Psychosis" (see Fig. 19.2). The only difference is that we have added the term "confusion" alongside "fear" in the intrapersonal section, as it can be assumed that the client lacks clarity in terms of emotional perception.

A Note on the Use of Physical Contact

In the scene between Matt and the family support worker, the latter uses physical contact (taking Matt's hand and leading him) to enhance his offer of clear guidance and leadership. In our reflections, it was clear that this was done following an impulse on the part of the person playing the family support worker role. Like a parent with their child, he takes Matt by the hand. Matt is somewhat disconcerted by this, but at the same time, because of the natural quality of the interaction, it gives him a sense of security. Another possibility would be to ask beforehand whether the client would welcome physical contact. In general, it is important to proceed with caution in this regard. For a person with acute psychosis, such a direct approach could at times be counterproductive. The acceptability and appropriateness of physical contact in social work in general, and in this situation specifically, can be critically discussed.

Discussion

The information that the family support worker received from Matt's wife had already indicated that there is a risk of self-harm as he was not drinking any fluids. This is grounds enough to necessitate considering psychiatric admission. According to German federal law, treatment without the consent of the addressee is indicated, "if and as long as [the person] is significantly and currently endangering their life or health or poses a significant and current danger to significant legal goods of others and the danger cannot be averted in any other way" (Sächsische Staatskanzlei, 2022, using the example of Saxony).

The family support worker did a risk-assessment before the visit; based on the information he had, he felt that aggressive behaviour was unlikely, given the reported tendency towards withdrawal. Nevertheless, it makes sense to carry out such an operation in pairs. There are also other protective aspects to be considered, such as the ensuring the constant availability of an escape route.

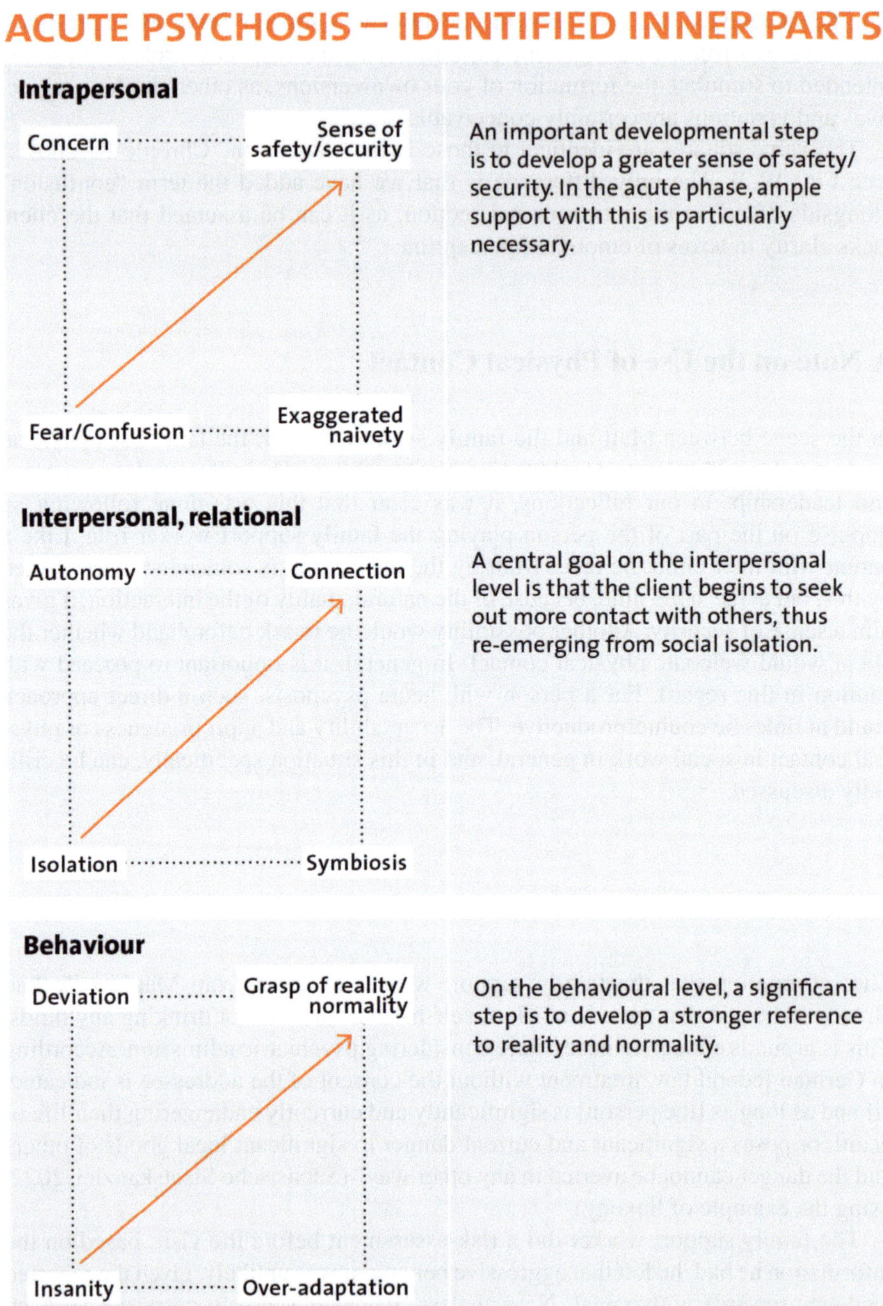

Fig. 19.2 Value squares for "acute psychosis"

It was noticeable in the role of the client that very little of the spoken content really got through, and that the decision about whether to wait for the police or go with the social worker represented an overload. He was genuinely unsure, from which we conclude that in such a case, clear guidance on the part of the professional is helpful. It is important to formulate offers of action rather than instructions, and to stay close to the client's subjective experience of reality (**Phenomenology**). In this case, this meant naming Matt's basic body movements rather than addressing his emotional inner life, to which he had only very limited access. The continuous naming of what is happening maintains the contact between both people; in contrast, longer pauses could lead to the client disappearing back into their inner world and no longer being able to follow the guidance.

Our experiences from the role-plays correspond to the "Contact Work" approach, a form of pre-therapy that can bring people back into interpersonal contact (Sanders, 2007, 14). This methodological approach goes back to Prouty (1994), who was strongly influenced by both Rogers and Perls. It is used with people who are in psychotic and/or dissociative states (ibid., 7 ff. Prouty, 1994). Through basic contact work, it is possible to free clients from the isolation they may often experience and establish contact with them (Sanders, 2007, 18). This form of relational work is especially effective at reducing stress levels and strengthening trust in the professional when working with psychotic clients who engage a high degree of withdrawal (ibid., 22, 23). It can also reduce perceptual disorders such as hallucinations (ibid.).

This method has also been applied in clinical studies that investigated the effects of humanistic, experiential approaches. To this end, perception experiments were conducted: "The stated purpose of these exercises was to create experiences in which the participants would relate to concrete elements in their surroundings. The exercises enabled differentiation between elements of the experience, organization of the elements into a whole, and differentiation between important elements and less important ones. An example of such an exercise involved the experience of closing one's eyes and describing the seating order in the circle, clothing worn by the participants, etc. Another exercise requested a detailed description of the immediate surroundings and the more distant surroundings, such as the garden or the doctor's office" (Serok & Zemet, 1983).

This approach corresponds to the methodological basic principles of phenomenological work. Directing attention to the obvious can provide psychotic clients with orientation and security.

Summary Graphic (Fig. 19.3): Client Experience and Key Interventions

ACUTE PSYCHOSIS

Interventions

A

- Accept psychotic events (pressure, fear, helplessness)
- Radiate calm
- Present a different perspective
- Lead calmly and clearly

B

- Name the longing for calm
- Keep returning to this

C

- Offer contact: safety and security through relationship

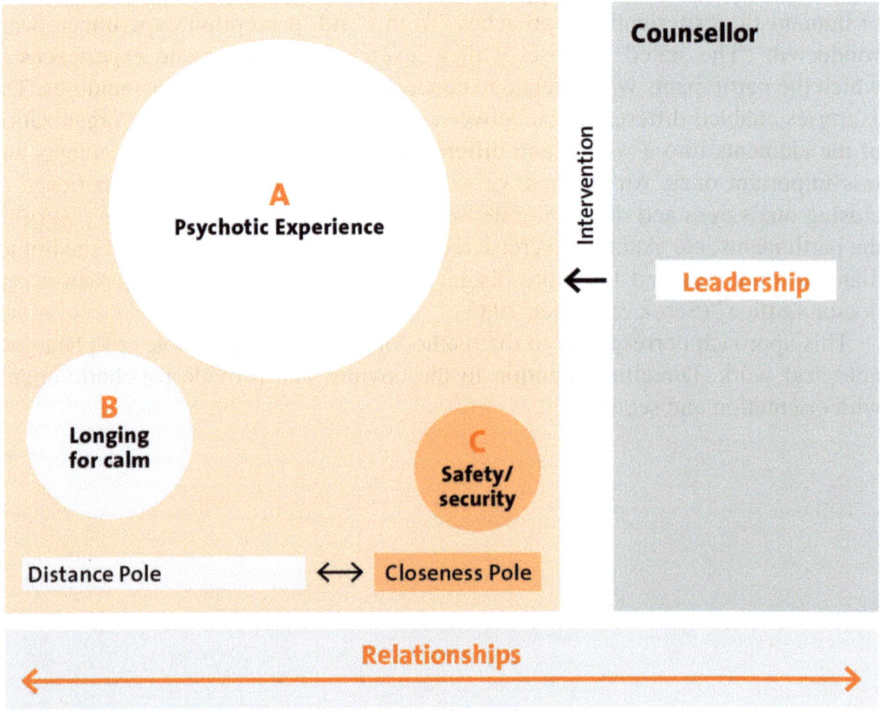

Fig. 19.3 "Acute psychosis"—summary graphic

References

BfArM. (Ed.). (2022). *ICD-10-GM: F20-F29 Schizophrenie, schizotype und wahnhafte Störungen*. Retrieved October 04, 2023, from https://www.icd-code.de/icd/code/F20.0.html

Prouty, G. F. (1994). *Theoretical evolutions in person-centered/experiential therapy: Applications to schizophrenic and retarded psychoses*. Praeger.

Sächsische Staatskanzlei. (Ed.). (2022). *REVOSax. Sächsisches Psychisch-Kranken-Gesetz*. Retrieved November 22, 2022, from https://www.revosax.sachsen.de/vorschrift/2015-Saechsisches-Psychisch-Kranken-Gesetz#p10

Sanders, P. (2007). *The contact work*. PCCS Books.

Serok, S., & Zemet, R. M. (1983). An experiment of gestalt group therapy with hospitalized schizophrenics. *Psychotherapy: Theory, Research and Practice, 20*(4), 417–424.

Chapter 20
Parent Counselling

The following example focuses on a single father who has been experiencing conflict with his son. The father wants to send his son to counselling, because in his opinion, the problem lies with him, and he is the one who should change.

Case Summary

Charlie is 45 years old, has separated from his ex-partner, and is solely responsible for their 10-year-old son. He is having a lot of difficulties with him, as he repeatedly refuses to attend school. There are phases when things 'work well', but again and again, the son refuses to go to school. Charlie is desperate, as he has already tried a variety of things: from 'raising his voice', trying to 'persuade', threatening and implementing punishments such as television bans. None of these methods have been successful. The school has already contacted him and threatened consequences if there are further absences. Subsequently, Charlie sent his son to the school psychologist, who conducted several counselling sessions with the boy. Neither this, nor participation in a therapeutic group for children led to noticeable changes. Now he is trying another educational counselling centre.

This particular educational counselling centre uses the multidimensional family therapy approach (Gantner et al., 2011), which works with both the child or adolescent and the parent(s), and in some cases with the family as a whole. However, the centre stipulates that the parent(s) attend for the first five hours without the child, and only after this time does the child attend.

Please watch the video entitled "Parent Counselling" for more information (www.gestalt-socialwork.com).

A. Schachameier et al., *Gestalt in Social Work*, https://doi.org/10.1007/978-3-031-95528-0_20

Experiences in the Client Role

Cognitive

Charlie wants his son to start "functioning" again, so that the difficulties finally come to end. He hopes that an expert can solve the problem.

Emotional

He feels very frustrated and desperate. He feels as though he has failed in his role as a father.

Physical

Due to his sense of overload, he is physically very tense.

Longing

His actual longing is to have a good relationship with his son, characterised by love, respect, and a harmonious dynamic. He wants to be a good father.

Action and Avoidance and Contact with the Outside World

He doesn't initially want to engage with himself and hands over the responsibility for the outcome to the counsellor. Charlie sees his son as being the cause of the problems and has given up on trying to influence his son himself. The impulse to do so does however still exist, but he suppresses it (**Retroflection**).

Identified Inner Parts

A: "Behaviour": "I take responsibility as a father." Charlie is or was trying to actively shape his son's upbringing.

B: "Problem": "I can't do it, I keep failing." Charlie devalues himself.

C: "Delegation of responsibility": "I need professionals to help my son."

D: "Longing": "I want a harmonious relationship with my child." Longing for relaxation and a loving relationship.

The inner dialogue could be depicted as shown in Fig. 20.1:

Case Transcript: Parent Counselling

00:00:00
SW: Charlie.

00:00:01
C: Yes.

00:00:02
SW: Good to see you here. We've already talked a bit on the phone. It's about your son, isn't it? He's not going to school, or keeps having phases where he doesn't go. And he has trouble in the mornings.

00:00:13
C: Yes.

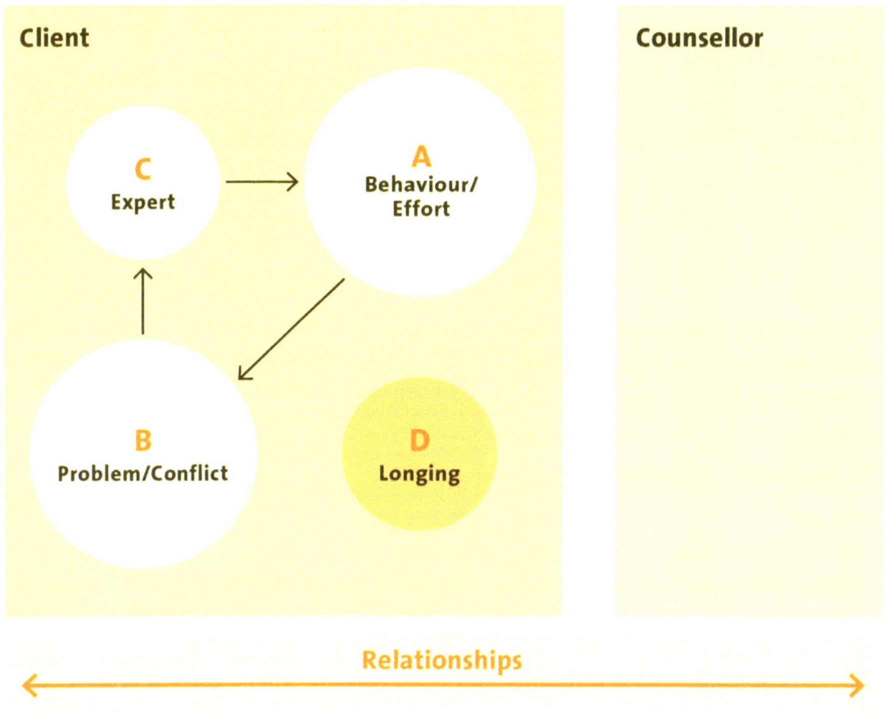

Fig. 20.1 "Parent Counselling"—identified inner parts

00:00:13
SW: Okay, so tell me more//

00:00:14
C: Well, it's a total disaster. I mean, it's been going on like this for almost a year now. There are phases when he goes to school and then there are phases when he just won't go. I'm a single parent, so…I don't really have any help.

00:00:29
SW: Mmm (affirming).

00:00:30
C: I've tried to talk him into it, I've threatened him with all sorts of punishments. But sometimes just…nothing works.

00:00:39
SW: You've already tried a lot. It sounds as though you're at your wit's end.

00:00:43
C: Yeah, I just don't know what to do anymore. I've already been to a couple of/I've already been to a school psychologist//

00:00:49
SW: Okay.

Effect on the client	Intervention and resonance
The client feels understood.	The counsellor initially listens, shows understanding for the situation and reflects back Charlie's state of mind (**Dialogical attitude** and **Phenomenology**). Part A is appreciated.

00:00:49
C: …for a few hours. And to a group, I went to this other parent counselling centre/ It didn't really help, you know? The school's breathing down my neck. They're putting on the pressure, saying he can't miss school that often.

00:01:01
SW: So that's extra pressure.

00:01:02
C: Yeah, yeah, exactly. Yeah, so…something has to change. I was hoping that I could just send him to you for a few hours, and that things would start working again.

00:01:12
SW: Mmm, so that would be your hope: that you send your son to us and then things start going smoothly again. Right?

00:01:18
C: Yeah, yeah, exactly; that would be great, yeah.

Charlie feels understood.	The counsellor paraphrases Charlie's concern, namely that his son receives professional support (Part C – "Delegation of responsibility").

00:01:22
SW: I can understand that. So…there are a few things I'd like to clarify: how are *you* doing? You say it's been a year. How are you dealing with it?

00:01:32
C: Me? (groans). Well, I mean it's…it's totally frustrating and I'm literally running out of steam. I'm exhausted//

00:01:42
SW: Exhausted, out of steam, mmm (affirming).

00:01:49
C:// …and, well…I'm worn down, to be honest (groans) I just don't know what to do next.

00:01:51
SW: Mmm, so…/You're helpless, exhausted. There's pressure coming from the outside too, you said.

00:01:57
C: Yeah, yeah, they're really breathing down my neck.

00:01:58
SW: Exactly, the school's breathing down your neck and you don't know what you should do, and you're exhausted from the long haul. It's been a year now.

00:02:05
C: Yeah.

00:02:07
SW: And you've really been giving it everything. You've been trying everything. And you don't know how to move forward.

00:02:12
C: Yeah, exactly…and all the trying, somehow it's getting worse rather than better.

00:02:19
SW: Mmm, you're carrying quite a burden right now.

00:02:22
C: Yeah.

00:02:23
SW: Mmm. And it sounds like it's getting heavier, the longer this goes on; you're getting more and more exhausted.

00:02:28
C: Yeah, yeah. The longer it goes on, the more wiped out I get, yeah.

Charlie describes the pressure, frustration, and exhaustion he is experiencing.

The counsellor does not address Charlie's concern directly, but rather explains that he is interested right now in how Charlie himself is dealing with the situation.

The counsellor reflects back Charlie's description of his experience and tries to put himself in Charlie's shoes. (Part B "Behaviour") (**Dialogical attitude, Inclusion** and **confirmation**).

00:02:33
SW: Yeah, yeah, yeah (affirming). How would you *like* it to be, if you can imagine waking up in the morning, and you could choose: how would you like things to be? In an ideal world? Can you describe that?

00:02:48
C: Mmm… I can hardly imagine anymore. I mean…I guess it would be great if things just worked, if I came into his room in the morning and he just cooperated, you know? And just got on with things like a normal child, no big fuss…yeah, if he just got on with it.

00:03:05
SW: What would it be like if things *did* start to work better, these next few weeks say? How would that be for you?

00:03:13
C: It'd be a huge relief.

00:03:16
SW: Mmm, yes.

00:03:18
C: I'd be really happy.

00:03:18
SW: (interrupting) …happy, yes, yeah. It'd be like a weight had lifted off you.

00:03:24
C: Yeah, yeah, totally. A huge load of stress would be gone. It'd be such a relief.

The client finds it difficult to imagine or describe a positive development, or what a successful outcome for their everyday life might look or feel like.

Nevertheless, he engages in the 'experiment' and feels that it would be a very great relief.

The counsellor asks Charlie what kind of solution he would wish for. This addresses his longing.

The follow-up question about how Charlie would feel about a positive development of the situation is especially important. This brings him into contact with his longing and lets him feel what effect its fulfillment would have on him (**Stagnation/Polarisation**).

SW: Yeah (exhaling). I can really understand that. And apart from all the stress that would be gone, how about when you visualise your child for a moment. What would change there? In terms of your relationship with him, too? Because I'm assuming that there's a lot of struggle at the moment…so if things started to work out, what would things be like between you? If you look from the perspective of a father at your son, and at your relationship?
00:03:57
C: Mmm, it would just be harmonious again. There might be space for love, rather than just so much struggle and frustration that I barely enjoy life anymore. I can hardly imagine it, to be honest, but if things were working out, it would be amazing, just coexisting harmoniously. We'd look forward to seeing each other.

A relationship relieved of constant struggle would mean more love, more harmony and more joy.

However, this is hard for Charlie to even imagine (Part D "Longing").

The counsellor imagines that the client is in a conflict situation with his son and asks what the effects of a successful everyday life between father and son would be.

He inquires how the relationship with the son would change and puts himself in Charlie's shoes. He suspects that a 'fight' dynamic is currently in the foreground (**real fantasy**).

00:04:20
SW: You'd look forward to seeing your son?

00:04:21
C: Yeah.

00:04:23
SW: Yeah, it sounds as though you still have a lot of love for him, which you don't get to feel so often at the moment because there's so much struggle in the foreground?

00:04:29
C: Yeah, yeah, that's what it's like.

00:04:33
SW: This last year has been a real low, hasn't it?

00:04:34
C: Yeah, it's a shame…it's sad.

Charlie feels his sadness about the "failure" and the difficult relationship / situation (Part B "Problems").	The counsellor once again addresses Charlie's experience, and that it differs from what he longs for. With this, he addresses Part B ("Problems") (**Polarisation**).

00:04:38
SW: Sad, yeah. Hmm (exhaling). And you'd be willing to invest quite a bit to change things?

00:04:48
C: Yeah, anything.

00:04:49
SW: Anything.

00:04:50
C: Anything, honestly I'd do anything to make it work again.

00:04:55
SW: Mmm, so that the whole relationship with your son would be better, more harmonious as you said, right?

00:05:00
C: Yeah, I mean when you say that…/Yeah, that would be so good. Yeah, I'd do a lot for that.

Charlie agrees that he would be willing to invest a lot to bring about a positive change in his relationship with his son.	The counsellor now addresses Part D ("Longing") directly. He reminds Charlie of the emotional experience of his longing (**Polarisation**).

00:05:09
SW: Okay. It was important to me to find out where *you're* at, what your hopes are. Our concept here is that we work with the adult first for five hours, and only then invite the child in after that.

00:05:27
C: Okay.

00:05:29
SW: To explain that briefly, one aspect is that experience shows/Well, that it works well that way, and another aspect is that *that* way, adults also get time to really talk about everything that's weighing on them, what their hopes are, but also… We've noticed that often, some form of change arises from these dialogues, we uncover things that weren't visible anymore in the midst of all the struggle. That's why we do it this way, and I heard you when you said you'd do anything to make a difference, right?

Charlie is somewhat perturbed. He now realises that he actually had a different concern, namely to send his son to counselling.

The counsellor presents the counselling centre's approach and explains why the first five hours are spent working with adults.

He refers to Charlie's previous statement, namely that he would be willing to do anything to improve his relationship with his son. This activates Part D ("Longing").

00:06:00
C: Yeah, yeah, I can understand that somehow, as you say… But I was thinking I might just be able to send him straight in to you. I mean…I'm kind of tight on time, you know?

00:06:17
SW: Yeah, that's actually very common, and I can understand you there I think. We really often have parents who say: can I just send my child to you and then—you know? And—that's how our concept is, and we've seen time and again here that it does make sense that way; *and* I can understand if it's not what you were hoping for. And I also heard that you have a strong wish for things to be more harmonious again and that you're really willing to work towards that.

00:06:40
C: Yeah.

00:06:45
SW: And it sounds like that might be new, that experience?

00:06:47
C: Yeah, I mean as I said, I'm a bit confused, but the way you say it, if things would start working again somehow then, like we were talking about just now. So I mean yes, I think I could give it a try. We could try it out.

The client continues to be a little disconcerted, but also feels hopeful; his desire for a good relationship with his son serves as motivation for committing to the first five counselling sessions.

The counsellor shares his experience of this approach, thereby reinforcing its fruitfulness whilst simultaneously expressing that he can understand the confusion; he repeatedly addresses the longing (Part D).

00:07:07
SW: Mmm (agreeing). Good. Okay, then I think it would be good if we had another appointment in a week or two and met again, and then we can take another look at how you're doing, what change you'd like to see, and how you're doing things so far. How does that sound?

00:07:23
C: Okay, we can do that.

00:07:24
SW: Great.

00:07:25
C: I'll be in touch.

00:07:26
SW: Mmm, and thank you for your openness. I look forward to seeing you next time.

00:07:28
C: Yeah.

00:07:29
SW: Okay.

Value Squares

The value squares in Fig. 20.2 are designed to show directions of development for Charlie. We wish to illuminate three levels. The first is the "intrapsychic" perspective, which refers to internal, cognitive-emotional processes of evaluation. The second, "interpersonal, relational", refers to internal dynamics that are important in dealing with other people. The third level, "behaviour", is ultimately the result of the preceding thoughts and feelings.

Such differentiation among the three categories is ultimately only possible to a limited extent, as the levels are mutually dependent. Nevertheless, we see the distinction between these perspectives as advantageous, as it allows us to recognise significant tendencies. The following development squares serve as suggestions, and were constructed through our exploration in the respective roles. These are intended to stimulate the formation of your own versions, as other similar perspectives and variations are certainly conceivable.

PARENT COUNSELLING

Intrapsychic

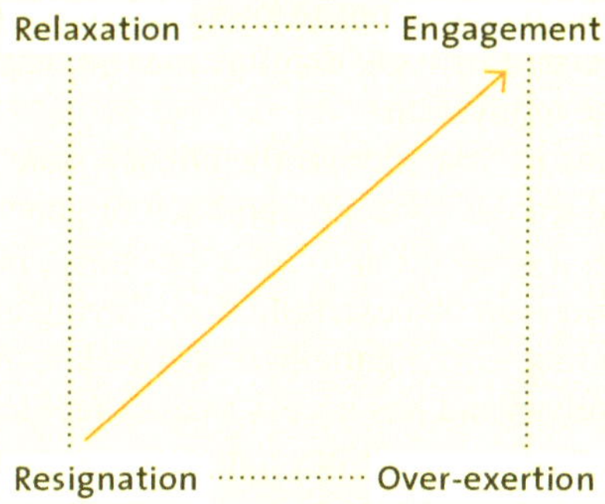

Firstly, Charlie must first change his inner attitude towards the conflict situation. The goal is to regain a sense of hope, begin to take responsibility, and develop a willingness to improve the relationship with his son.
This is what is meant by the term 'engagement'.

Interpersonal, relational

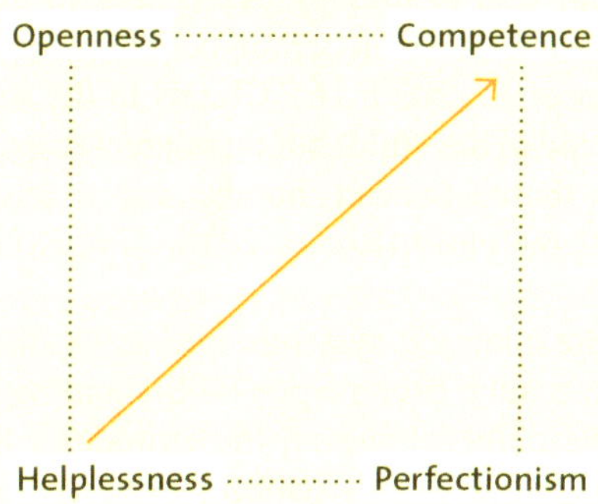

In order to improve the relationship between himself and his son, Charlie must develop appropriate social skills.

Behaviour

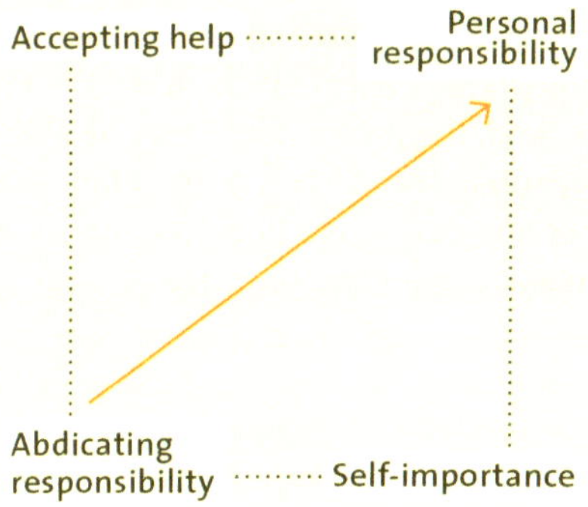

To really develop alternative behaviours, Charlie must take responsibility and initiative in engaging with his son.

Fig. 20.2 Value squares for "Parent Counselling"

Discussion

In the role-plays, we have repeatedly experienced that coming into contact with a deep longing leads to a willingness to examine and confront one's own behaviour. This motivation comes from the emotion associated with the longing, idea or vision. The more intensely this is felt, the stronger the motivation.

We suspect that it is generally advantageous to first address the client's state of mind, then their longing, and only then introduce the concept, approach or general framework. This allows the client to establish a connection to their emotions, particularly those associated with the inner longing—in this example, for a loving and harmonious relationship. The prerequisite for this working method approach is that the client has the capacity to reflect on themselves and has access to their feelings. For clients who have had many negative experiences and have shut down to the extent that they can no longer develop positive ideas on their own, it is necessary to offer images.

The inner dynamics of the client show parallels to the "submission pattern", as described in Biene's systemic interaction approach to therapy. According to this, parents act according to certain patterns. These are based on certain beliefs, ways of thinking, and behavioural patterns (Euteneuer et al., 2020, 16). Clients in the submission pattern see the problems as being related to the child, but do not feel responsible or competent enough to deal with these, instead hoping for external interventions such as experts who can 'treat' the child (Rhein, 2018, 134; Koller Stuber & Biene, 2009, 44).

When it comes to clarifying the therapeutic contract, systemic interaction therapy and counselling aim to help parents learn to take back responsibility and begin to reflect on their own behaviour towards the child. However, the attitude of the professional and the role this plays in influencing a client's patterns of perception and interaction is of particular importance (Rhein, 2018, 134). In our example, the counsellor assumes a belief that the client has the skills and abilities to change their situation. This has a very important effect on the support process.

Social workers who work in parent counselling usually have additional qualifications in therapy or counselling. Some clients may bring concerns which require both skill sets ideally, and if both qualifications are held, the professional may be able to employ both. The focus of therapeutic interventions should be on the relationship between parents and children. If diagnosed or suspected psychological issues are detected in the foreground, the professional may recommend the client to seek out additional psychotherapy (DGVT,[1] 2007).

[1] German Society for Behavioural Therapy.

Summary Graphic (Figs. 20.3 and 20.4): Client Experience and Key Interventions

Step 1

PARENT COUNSELLING – STEP 1

Interventions

A

- Enquire 'diagnostically' about efforting
- Explore the emotional aspect of effort non-judgmentally

B

- Ask about conflicts
- Explore emotional conflicts non-judgmentally (failure, frustration, exhaustion)

C

- Enquire about expectations of expert/child and explore non-judgmentally

D

- Explore longing, possibly offer images

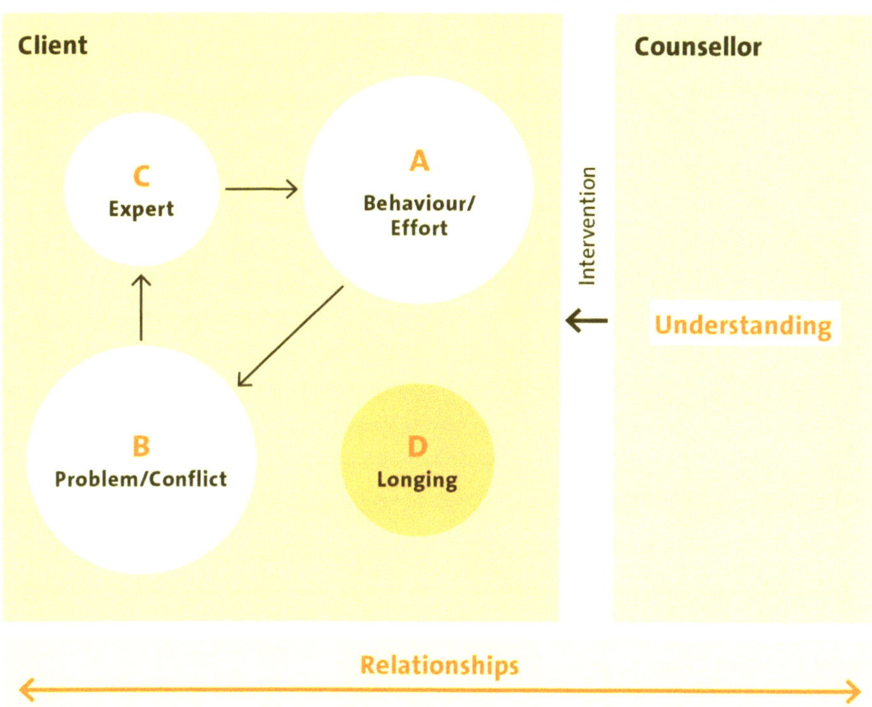

Fig. 20.3 "Parent Counselling/Step 1"—summary graphic

Step 2

PARENT COUNSELLING – STEP 2

Interventions

D

- Bring the longing component into focus and explore this

E

- Consistently confront the abdication of responsibility to the expert

F

- Make clear how the combination of behaviour A and conflict B block longing D (polarisation)

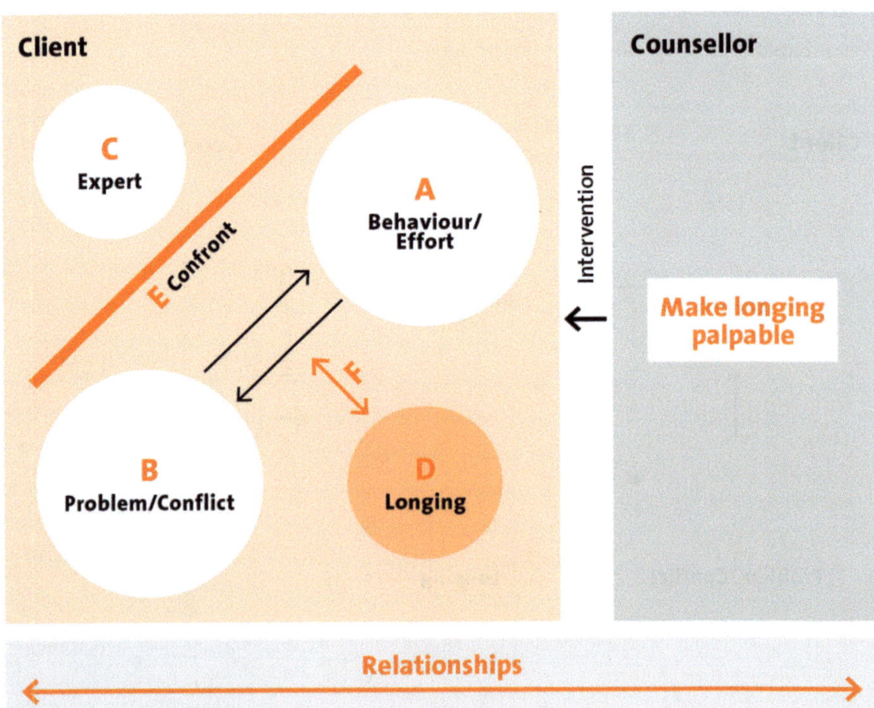

Fig. 20.4 "Parent Counselling/Step 2"—summary graphic

References

DGVT. (2007). *Erziehungsberatung und Psychotherapie. Eine Stellungnahme der Bundeskonferenz für Erziehungsberatung*. Retrieved January 08, 2024, from https://www.dgvt.de/aktuelles/news-details/erziehungsberatung-und-psychotherapie-2

Euteneuer, M., Schwabe, M., Uhlendorff, U., & Vust, D. (2020). *Die Systemische Interaktionstherapie und -beratung in den Erziehungshilfen. Theorie und Praxis eines elternaktivierenden Ansatzes*. Beltz Juventa.

Gantner, A., Spohr, B., Bobbink, J., & Liddle, H. A. (2011). *Multidimensionale Familientherapie: Jugendliche bei Drogenmissbrauch und Verhaltensproblemen wirksam behandeln*. Vandenhoeck & Ruprecht.

Koller Stuber, E., & Biene, M. (2009). SIT – Systemische Interaktionstherapie und -beratung. Ein Modell für die Elternarbeit in der Heilpädagogischen Früherziehung? *Schweizerische Zeitung für Heilpädagogik, 15*(1), 40–47.

Rhein, V. (2018). *Moderne Heimerziehung heute. Bd. 7, 8. Evaluation der Systemischen Interaktionstherapie und -beratung*. Frisch Texte Verlag.

Chapter 21
Trauma/Dissociation

Case Summary

Ali (35) has fled from Syria. He has been living in supervised accommodation for people with a background of migration for half a year. His roommate has noticed that he is visibly absent, barely responsive to conversation, and spending most of his time sitting in his chair irritably. The social worker who is responsible for Ali is notified to check on him. He has known Ali for half a year and has built a trusting working relationship with him.

Ali's behaviour and experiences can be diagnostically classified as post-traumatic stress disorder (PTSD) with dissociative symptoms. He suffers from flashbacks and derealisation. Concretely, he sees scenes from the war in his mind's eye and perceives himself as 'far away' from the environment and the people around him. The "feeling of detachment or alienation from others" (Fiedler, 2013, 17) can occur in connection with recurring and intrusive distressing memories of a traumatic event. Fiedler refers to these as "dissociative flashback episodes", which are accompanied by self-alienation and "detachment". These symptoms can be classified as depersonalisation and derealisation (ibid., 6).

Please watch the video entitled "Trauma/Dissociation", for more information (www.gestalt-socialwork.com).

Experiences in the Client Role

Cognitive

Ali cannot form clear thoughts. He experiences a foggy mental state, with fragments of thoughts only.

A. Schachameier et al., *Gestalt in Social Work*,
https://doi.org/10.1007/978-3-031-95528-0_21

Emotional

Ali is afraid and feels under stress. On one hand, this is because he sees images of traumatic situations from the war in his mind's eye; on the other hand, it is because he is afraid that this state of 'disconnection' from the environment will continue indefinitely.

Physical

Ali has little access to his bodily sensations; he is trapped in a bombardment of 'fragments of images' and his sense of detachment.

Longing

He longs primarily for this state to be over, and for a sense of safety.

Action and Avoidance and Contact with the Outside World

He lets himself be drawn into the 'vortex' that comes with this state. So far, he has not developed strategies to deal with emotionally unstable states. It feels exhausting both to turn to the outside world and to feel his own body.

Identified Inner Parts

A: "Dissociative Experience": "I am trapped in this state, far away and detached from the environment. There is a vortex that scares me and makes me feel helpless."

B: "Body": "I make contact with my body perception to get out of the vortex."

C: "Longing": "I make contact with other people to feel safe in their presence and to get out of this state."

The internal dialogue could be depicted as shown in Fig. 21.1:

Case Transcript: Trauma/Dissociation

00:00:00

SW: Ali? Your neighbour called me, and said I should come over, he said you're not feeling well. What's wrong?

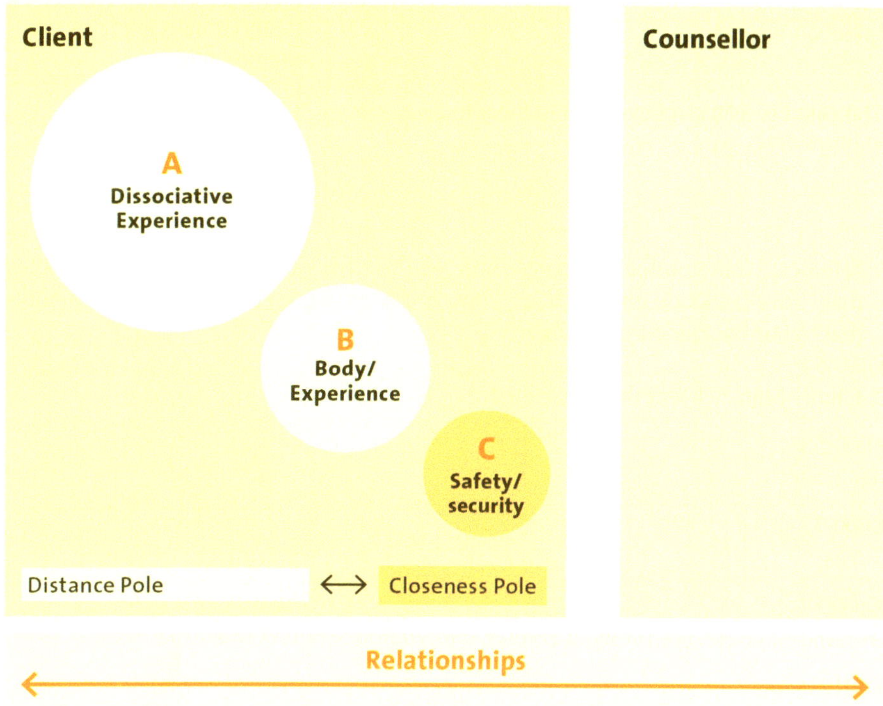

Fig. 21.1 "Trauma/Dissociation"—identified internal parts

00:00:18
C: (Silence 00:00:14–00:00:22) (sighs) I'm—I'm somehow not here,//

00:00:28
SW: You're not here?

00:00:28
C: // there are these… there are terrible images of the war.

00:00:39
SW: Yeah. You're not here and you're seeing terrible images of the war? Mmm (listening). (Silence 00:00:33–00:00:38)

Effect on the client	Intervention and resonance
The client is a little relieved not to have to be alone in this state.	The counsellor asks what's going on and how Ali is doing.

T: Tell me… Can you feel right now how you're sitting on your chair? Can you feel that? Your backside on the chair? How you're sitting on the chair? Do you notice that? Your backside on the chair?

00:00:54
C: Chair, yeah… I feel the chair, yeah.

00:00:55
SW: Yeah?

00:00:57
C: Yes.

00:00:57
SW: And your elbows on the armrests, can you/do you feel that too?

00:01:04
C: (Silence 00:01:00–00:01:04) Yeah.

00:01:05
SW: Your elbows, yes?

00:01:06
C: Yeah.

00:01:06
SW: And your back, the way it's leaning against the chair, can you feel that too? Mmm, your back against the chair?

00:01:13
C: Yeah.

The client notices that focusing on his body does bring him out of his dissociative state to some degree. At the same time, he continues to feel the strong pull of the dissociation.	The counsellor directs attention to Ali's body to help bring him back in contact with a real sensation in the here and now (**Phenomenology, Dialogical attitude**).

00:01:14
SW: Yeah, right? And your backside, do you still feel that on the chair?

00:01:19
C: I think it's pulling me back in. It's…//

00:01:20
SW: Yeah, uh-huh, it keeps pulling you back in. But stay noticing your backside on the chair, and how you're sitting just now. Exactly, and feel your feet on the ground. Can you feel them? Your feet on the ground? Uh-huh. Can you move your feet? Mmm, and your hands too. See if you can feel your hands. Exactly. Move them a bit, make a fist. Exactly. Or you can bring them together/Feel how that is. Can you feel your hands now? Try moving them around. Yeah, just like that. Can you feel your hands a bit more?

00:01:52
C: Yeah, yeah.

00:01:54
SW: Yes? Okay.

00:01:54
C: Yeah.

00:01:55
SW: Exactly…and you're still sitting on the chair?

00:01:57
C: I'm sitting on the chair, but it's…it's just pulling me away again.

00:01:59
SW: Yeah, yeah, there's like a strong pull, but stay with your hands. It helps you to come back here a bit when you feel your hands. Exactly. Stay with your hands and see if you can…maybe you can take me in, as well. Do you know what colour my sweater is? Take a look. Look//

> The client is relieved that the counsellor has understood that there is a sort of 'pull' into the dissociation, and he understands the explanation that in order to come out of this state, it is important not to follow this pull. However, it is not easy to resist it.

> The counsellor continuously guides Ali to focus on the perception of his bodily sensations.
>
> He explains that it's important not to give in to the inward pull, but to stay with his bodily sensations (**Phenomenology**).

00:02:17
C: It's blue. It's exhausting.

00:02:19
SW: It's exhausting?

00:02:20
C: It's exhausting and//

00:02:21
SW: Mmm, I can believe it's exhausting. You keep getting pulled back there, don't you?

00:02:25
C: Yeah.

00:02:26
SW: Yeah, and still—stay with the hands. It helps to bring you back, to be more here, to get away from the images a bit, even if they're pulling you back. I get that. Hands. Can you still feel your backside?

00:02:39
C: Yeah.

00:02:39
SW: And your back?

00:02:40
C: Yeah.

00:02:41
SW: Your back, yeah?

00:02:41
C: Yeah.

00:02:42
SW: And your feet on the ground? Yes? Your body? And I want to ask you again. Can you focus on me a bit better now?

00:02:49
C: Bit better. Tiny bit better.

00:02:52
SW: My eyes, what colour are they?

00:02:54
C: Mmm, that's too difficult.

00:02:55
SW: Yeah? I know it's a challenge, but try it! Really try, even if it feels exhausting. Try to say my eye colour, what colour they are. And?

00:03:08
C: (sighs) Blue.

Ali senses himself coming out of his dissociative state when he focuses on concrete environmental objects but it is still very exhausting for him.

The counsellor now directs Ali's attention to him, supporting him to distance his perception away from the inner pull of the dissociation (**Phenomenology**).

00:03:09
SW: They're blue. Yeah, exactly. Blue. Hmm, there's a really strong pull away, isn't there? But right now you're a bit more here, compared to when I arrived. (Talking over each other 00:03:16–00:03:18)

00:03:19
C: Just tiny bit better//

00:03:19
SW: But you really have to work for it, right?

00:03:22
C: Yeah.

SW: Yeah.

Ali is pleased with his progress and understands that it is within his ability and his responsibility to get out of his state.

He continues to follow the counsellor's instructions.

The counsellor clearly points out Ali's progress and explains that it is important to keep focusing on directing his attention to reality and not giving in to the pull (**Phenomenology, Dialogical attitude**). He continues to lead clearly, staying close to the client's experience.

00:03:22
SW: Yeah, great… And your hands, are they still good?

00:03:25
C: Yeah.

00:03:25
SW: You can feel them still? Okay, I have another question: have you had breakfast yet today?

00:03:31
C: Breakfast? No, no.

00:03:33
SW: You haven't had anything yet?//

00:03:34
C: I haven't had breakfast.

00:03:34
SW: What do you normally have for breakfast?

00:03:38
C: Uh, toast.

00:03:38
SW: Toast. What do you have with that?

00:03:40
C: With, um, butter and jam, yeah.

00:03:43
SW: Mmm, toast with butter and jam, sounds good, I like that too. And how about going off now to have some breakfast? We can go together.

00:03:50
C: Mmm, breakfast is good.

00:03:53
SW: Breakfast'd be good, right?

00:03:54
C: Breakfast's good, yeah.

00:03:55
SW: Yeah, and it's a chance to get up and move about a bit too, and I think//

00:03:57
C: Yeah.

00:03:58
SW: // it'd be good to go and get some breakfast, no? And do you notice how you're a bit more here again now?

00:04:02
C: Yeah.

Ali notices that focusing on something everyday like breakfast is beneficial. He is willing and motivated to go along.

When he checks, he realises that he is more present again. This brings some relief.

The counsellor directs Ali's attention to the topic of breakfast; this is because simple, everyday activities can help a person to further land in external reality.

In dialogue, the counsellor voices his sense that Ali is more present again and asks whether Ali feels that way too (**real fantasy** and **dialogical attitude**).

00:04:03
SW: Yeah, right? It's good to physically feel yourself getting up as we go off to eat something, okay? That helps you to come back a bit more too, okay?

00:04:10
C: Yeah.

00:04:11
SW: Good//

00:04:12
C: Yeah.

00:04:12
SW: // then I would say//

00:04:12
C: Mmm, okay, I go.

00:04:12
SW: // I'm going to stand up, are you going to come with me?

00:04:13
C: Mmm (affirmative).

Value Squares

The value squares in Fig. 21.2 are designed to show directions of development for Ali. We wish to illuminate three levels. The first is the "intrapsychic" perspective, which refers to internal, cognitive-emotional processes of evaluation. The second, "interpersonal, relational", refers to internal dynamics that are important in dealing with other people. The third level, "behaviour", is ultimately the result of the preceding thoughts and feelings.

Such differentiation between the three categories is ultimately only possible to a limited extent, as the levels are mutually dependent. Nevertheless, we see the distinction between these perspectives as advantageous, as it allows us to recognise significant tendencies. The following development squares serve as suggestions, and were constructed through our exploration in the respective roles. These are intended to stimulate the formation of your own versions, as other similar perspectives and variations are certainly conceivable.

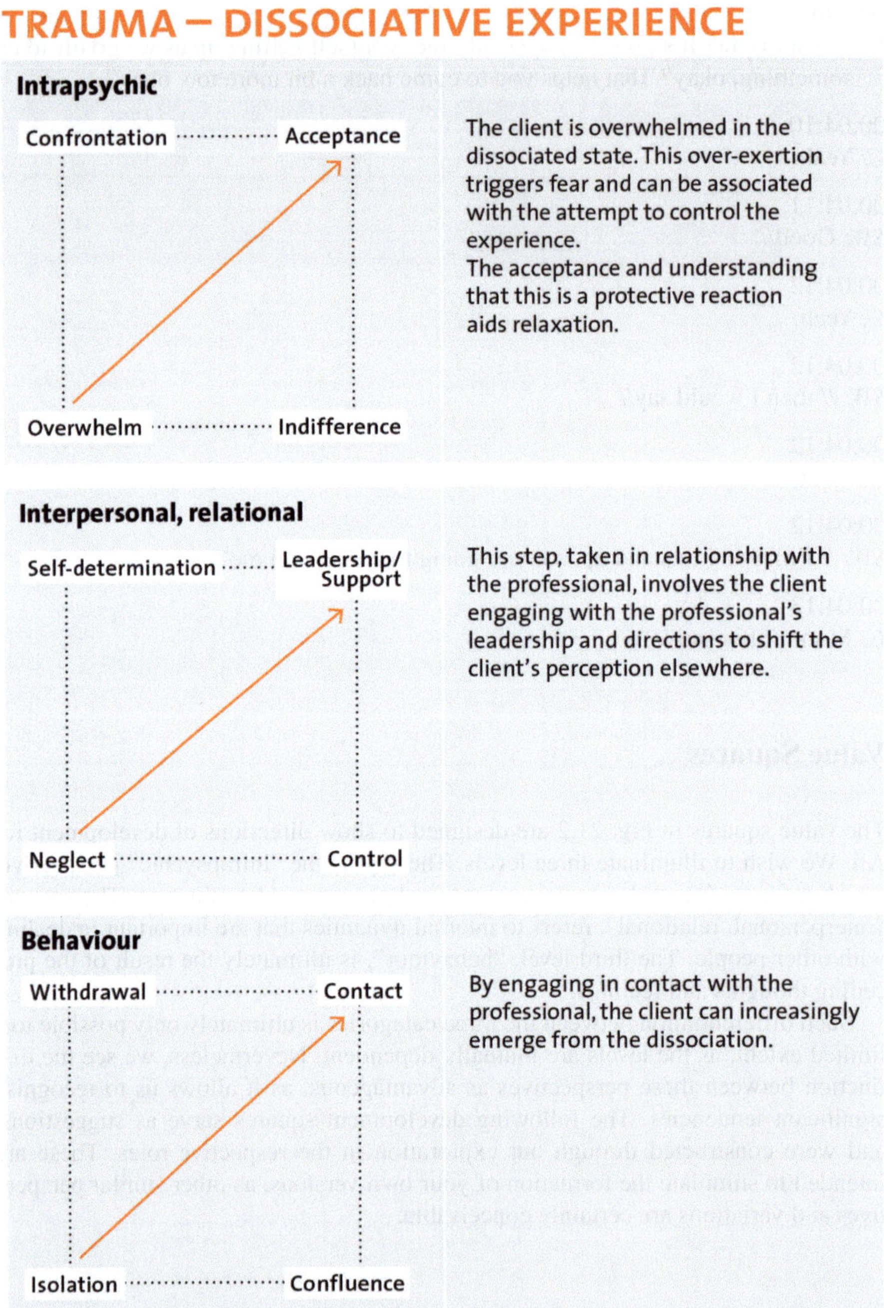

Fig. 21.2 Value squares for "Trauma/Dissociation"

Discussion

In a situation such as this, which is a likely occurrence within the everyday life of many social workers, it is first of all important to remain calm and simply recognise that the client is in a dissociative state. The pathway out of dissociation, back to 'reality' or normal perception, is through perceiving the body, re-engaging in contact with the environment and other people, and turning towards everyday tasks. In this example, as is often the case, it was important that the counsellor took the lead, or else Ali would have 'fallen' back into the dissociative state again. The counsellor represents reality, and acts as a point of orientation for the client, thus lending stabilisation and security.

The foundation for any kind of trauma education or support should be a respectful and understanding attitude, especially with regard to the traumatised person's experiences and behaviours. Within the course of dialogue, the counsellor should emphasise that these are normal reactions to extreme levels of stress (Weiß, 2011, 92 cit. n. Gahleitner et al., 2017, 31). In our case example, once Ali had stabilised again, it would be appropriate to calmly explain more about the mechanism of dissociation, how it works, and how he can 'come back' out of it (Gahleitner et al., 2017, 60 ff.). Psychoeducation is particularly important for clients with trauma backgrounds; in particular, strategies can be taught or developed together in order to manage dissociation on their own (ibid. 63 ff.).

It is advantageous if a bond already exists between the social worker and client, and that the latter is familiar with the environment and the procedures of the institution. A safe framework and the experience of reliable relationships with staff members are fundamental for the stabilisation process (Gahleitner et al., 2017, 20). This requires a multidisciplinary, trauma-sensitive approach that provides comprehensive security (ibid. 30). A trauma-sensitive or trauma-aware everyday environment forms an important basis for stabilisation. Only once this ground has been paid can the trauma be processed, e.g. through psychotherapy.

The task of the social worker, as in this example, is the everyday contact with the clients in the institution. In moments of acute crisis, professionals must intervene and offer support with stabilisation. Such interventions cannot be distinguished methodologically from a therapeutic approach. However, as in this case example, the focus is on stabilisation and integration into the everyday routine of the institution. This might include one-on-one conversations, but not psychotherapeutic treatment, which can be recommended and mediated if necessary.

Summary Graphic (Fig. 21.3): Client Experience and Key Interventions

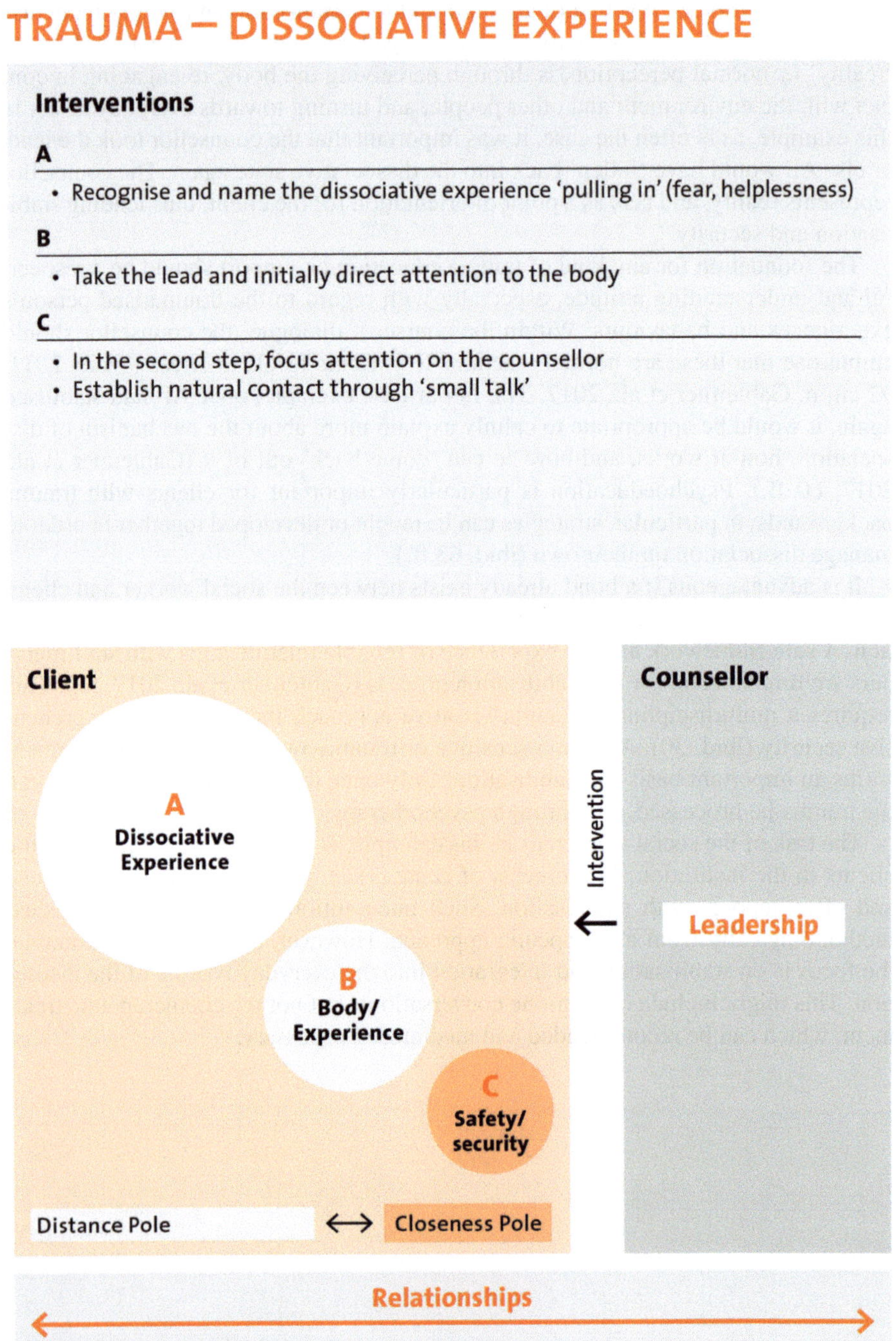

Fig. 21.3 "Trauma/Dissociation"—summary graphic

References

Fiedler, P. (2013). *Dissoziative Störungen*. Hogrefe.

Gahleitner, S. B., Zimmermann, D., & Zito, D. (2017). *Psychosoziale und traumapädagogische Arbeit mit geflüchteten Menschen*. Vandenhoeck & Ruprecht.

Weiß, W. (2011). *Philipp sucht sein Ich. Zum pädagogischen Umgang mit Traumata in den Erziehungshilfen*. Juventa.

Part IV
Summary and Outlook

Chapter 22
Methodological Commonalities and Their Importance for Social Work

The preceding chapters centred around reflections on a variety of different practical situations within social work. These included interactions with clients who were chronically depressed, suicidal, substance-dependent, co-dependent, psychotic, experiencing trauma-related dissociation, or having parenting difficulties. We also discussed the peculiarities of mandatory contexts, e.g., in the fields of addiction counselling or acute psychosis.

Looking back, it has become clear to us that in each of the relational contexts, Gestalt methods, techniques and perspectives were both relevant and supportive. We would like to end this book by revisiting the core of these Gestalt interventions here, as our experiences have proven them fundamental for the establishment of a professional working relationship. We summarise this methodological core under two umbrella terms, **phenomenology** and **responsibility and motivation**.

Phenomenology

By phenomenology, we mean the naming of the 'obvious' (or those phenomena which, for the counsellor, form the foreground of their awareness as pertaining to the client); we also mean supporting the client to name and explore their own subjective experience through explorative questioning and mirroring. Through our role-play experiences, we conclude that clients felt most understood when relevant inner parts were addressed. The crucial intervention was to ask how the client 'is doing' in the respective situation. When their emotional experience was accurately captured, they felt understood.

Fundamental to this 'capturing' is an attitude that recognises the potential or resources of the other, and believes in their ability to change (**Inclusion**). The more

A. Schachameier et al., *Gestalt in Social Work*,
https://doi.org/10.1007/978-3-031-95528-0_22

professionals—or students—know about the inner experience of the client and can empathise with it, the more easily such an attitude can be developed. Taking on the client role and exploring it 'from the inside' through role-play is an effective way of doing exactly that.

This even allows the recognition of inner parts that are not initially obvious or in the foreground, but can nevertheless be relevant. Often the inner part that wants to grow and take on the problem in a self-determined way is very small, and perhaps virtually invisible from the outside, but is obviously present on the 'inside'. This motivational part is connected with a longing, or a fundamental need. Phenomenological work in this context means exploring and understanding this all-important part too, and finding out, mutually, how the client currently relates to their underlying needs. Change processes are initiated through these steps of increasing awareness, which is a matter of naming what is.

Exploring the obvious includes, by its very nature, naming the lack of something. "Absent" parts and perspectives are also to be explored, and thus made more present and tangible (Francesetti, 2022, 11). This includes aspects related to the 'special circumstances' of the respective situation; in the example of the mandatory addiction counselling context, this was done by ensuring transparency around the control elements of the situation, and by creating a safe relationship within which the client could explore their reaction to this context. Dialogical exploration of any relevant situation acts as the basis for possible change, both in the counsellor and the client.

Another important aspect is showcased by the examples of a client with acute psychosis and the client with trauma-related dissociative symptoms. Here, the phenomenological work was related to their sensory perception and physical action in the here and now, through which the client was able to re-establish contact with external reality. This provided orientation, offered the client support in gradually restoring contact with their environment, including with the counsellor themselves, and enabled the client to move beyond their delusional thought structures.

On the one hand, engaging with clients in a phenomenologic, dialogical way can mean staying close to their foreground experience and supporting them to explore it. On the other hand, it is also possible to direct their attention towards parts or situational circumstances that are more 'hidden' and are not initially accessible. As a rule, such parts are often 'problematic' and take up a very large space in a person's consciousness. In order to explore these less 'hidden' parts, the counsellor must guide and direct the client towards where their longing, and therefore motivation, lie.

Responsibility and Motivation

As we have just described, the first step of any change process is to support clients, in a dialogical way, to become aware of and explore the *status quo* of their inner experience. When the relevant inner parts have become conscious, both the ones which are suffering from the problem *and* the ones which hold the person's longing and their personal drive to bring about change (usually less accessible initially), the prerequisite is created for the person to take back responsibility for their life—for the situation they are in, and the way in which they cope with it.

To be motivated ultimately means deciding to want to change something and being willing to look for possible solutions. As we have seen in the case examples in various chapters, clients usually experience the status quo from a "victim perspective"; they suffer, but do not see themselves as able to solve or cope with the problem independently. They do not recognise initially that they themselves have a range of behavioural options at their disposal. However, when the relevant situational circumstances and inner parts—including their wish for change—have been addressed, not only cognitively but especially in terms of the associated emotional experience, then the client can choose; they may choose to accept the professional's offer of support to change, or they may choose *not* to change anything.

Either way, supporting clients to make this decision for themselves means that they start a reflection process. Crucially, this necessitates an attitude that always locates the responsibility for making this decision with the client. Even in a mandatory context, such as our example of addiction counselling, the client can choose whether to accept the conditions or to reject them and live with the associated consequences. Even in the case example of acute psychosis, the client has some room for maneuver: ultimately, he chooses whether or not to accept the offer of guidance. It is only the client who can truly take responsibility for a change. For the professional, to know this, and to internalise this knowledge through a correspondingly respectful attitude, is fundamental for the establishment and development of a successful working relationship.

The Gestalt approach is particularly suitable in dealing with conflictual situations and conversations. In mandatory contexts in particular, clients may have very strong emotions. The capacity to accompany the client through these in a de-escalating way is a strength of the humanistic, emotion-focused approaches.

In summary, the dialogical and phenomenological working method that we have described and exemplified in the role-plays, and which represents the foundations of Gestalt methodology, can be seen as a guiding principle that orients towards the client's experience, creates awareness of relevant inner parts and dynamics, and guides the client in a change process. Equally fundamental is the attitude associated with this, which sees the responsibility for behavioural change as lying with the clients themselves.

Outlook: The Significance of Gestalt for Social Work

Our aim in writing this book was to take key scenes from social work contexts and illuminate them from a humanistic, Gestalt-methodological perspective. On the basis of case role-plays, with their iterative, experiential and experimental character, we have identified useful methods and techniques and shown how these can be applied in practice. As we have repeatedly pointed out, our video examples are not to be understood as 'one size fits all' solutions; in practice, each person has acquired and developed their individual patterns of action in the context of their own specific biographical background. In addition, each case has its own particular situational circumstances which must be taken into account.

Nevertheless, it can be assumed that in certain cases, fundamentally similar dynamics arise. Exploring these 'typical cases', especially through the attempt to understand the client's inner experience through role-play, can be very helpful in developing the ability to empathise with 'real' clients. In addition, it offers opportunities to try out and practise new or unfamiliar approaches and strategies, thus expanding the student's or professional's methodological repertoire. Role-play can be used flexibly within professional practice to reflect on encounters with clients, while taking into account the respective peculiarities of the individuals and the given situations.

Essential for this work is an attitude of cultivated uncertainty (see "**Cultivated Uncertainty**"), thus maintaining an openness to the uniqueness of human experience; this is why moment-to-moment dialogical exploration is necessary at all times. Nevertheless, the described combination of practice and reflection can lead to an increased sense of security in professional practice; it becomes easier to assess which inner parts and dynamics are relevant for which topics, which reactions can be expected, and which methods and techniques might be effective.

Our principle of exploratory reflection can also be applied in practice in team meeting and/or supervision contexts. This is already being practiced in some contexts; for example, 'Socianos', a child and youth welfare organisation in Berlin, Germany, regularly integrates role-play into their team meetings to find application-friendly solutions for difficult practice interactions. Although the work is not grounded in Gestalt therapy, but rather in systemic interaction therapy and counselling (Biene, 2014), it shares a common focus on understanding clients and building relationships.

Another aspect which is important for the development of social work degree programs has emerged over the course of our project. The selected topics covered by our case examples are significant for many fields of practice in social work. Social workers are almost guaranteed to encounter people who are depressed, suicidal, suffer from addictions, dissociation or psychosis, as well as people who are struggling to find motivation for change or confronted with legal requirements. These are cross-sectional issues that social workers face in multiple contexts in their practice. We therefore believe that it is appropriate and necessary that social work study programmes offer spaces within which students can practise and to some extent learn how to deal with certain fundamental case patterns. The focus should not only be on the transmission of theoretical background knowledge; training in skills and reflecting on one's own actions are equally important. Ideally, what has been practised through role-play can also be applied in real-life practice, and the experiences here can then be reflected upon again. This transfer between theory and practice and vice versa is particularly suited to dual degree programs.

Of course, it is also necessary to test the skills which are being promoted and to develop competence-oriented formats which correspond to the learning needs of the students. If the goal, when planning the modules of a social work degree program, is a cohort of competent social workers, then the relevant and desirable knowledge and skills must be defined and anchored in the study programme in didactic terms in a systematic way. Given that the case examples described in this book are relevant for almost all fields of social work practice, we advocate for their inclusion in general, entry-level social work training. We suggest defining basic abilities and knowledge for social work degree programmes, optimising this in close relationship to practice, and making this skill and knowledge base the subject of research. In this way, social work can grow, both as a discipline and a profession, and deliver better training for better professionals—not only academically or theoretically, but also most importantly in the field of practice.

References

Biene, M. (2014). Systemische Interaktionsberatung - Einführung. In V. Rhein (Ed.), *Moderne Heimerziehung heute. Band 2 und Band 3* (pp. 14–139). Frischtexte Verlag.

Francesetti, G. (2022). *Grundlagen einer phänomenologisch-gestalttherapeutischen Psychopathologie*. EHP; Originalausgabe (2022). Fondamenti di psicopatologia fenomenologico-gestaltica: una introduzione leggera. Libri Giovanni Fioriti.

Index

A. Schachameier et al., *Gestalt in Social Work*,
https://doi.org/10.1007/978-3-031-95528-0

MIX
Papier aus verantwortungsvollen Quellen
Paper from responsible sources
FSC® C105338

If you have any concerns about our products,
you can contact us on
ProductSafety@springernature.com

In case Publisher is established outside the EU,
the EU authorized representative is:
Springer Nature Customer Service Center GmbH
Europaplatz 3, 69115 Heidelberg, Germany

Printed by Libri Plureos GmbH
in Hamburg, Germany